GIVE MY HEART

Give My Heart

The Dr. Marion Hilliard Story

MARION O. ROBINSON

Garden City, New York

DOUBLEDAY & COMPANY, INC.

1964

If I were a shepherd
I would bring a lamb;
If I were a wise man
I would do my part;
Yet what can I give him —
Give my heart.

—from the carol "Mid-Winter," by Christina G. Rossetti

CONTENTS

Illustrations

GIVE MY HEART

The Birth of a Baby

It is just 12:30 by the big clock high up on the wall of the delivery room, as two nurses wheel the patient through the door from the quiet corridor. Outside in the summer darkness the city is slowing down. The daytime roar of traffic has become an intermittent murmur. Nearby office buildings are dark except for windows here and there where the night cleaning crew is at work. A revolving searchlight atop a downtown building briefly silhouettes the massive houses of Parliament at intervals against the night sky.

Here in this room it is another world: bright lights on white walls and green tiling, the gleaming metal of instruments, spotless glass doors of wall cabinets; from the adjoining scrub room the swish of running water, the bump of the foot pedal as it turns off and on, the shush-shush-shush of the brush; swift, sure, rubber-soled steps; cheerful voices, talking about ordinary things: "a picnic Saturday," "good fishing up north," "mow the lawn tomorrow." But under it all flows a current of tension and excitement.

Quietly nurses move into position. The pale young woman on the delivery table turns her head to look up at the nurse at her side.

"You don't know me this morning, do you?" says the nurse, smiling.

"Morning? What time is it?" Her voice is faint, sleepy.

"It's early Tuesday now," replies the nurse gently, and then, as a new contraction claims the young patient, "Here, hold tight to my arm—like this."

The clock says 12:34.

At the patient's head the anesthetist, a handsome, high cheek-boned woman in a white doctor's coat, arranges her equipment on a small table, then comes around and helps the patient roll on her side, talking quietly to her. "This is going to feel a bit cold for a moment." She swabs the lower back. "Now a little prick—hold as still as you can." With steady hands she marks the spot; the needle goes in, the solution injected, then swiftly out again.

"Gradually now you'll begin to feel numb. Your toes will feel tingly. Then you will feel no pain." Left hand in pocket, she uses her right hand to feel the contractions of the young patient's abdomen. Then, with her stethoscope, she listens for the fetal heartbeat.

The girl on the delivery table relaxes now and some color comes into her face. Half smiling, she looks toward the door to the scrub room, hearing above the sound of the water, the deep-throated laughter she knows so well.

Now the clock stands at 12:50.

There's a swish of an unfolding sterile gown, then brisk, firm footsteps, and the doctor—capped, masked, white-clad, and rubber-gloved—comes to the foot of the table, lifting both elbows to lean on the sheet-covered stirrups. Above the mask her great blue eyes are gentle and merry. "Well, Peggy, here we are at last. And everything's just fine." Her voice is bright, brisk, warm, confident.

Gently she examines Peggy to determine the baby's position, talking on, conversationally. "I saw Bill down there in the fathers' room—pretending to watch TV."

The girl laughs; then, with a new, joyous note in her voice, cries, "The baby's moving down!"

Doctor and anesthetist exchange a barely perceptible nod.

"You're doing beautifully, Peggy. Only a little while now. I'm going to be very busy and not very talkative now for a few minutes. Do just as Dr. Blatchford [the anesthetist] tells you."

It is 12:58.

Taking surgical scissors from the nurse, the doctor makes one swift, sure motion. Then her strong hands move on the forceps, and for a moment time seems to halt. Then the small dark head appears. Cradling the head in one hand, the doctor uses the other hand to insert a rubber tube in the tiny mouth, using suction to draw out mucous and clear the way for the baby's first breath.

And now here it comes: a breath of a wail, a gulp, then a real squall. Automatically everyone but the doctor and patient look at the clock.

It is 1:04, a minute of this August date that will forever belong in a special way to this new little person.

Slowly the rest of the small body appears.

"It's a girl, Peggy!" cries the doctor jubilantly, holding the red, squalling scrap high. The new mother, eyes shining, lifts her head to see.

Quickly, with the help of a nurse, the doctor cuts the cord, and, with a gesture of bestowal, lays the baby on the mother's breast. "You can start getting acquainted right away," she says, laughing.

Now the mood of the room has changed. The tension is gone. Each person goes about her job quickly, talking happily. Records are made out. The baby is cleaned with oil and wrapped in a blanket while the happy, tearful, smiling mother watches.

Now the doctor concentrates on bringing out the placenta, nature's outworn cocoon; making sure the mother is safe from hemorrhage; suturing the cut tissue that has facilitated the birth. The anesthetist stands by, keeping close watch of pulse and blood pressure of the young patient, now easing her with a whiff of gas, now wiping the beads of perspiration from her forehead.

The doctor strips off her gloves and leans over her patient. "You did wonderfully, Peggy. Have a good sleep. I'll see you tomorrow. Now I'll go put Father out of his misery." Half asleep, the girl smiles.

The doctor makes for the corridor, mask dangling, cap and gloves thrown aside, face alight. The tired young man pacing the fathers' room sees her coming and strides to meet her.

"It's a girl, Bill! And Peggy's splendid. Isn't that wonderful? I'm so happy for you." Their duet of laughter, bubbling out of relief, thankfulness, and delight, spills down the quiet hallway.

Another "Hilliard baby" has been born. It could have been the fifth, the five hundredth, or the five thousandth. Marion Hilliard never kept count of the number of babies she delivered, because she thought it would be boastful. Besides, who needs to keep count when each time brings the same feeling of joy at the miracle of new life? That was the way it always felt to her.

The baby is taken to the nursery, the mother to her room. After a few minutes with his wife the young father goes home. The doctor goes home too, perhaps to sleep the night out, perhaps to be called again once or twice before the sun comes up. At eight o'clock she is in the operating room; at ten she has coffee in the doctors' lounge before rounds of her patients in the hospital. Four days a week at her office she sees thirty to forty patients, some with gynecological ailments, many in various stages of pregnancy. By seven o'clock the last patient has left. The doctor goes home for dinner and a quiet evening, or to a party and sometimes on to a theater, concert, or to make a speech, always only a phone call away from the hospital.

She goes to sleep instantly, the telephone at her left hand, knowing that in an hour, or three hours, or perhaps only twenty minutes; a call will come. Sometimes she wakes in the still of the night, listening, and a moment later the phone rings. She scrambles into her clothes, her mind occupied with the patient who is even now being wheeled down the quiet corridor to the green and white, brightly lighted room where very shortly time will stand still for a moment and the miracle will happen again.

For thirty years this was Marion Hilliard's way of life. She loved every moment of it.

She was a teen-ager when she decided that she wanted to study medicine. On the verge of quitting medical school, she went into a delivery room for the first time and saw a baby being born. She knew instantly that, for her, this was what life was all about.

From the beginning her natural endowments—a sturdy constitution, native intelligence and abounding energy—combined admirably with her gifts of personality and her abundantly generous heart.

Her patients and their husbands treasured their relationship with her, and thought of her as a special member of the family, an unusual kind of friend. Her colleagues looked upon her as an artist in the practice of medicine. She won her goal of being known as "not just a good woman doctor, but a good doctor."

She came to know intimately the female fears and doubts that by ancient tradition are supposed to be kept secret, or, at most, whispered from woman to woman. With her own unique combination of briskness, cheerful confidence, and humorous warmth she helped to dispel confusion and fear in her patients, to wipe away doubts, and to give some of her own joy of living.

After thirty years she wrote of her clinical experience with wit, wisdom, and vigor, bestowing the same gift of cheerful enlightenment that she had given her patients, upon thousands of women and men all over the world.

A happy crusader, she helped build on the work of the pioneers among women in medicine. It was a source of "delirious pride" to her to have been one of the moving spirits in the spectacular development of the women's hospital that she entered as a junior intern and left as retiring chief of the department of obstetrics and gynecology.

The story of her fifty-six years tells of a joyful member of the family of man, a woman who deeply believed that "we are born to love—and we are loved." It ends abruptly, just as she is eagerly planning for a new chapter of life. The simple legend "Marion Hilliard—Beloved Physician" marks the place of her burial in a small cemetery at the edge of the St. Lawrence Seaway, only a short distance from the village house where her story begins.

The Glorious Years

> "I'll give you a silver spoon
> To feed your babes in the afternoon,
> If you'll marry me, me, me . . . ,"

sang the redheaded moppet at the top of his lungs. The mammas in the audience smiled and shifted in mild discomfort on the makeshift chairs, but the young ones, sitting on the barn floor, laughed and hugged themselves gleefully. They had heard the song a hundred times and knew every word to follow.

The nine-year-old blonde in the gingham dress, who was the other half of the duet, cleared her throat, rolled her enormous blue eyes up to where the summer sun sifted in through the rafters, and belted out the anticipated next verse:

> "I'll not accept the silver spoon
> To feed my babes in the afternoon
> For I won't marry you, you, you . . ."

Then, while the story unfolded through succeeding verses, she flashed a silent message to the stage crew hidden behind the old carriage robe that served as a curtain: *Get ready for the acrobatics next!*

The duet ended in a crash of applause. The singers ran behind the curtain, reappearing almost immediately in a foursome of acrobats. Hand over hand the youngsters tugged themselves up the ropes suspended from the huge beam. The mammas held their breath while the young fry called for, "Skin the cat! Skin the cat!"

It was an early summer Saturday afternoon of the year 1911 and another big show was in full swing in the Hilliard barn, in the St. Lawrence River town of Morrisburg, Ontario.

For two cents' admission the neighborhood audience could expect a full program, planned, produced, and directed by nine-year-old Marion Hilliard, assisted by her best friends, Marjorie, the tall, dark-haired one, and Clint, the redheaded singer. As everyone knew in advance that it would, the afternoon ended with Marion's and Clint's special interpretation of "Silver Threads among the Gold."

The Hilliards liked to put names to their houses. The yellow frame house where Marion was born had been named Piety Cottage, in honor of Mrs. Hilliard's father, a retired Methodist minister who now lived in the house with his wife and a widowed daughter. When, in Marion's first year, her family moved into the old red brick house with its twelve rooms, enormous veranda, spacious garden, and big barn they named it Oak Hall, for the huge, ancient tree that stood on the west lawn. Here Marion lived what she later called "those glorious childhood years."

Glory began at home, where Marion lived with her parents and four brothers and sisters, and spread outward through a neighborhood where every child was known and welcomed in every home, and through the bustling yet tranquil Canadian town on the edge of what Charles Dickens had called "this noble stream."

In this year of 1911 Marion's father, a man of medium height, blue eyes, and great dark beetling eyebrows, was in his late forties. In order of importance to his wife, he was superintendent of the Methodist Sunday school, a member of the town council, and a lawyer with an office downtown, a few blocks from home. Mrs. Hilliard, ten years younger than her husband, was slim, dark, and by turns intense, serene, and full of laughter. She was the Methodist minister's right-hand woman, the moving spirit of foreign missionary work of the church, and a member of the local school board.

Marion was a middle child, with a big brother and sister on one side, and a younger sister and brother on the other. Foster, who was going to be either a pianist or a minister, and pretty, gay Ruth were teen-agers. Helen Barbara, a dark-haired toddler, and Irwin, the frail, big-eyed baby, were often Marion's special charges, and she loved them devotedly. They called her "Ma," pronouncing the "a" as in "actor," the nearest they could get to saying her name.

Marion went often to the house where she had been born to see her grandparents and Aunt Laura, a young widow. Downtown she visited tiny, twinkly Aunt Sue Hilliard, who had a millinery shop with a cozy place upstairs to live in. Grandmother Hilliard used to live there too, but she had died when Marion was still a very little girl. Marion remembered the tall, strong-faced woman, whom everyone addressed with much respect, and how she talked with an Irish brogue. An hour's ride back in the country, Uncle Jim and the grown-up Hilliard cousins lived on a farm, where there were always new little kittens to play with; and down the river there were other cousins whom the Hilliards often visited at New Year's for dinner and a skating party.

Other uncles and aunts came to visit and wrote letters. Some of the most exciting letters came from Uncle Rob, Mrs. Hilliard's brother. He and his wife were missionaries in China, and Marion's mother was very proud of them. When he came home on furlough Uncle Rob had taught the children to sing "Jesus Loves Me" in Chinese, and Marion had sung it as part of an entertainment program of the Loyal Temperance League of Morrisburg.

Marion went to school in a little red schoolhouse, a five-minute walk away. (Some days, when family prayers ran overtime, it had to be a two-minute run, across the neighbors' lawns.) She took piano lessons every week and practiced every day. She and her family went to church every Sunday and sat in the same pew each week, just as they sat in the same reserved seats each time there was a concert at Merkley Hall. When school was out for the summer the whole family moved eight miles up the river to Iroquois Point to their cottage named Irwanna, a combination of Irwin and Anna, her father's and mother's first names.

At Oak Hall the barn was the children's favorite playground. It was occupied by Tommy Kay, the sleek black horse that had once run a mile in 2.2 minutes, a flock of chickens, and Daisy, the Jersey cow. The only drawback in the barn was the rooster; he liked to chase the children and once "caught" Marion and Marjorie, who shrieked for Mrs. Hilliard to come rescue them.

The big double doors opened onto the space for two carriages: a one-horse surrey with a fringe on top, and a buggy used for out-of-town business trips by Mr. Hilliard. These were replaced in the winter by two cutters that in summertime were stored in the rafters, covered with cotton dust covers, ideal for stage curtains. Ladders laid across the barn beams were natural trapezes. When the play called for costumes, the little girls raided Oak Hall's attic for Mrs. Hilliard's old hats and dresses.

Oak Hall's lawn allowed for a place to play croquet and a grass tennis court that, in wintertime, became a hockey rink.

"My father reasoned astutely that sports taught the value of a direct approach, concentrated energy and nobility in defeat or victory," wrote Marion in an article about her childhood days. "My mother saw the advantage of sport as a distraction from sin. They both played with us and so did every child in town."

Marion began to skate when she was so little that she almost skated on her ankles. When she and Marjorie thought they were good enough to play hockey they found that the boys did not agree. Marion sat on the puck to keep them from playing. The boys were furious. Six times they pulled her off; six times she fought her way back on. Finally Mrs. Hilliard was appealed to for a ruling, and she decided that any child who could really skate could be in the game.

Only a few clouds hovered over Marion in these glorious years.

She was afraid of the dark, hated the task of brushing bugs off the potato vines, and she and her younger sister were just like their mother when it came to thunderstorms—terrified. At the first clap of thunder Marion huddled on the couch and Helen made for the clothes closet.

Then there was Daisy the cow. Daisy provided milk for the Hilliards and some of their neighbors, so was worth her keep, but she was a thorn in the flesh of the Hilliard youngsters because she had to be escorted to and from the pasture. She was not mean, just a stubborn cow with a mind of her own.

"I hated the job of bringing the cow in from the fields in the evening," wrote Marion many years later, "because I was afraid of the dark and a little afraid of the cow. I tried getting someone to go with me, I tried to change jobs with someone else, and I tried putting it off so that someone would go in my place. Nothing worked. No matter how I twisted and tried, I always had to get that cow. Eventually I learned the great truth. The best way, the only way, was to get the cow right on time and get the job over with. I have been applying that same knowledge all my life to jobs I didn't want to do. It was the most useful lesson I ever learned."

Life at Oak Hall was full and fascinating. Marion and Marjorie played house with their dolls on the little porch Mr. Hilliard had built for them, and Marion told everyone that she intended to be "a married lady with six children." She and her small friends practiced writing on old pieces of slate, snitched rubber boots from the attic to go wading in the spring freshet, played tag on the tennis court, made skis out of barrel staves and kept them on with old suspenders fastened with carpet tacks. On the way home from school they stopped to "skin the cat" on Aunty Gale's fence, which was admirably suited for the purpose. On a winter day they sometimes hopped a ride with Frank, who drove the sled for the bakery; when he opened his stores at a customer's door they swooned with hunger at the steamy smell of hot bread on the cold air. If they had a penny or two they went around to the bakeshop to see if Mr. Cameron had made any of his special sidelines; if he had, they could choose a chocolate pig, a licorice stick, or an all-day sucker.

Now and then Marion would scamper up the side steps of Molson's Bank Building to her father's office where she would have a chat with his secretary, whom all the family called Mylilly, because that was the way he always referred to her. Nearly every day she called on the Von Dorans, who lived near Oak Hall. The Von Dorans' daughter, Georgeanna, a handsome young lady who wore dashing sports clothes, and was a fine horse-woman and a crack shot, was Marion's special friend. "Vonnie," as Marion called her, always talked with Marion as though she too were a grown-up person. They had many good chats and some jokes together. Because Vonnie's birthday was just two days before Marion's it was their tradition to have a special celebration together, when they would have ice cream and cake and make good wishes for each other.

In sun, cloud, rain, fog, and snow, through all the days of the seasons, the river played its own accompaniment to life. The sound and sight of river traffic as it creaked through the locks along Canal Street were in the background of the daytime hours. At night, when they were snugly in bed, the children could hear the river sounds in their dreams. From their elders they learned to say "down" to Montreal, "up" to Toronto, and "back" to Ottawa, as earlier folk had said when the river was still the only highway into Canada.

Now sparkling and beautiful, now turbulent and dangerous, now purring, now roaring, always hurrying on its endless journey, always mysterious, there was the river, always the river.

CHAPTER 3

River Town

For more than two hundred years after Jacques Cartier was swept by a storm into the river's mouth—one historian reports that it was August tenth, a day sacred to the memory of Laurentius—half of the St. Lawrence's seven hundred miles of shore line lay in silence. Thick forests of pines reaching a hundred feet into the sky crowded close to the water's edge, and in the dense, hidden places moose, deer, beaver, wolves, panthers, bears, and foxes lived out the seasons.

Flowing northeast to the Atlantic from the beautiful lake named Ontario by the Indians, the river widened in slow circles for fifty miles to pass around the hundreds of islands that lay as though flung there by a giant weeding out handfuls of northern wilderness and throwing them over his shoulder. When the river passed the headland chosen by the Iroquois for their councils of war, because it commanded a clear view in all directions, it narrowed to a third of a mile from shore to shore. Opposite the headland the rapids began, and the spine of the swiftly moving stream frothed and bubbled at intervals for sixty miles.

When the French penetrated the country they put names to these mad swirls of water—Rapide du Galop, Rapide du Plat, the Longue Sault.

With the outbreak of the American Revolution the river became a political dividing line; over its waters fled those of the colonies to the south whose fidelity to the crown of England earned them the name Loyalist. Among their number were the descendants of a group of Germans who had led a rootless life

since the early days of the eighteenth century. Adherents of
Calvin and Luther, they had escaped to England when their
homeland, the Palatine, became a theater of war between Louis
XIV and nearly all the rest of Europe. From England they had
come to America, fanning out into the rich, agricultural lands
of Pennsylvania and New York. Most of those in Upper New
York State had followed the leadership of Sir William Johnston
and his son John, and were among the two hundred Loyalists
who walked nineteen days through the forest to Montreal in
December, 1775, to escape capture by the American rebels, and
there joined the King's Royal Regiment of New York.

Nine years later, the war having ended, six hundred Germans
were among those entitled to crown lands to recompense them
for the farms they had left south of the border. Each soldier was
allowed one hundred acres on the river, with additional allot-
ments for wife and children. Allocations were made in an orderly
fashion, with an eye to congeniality of these pioneers who would
carve homes and communities out of the forest lands. To the far
east, bordering the Catholic province of Quebec, the Roman
Catholic Highlanders were placed; next to them came the Scotch
Presbyterians, whose place of birth, if not religious persuasion,
was the same, and west of the Scots the German Lutherans were
assigned to the land opposite the rapids.

In June of 1784 the German soldiers met the government
agent, drew lots out of a hat for their river-front property, and
ascended the river, each dropping off at the spot designated as
the boundary of his property. By the time winter set in, each had
cleared three-quarters of an acre of land and built a one-story log
cabin roofed with overlapping strips of elm bark, and together
they had built the first Protestant church in Ontario.

The great pine trees of Dundas, as the county was named in
1792, proved a mine of wealth to these pioneers. Destined for
ships' masts, logs measuring ninety to a hundred and twenty
feet long and forty to forty-eight inches in diameter were dragged
from the forests by teams of a dozen pairs of horses and rafted
down the river close to shore to avoid the rapids. Opposite

Rapide du Plat a trading post sprang up, later to be incorporated as a village and named Morrisburg.

A former schoolmaster was employed by the German community to act as visiting tutor, going from house to house to teach the young.

Then once again war came to this group of emigrants who had for the second time tried to settle themselves in the New World. Battle action in the first year of the War of 1812 had taken place far to the west of the settlement, but in the fall of 1813 the American army began to sweep down the river with the intention of knocking out all forts as far as Montreal. Warned by Lieutenant Duncan Clark, a Canadian Paul Revere, the British and Canadians mustered eight hundred and fifty men to make a stand at Chrysler's Farms, a few miles east of Morrisburg. From daybreak of November eleventh until late afternoon a battle was fought "with the most resolute bravery by both combatants," according to a Canadian historian. The Americans withdrew across the river, and the tides of war flowed in another direction.

Some years later, when Queen Victoria awarded medals to those who had acquitted themselves well, a special medal was struck for Canadians who had fought at Chrysler's Farms.

By this time emigrants had poured in from the British Isles and several new generations had been born on Canadian soil; indeed, in the twenty-seven years preceding the unification of Upper and Lower Canada in 1840, the population of Ontario, then known as Upper Canada, increased fivefold.

In the social order of nineteenth-century Canada none ranked higher than the descendants of a genuine United Empire Loyalist who was also a "medal man," a holder of the queen's award.

A few years after the end of the American Revolutionary War an unordained missionary from the Methodist Conference of New York State came across the border and set about converting the rural and village folk between Niagara and the river town of Cornwall. On horseback, sometimes on foot, he and his followers made their way to remote cabins, farmhouses, and settlements, carrying their gospel of repentance and seeking salvation to avoid the fires of hell and insure a life in the hereafter.

Methodism swept through the Ontario countryside for the next seventy years, claiming a quarter of the population by the time of the 1861 census. In German Lutheran Dundas County, the first Methodist church was built in 1797 in a grove of pines atop the very headland on the river where, not long before, the Iroquois had held their councils of war. A half century later thirteen hundred of the county's fifty-five hundred souls belonged to Methodist churches.

The wave of conversion had not been unhampered by political events. During the War of 1812 and afterward, the Methodist movement that had originated in New York State was subject to close scrutiny by provincial authorities, lest the convert's loyalty to the crown be subverted while his soul was being saved. A Methodist minister's legal status was nil; one of them who unlawfully married a young couple was tried, found guilty of high misdemeanor, and sentenced to fourteen years' banishment—whereupon he and his family were placed in a canoe and ferried across the river to the United States.

England sent her own missionaries into Canada to compete with the brand of Methodism coming over the border. In 1820 the Wesleyan Methodist Church of Canada was established by these politically approved clergy, who succeeded in attracting the majority of Methodists into its fold. Shortly afterward the minority group formed the Methodist Episcopal Church. By the mid-1800s the "Wesleyans" outnumbered the "M.E.s" by slightly more than two to one.

Thomas Hilliard was a lad in his teens when he ran away from home in Enniskillen, the capital of Fermanagh County, in the north of Ireland and came to Canada in 1837. To earn the money to buy a bush farm—a tract of uncleared land—he drove a stagecoach between rural Ontario towns. On the run into the river trading center later named Morrisburg one of his regular passengers was a compatriot. Charlotte Gillespie, a robust, dignified young woman had emigrated with her father, a captain in the Royal Engineers, and her brother James. She divided her time between her father's farm and her brother's home in the village where he had established himself as a builder.

Both young people were of mixed English and Irish descent and members of the Church of England. Thomas Hilliard's ancestors had come from Yorkshire to Ireland with Cromwell's armies. Captain Gillespie traced his family line to the Tudors.

After their marriage in 1843, Thomas bought his farm in Osnabruck Township, several miles back in the country from the river. There they brought up a family of eleven children, of which Marion Hilliard's father, born February second, 1863, and christened Thomas Irvine Foster, was the eighth. Although the children were christened in the Anglican Church, the family attended Methodist services that had been made easily accessible by the early missionaries and their followers, and one of the children was named for John Wesley.

The life of the bush farm was a harsh one. All the sons except one, James, left home early to seek their fortunes elsewhere in Canada or in the States; even their father gave over the farming to James and spent his last years before his death in the late 1880s working as tax collector for the township. Susan, the one daughter who did not marry, went to Morrisburg and opened a millinery shop.

Encouraged by his good record in the country grammar school, Marion's father went to Morrisburg at the age of thirteen. The public-school system, begun by the German founders of Dundas in 1807, now boasted a first-rate high school, and young Irwin (not liking any of his three names, he discarded two of them and changed the Irvine to Irwin) enrolled, after arranging with a town family to earn his keep by fetching water and wood and running errands. Three years later he graduated with honors, having made a special contribution to school life by helping to start the high school's first newspaper.

After matriculation at Osgoode Hall, the Ontario law school in Toronto, he returned to Morrisburg to read law in the office of

James Pliny Whitney, a tower of Conservative strength in Dundas County, who imparted an interest in politics as well as a knowledge of law to his young protégé. In 1885, when he was twenty-two, Irwin Hilliard passed examinations for barrister and solicitor and began work in the office of Frank Tyrrell, another Morrisburg barrister. When Mr. Tyrrell died in 1898, Mr. Hilliard took over the practice.

The year Irwin Hilliard was born two young sons of a Bytown (later Ottawa) innkeeper, Thomas and Foster McAmmond, were converted to Methodism—the family was Presbyterian by tradition—and made a pact to go into the ministry. They were the second generation of the McAmmond family to be born in Canada, their paternal grandfather having come from the north of Ireland at the turn of the century; their mother, a woman of Scotch descent, had come from Ireland as a girl.

Along with their nine brothers and sisters the two boys had been brought up to help with the family enterprise, which catered to farmers coming into the Bytown market with their produce. They waited on table, then sang to entertain the customers in the evening. Spirited young men with fine tenor voices, they had a full repertoire of old-fashioned songs from their grandfather's home country.

On the eve of his departure for his first charge as a Methodist missionary to the lumber country of northern Ontario young Thomas McAmmond wooed and won Ann Jane Hare, a handsome, well-born girl whose parents had emigrated from England. Anna Caroline McAmmond, Marion Hilliard's mother, was the fifth of their eight children.

Life in the rugged, sometimes dangerous wilderness was a far cry from Ann Jane's comfortable, protected girlhood, but she packed away her fine trousseau in favor of a wardrobe of sturdy homespun dresses like those of the women in her husband's congregations. (Later she dug into the trunks for her riding silks to make dresses for her little girls.) Poverty was their constant companion, and storms of the long winter increased the hardship. While her husband rode his circuit on horseback Ann Jane cheerfully stretched their meager provisions, stoutly maintaining that "God will never see us want."

Once, marooned by a storm while her husband was away, she played surgeon for herself, cutting off a festering and infected thumb down to the joint with a butcher knife.

For forty years, following Reverend McAmmond's brief period of study at Albert College, a Methodist seminary on Lake Ontario, the family moved from one small Ontario town to another, spending two or three years in each pastorate, in the Methodist fashion.

The Reverend McAmmond was a high-strung man; he nearly always suffered from spasms of nausea before preaching a sermon. Though disposed to be fair, he had a temper. Once, after chiding a parishioner about his habit of going to sleep during services, he hurled a hymnbook at the heedless transgressor as he slept in the front pew. He loved fast horses. With his favorite, Old Mag, he liked to race trains to the railroad crossing. He believed that pride was woman's besetting sin and forbade his womenfolk to wear jewelry or feathers in their hats. Until after his death in 1912, Marion's mother respected her father's wishes and did not even wear her wedding ring.

The stouthearted Ann Jane was a whirlwind of energy and competence. It was suspected by some parishioners that occasionally she wrote her husband's sermons. The village doctor in one of the towns where they had lived, a man grown old and retired, met Marion Hilliard in Toronto at the peak of her career. After a spirited conversation in which she pleased the old man by talking "medical talk" she ran off in a hurry, as usual, and when she had gone he smiled and said, "She's just like her grandmother."

True to the brothers' pact, Foster McAmmond entered the Methodist ministry, and the tie between them became closer when he married Ann Jane's younger sister, Barbara Caroline Hare. After filling several pulpits in Quebec and eastern Ontario he became principal of Stanstead Wesleyan College on the

Quebec-Vermont border. Though geographically separated, the two couples kept closely in touch, and after the death of Foster's and Barbara's only child they lavished their love and interest upon Thomas's and Ann Jane's children.

One of their favorites was Anna Caroline, born October twenty-second, 1873, and named partly for her aunt. Anna was a fast-developing child who very early began to play the little mother with the younger children and help with the extra duties of the Methodist parsonage. She showed musical aptitude as a child and by the age of twelve played the organ for Sunday school. Later she played the accompaniment when she and her younger sisters, Laura and Luella, sang together. Taught by their father and Uncle Foster, they learned the old songs once enjoyed by the guests at Mr. McAmmond's Inn at Bytown. "The McAmmond sisters" were known over the countryside for their lovely singing voices and comely vivacity.

Although Reverend McAmmond's earnings were small, he and his wife were determined upon a higher education for the five of their children who survived babyhood. When Anna was fifteen her older brother, Fletcher, had completed medical school at Queen's University, and a second brother, Robert, was studying at Wesleyan Theological Seminary. The resources of the Methodist preacher had been stretched about as far as they would go.

From Quebec his brother and sister-in-law wrote to propose that Anna come to them at Stanstead, where she could earn part of her expenses teaching music and make her home with them. It was just the lift that was needed, and eventually it was possible to send the two younger girls to Ontario Ladies' College to prepare for teaching, thus fulfilling the parents' dreams for their children.

Three years later Anna graduated from Stanstead, winning a gold medal for scholarship and proficiency in music. One of her most prized possessions was the volume of Chopin that was presented to her; it was printed in Leipzig and upon the cover her name was inscribed in gold.

At eighteen Anna came home to the parsonage in Elma, Ontario, a village a few miles north of Morrisburg, and plunged in to help her father and mother with church and Sunday-school affairs. The pastor of the Morrisburg Methodist Church, paying a visit to his colleague in Elma, took a good look at her and went home to tell the young lawyer who was such a mainstay in the Morrisburg Methodist Sunday school that it was time he got married and there was just the girl for him at the Elma parsonage.

Irwin Hilliard had just turned thirty. He lived with his sister Susan, the Morrisburg milliner, and divided his time between the law office and the Sunday-school work in which he was so deeply interested. That fall he was invited to present a paper on some of his ideas about Sunday-school programs at a regional convention. In his audience were Reverend Thomas McAmmond and his daughter Anna.

Many years later Mrs. Hilliard told her daughter, "The minute I heard your father speak, I knew this was the man I would like to marry. The thing about him that attracted me right from the start was that he would say what he felt and thought with great conviction, regardless of how popular or unpopular it might be. Of course he was sometimes wrong about things, but when he discovered it, he would always admit it—after a couple of days."

On the second day of the convention the two young people met. Anna congratulated Irwin on the excellent paper he had given. This was the girl his pastor had told him about, he realized. He invited her to go driving, and the courtship began. The following June fourteenth they were married by Reverend McAmmond at the Elma church. After a honeymoon spent mountain climbing in the Adirondacks they settled down in Morrisburg.

The villages and pleasant farmlands along the St. Lawrence were only a hundred years beyond their pioneer days. The erstwhile trading post had been incorporated as a village just thirty years before. The past fifty years had seen construction of a string of forty-seven canals to circumvent the dangerous rapids; the opening run of the first steam-driven mail boat, the *Lord Elgin*; and the building of the Grand Trunk Railroad that ran across the northern boundary of Morrisburg on its way between Montreal and Toronto. The War of 1812 had faded into history, and between the Morrisburg dock and Waddington, New York, across the river, a ferry line was doing a brisk business.

The German founding fathers had chosen English place names. The county was named for Henry Dundas, Lord Melville, the English colonial secretary in the 1790s. The township, Williamsburgh, honored William Henry, son of George III, who as William IV came to the throne in 1831. His sister, Princess Charlotte Augusta Matilda, was similarly celebrated by namesake townships and villages.

Morrisburg itself had followed no such historic sentiment. In the spring of 1864, four years after its incorporation as a village, it simply adopted the name "out of compliment to an honorable gentleman," James Morris, one of its residents. Mr. Morris had shown his appreciation by the gift of a hundred dollars for the purchase of a clock for the town hall.

The river was still the center of all life. Lock 23 on the run from Montreal to Kingston, named the Rapide du Plat for the rapids opposite the town in the middle of the river, lay at the foot of the town's main street. Three miles long, ten feet deep, and a hundred feet wide, it was constructed of cut stone, with gates of solid timber eighteen inches thick. A stone retaining wall ran west from the business district, paralleling the choice residential streets, and on a small man-made island surrounding the lockmaster's house was a park with gay flowers and Lombardy poplars.

In earlier days of canal history great barges loaded with lumber were dragged through the lock by horses plodding along the towpath. Now many of the boats locking through were steam-driven and called in at Lock 23 for grains brought from the back country to the mill elevator at the foot of the canal, butter known the world over for its excellence, and apples from the orchards of Morrisburg and Iroquois, its western neighbor, where an orchardist named John McIntosh had had particularly notable success with his crops.

Mr. Hilliard's law office was on the second floor of Molson's Bank Building, part of a red-brick business block built by Captain Alexander Farlinger in 1872 when he retired from his successful career as river pilot and owner of the *Lord Elgin*. Not far away was the block built by H. G. Merkley, an industrialist. Not to be outdone by the captain, Mr. Merkley had included a large public hall whose regular winter schedule of concerts and lectures attracted audiences from all of eastern Ontario.

Most important to the newly married couple, Morrisburg was a churchgoing community, and a center of quite superior secondary education. The population of two thousand people supported, besides the Hilliards' own Methodist church, thriving congregations of Lutherans, Presbyterians, Baptists, Anglicans, and Roman Catholics. The Morrisburg Collegiate Institute, which had replaced the high school in 1890, boasted a faculty of qualified specialists in the major subjects taught, and was conducted somewhat like a junior college, with its separate departments of study. Promising young people came from some distance to board in the town during the school session so that they could graduate from the MCI, and a high proportion of them went on to Queen's University at Kingston, McGill in Montreal, or the University of Toronto.

The Hilliards' marriage was a love match firmly based on great mutual admiration and sharing of values. Often Mrs. Hilliard walked to meet her husband when he came home at noon, and it was a familiar sight to the neighbors to see them strolling, arm in arm, laughing and talking. She loved to go driving, and he loved to take her. She assumed that she was called to higher things than doing all her own cooking and housework, and he was in complete agreement. Until Marion and her sister were old enough to take over a good share of household responsibility there was always a maid of all work in the household, often a niece or cousin earning her room and board while attending the MCI. The neighbor to whom the laundry was trundled on wagon or sled each week and "Aunty Gale," the neighbor who did most of the dressmaking, were part of the way of life in which the Hilliard children grew up.

From their youngest days they were accustomed to their mother's many church and community activities. She filled the role of church deaconess, visiting the sick and praying with the troubled, always eager to make sure that they were "right with the Lord." She believed that the purpose of life was to serve others. When her daughters urged her to be more active in a woman's group whose program was educational and social rather than religious she explained, "There are so many other women who will support that, but not all of them are willing to do the things I do."

Foreign missions was her most consuming interest, and she strove to fire women of the church with a vision of "bringing Christ to people in the uttermost parts of the earth." She organized a Mission Band, a children's missionary group, to teach the young about the children of China and Japan and the work of the church missions schools. The flame of dedication burned bright in her, and her strength of purpose and surety of conviction put her in demand as a speaker.

"We must be women like Hannah," she cried in one speech to a missionary group, "and before our child is placed in our arms must dedicate that life to the Lord! Talk about Livingston at breakfast, Carey at dinner, Paton at supper—but that is not enough. There must be in our homes a Christian atmosphere which our children breathe into their souls, giving them the true value of life, the service of Jesus Christ being the only thing worth living for."

Her public activities never took precedence over her concern for her children, and she could be counted on to hear out their problems, to advise, comfort, and be definite about where the path of duty lay and what values were involved in a decision. She never lost an opportunity to encourage and inspire, not only her own children, but also others in the church and community.

A successful businessman in eastern Ontario recalls how, when he was a boy, she always took time to thank him and his friends when they helped her at church suppers.

"I can see her now," he reminisced, "looking at me with those great big eyes and saying, 'You've got the light of the Lord in your eyes. I know you'll be a fine man.' Gosh, I can hardly remember things my own mother and father said to me when I was that age, but I've never forgotten her words. She had a way of making you believe you amounted to something."

Marion always said that her mother's laughter and her acute sense of anticipation were among her loveliest memories of "the glorious years." Whether it was a birthday cake, a picnic, or the fun and happiness of Christmas morning Mrs. Hilliard always looked forward eagerly to life's small adventures.

"That sense of eagerness has come down to all of us," Marion once wrote. " 'Enter every open door,' my mother told us. We always have."

She loved to play games with the children and was a good example to them, teaching them how to lose gracefully. When they all trouped out onto the lawn for a round of croquet they knew that, win or lose, the game was the thing for Mother; on the other hand, Father minded losing terribly and didn't care who knew it!

As a parent Mr. Hilliard was "stern, insistent on obedience, but implacably just and fair," wrote Marion in a moment of reminiscence. Out of her years of experience as a counselor on marriage relations she added, "He was a wonderful husband, full of fire but gentle."

To save his weak eyes his wife read to him from his law books when he was preparing a case, and bore with him in the dilemma posed by his chronic indigestion and his love of indigestible foods, catering to his appetite for roast pork and rich desserts and taking tender care of him when it brought him to grief.

Though dutiful, she could be devious. He rather fancied the

beard and mustache he wore early in their marriage. She secretly thought they spoiled his looks. One day after they had entertained a bearded guest for dinner she remarked casually that it was too bad that Mr. X's beard was "so untidy," recalling that it got stained when he drank his coffee. The next day Mr. Hilliard shaved his face clean, and although many of his neighbors failed to recognize him at first, he enjoyed the approval he won at home.

Like his father-in-law, Mr. Hilliard loved fast horses, but, disapproving of horse races, he confined his exercise of Tommy Kay to brisk drives to and from the towns where he went to court, and taking his family for country drives.

He was all business when on the job. Other lawyers visiting the registry office might stop for a bit of gossip with the clerks, but he would make his request and leave immediately. He was prone to great mental absorption and once, lost in thought, passed his wife on the street without recognizing her.

His first important assignment was that of legal advisor to Georgeanna Von Doran. The young woman was appointed administrator of the Dardis estate, which involved a good-sized portion of Morrisburg property and a large collection of heirs. She and her mother and father, a descendant of a United Empire Loyalist and "medal man" from the Battle of Chrysler's Farms, lived near Oak Hall and took a neighborly interest in the young Hilliards.

The young woman's business acumen and straightforward friendliness impressed Mr. Hilliard, and she valued his integrity as well as his legal judgment. They became devoted friends, although their way of life was very different. She was as ardent a Liberal as he was a Conservative. She attended the church of her German Lutheran forebears and, subject to no such restrictions as those of her Methodist neighbors, was one of the lively, high-spirited leaders of Morrisburg's younger social set.

Mrs. Hilliard was fond of her good neighbor, but concerned about her immortal soul. Once, in an effort to suggest a way for Georgeanna to live what she felt would be a more useful life, she suggested to Mrs. Von Doran that her daughter adopt a child from a family left destitute by a deserting father.

Marion's parents deeply believed that as religious, educated people, their duty lay in giving freely of themselves for the betterment of church and community, and to equip their children to do the same. They bent their energies to the Sunday-school work that had brought them together, were in the forefront of the temperance movement, and held public office in the town.

Both offered their services in civic affairs when they felt strongly that something needed doing. Mrs. Hilliard ran for a position on the school board because she felt that the town's teachers were being underpaid and she wanted to work for salary raises for them. While she was on the board an economy-minded group moved to change the Collegiate Institute back to a high school staffed with generalists rather than specialists; she stayed on until the move was defeated. Although she lived by the philosophy of "turning the other cheek," she could be a fighter when a principle was at stake, and, to the Hilliards, providing the best possible education for the town's children held a very high priority.

Because their family was widely spaced—the oldest was sixteen when the youngest was born—one or more of the Hilliards' children was in the university over a period of twenty-three years. Once a neighbor asked Mr. Hilliard how he had managed to educate his family, which eventually included a minister, two doctors, and two schoolteachers. He said that he had once figured out the cost and mentioned a sizable sum, adding proudly, "And it was worth every cent."

Mr. Hilliard served a number of terms on the town council. Once he ran for the office because he and his wife were alarmed about the effect of poor lighting upon the children in their student years. A proposed system of electric meters that would bring sufficient revenue to repair the power plant and provide more adequate lighting was opposed by a majority of the townspeople because of the added cost. Though his stand was unpopular, Mr. Hilliard's sincere concern for the young people and his reputation as a man of integrity won him the election. He was asked to take charge of the plant, and the meter system was installed, after which he resigned from the council, feeling that his contribution had been made.

He was a staunch member of the Conservative Party, for which he worked devotedly in Dundas County from the time of his first association with Sir James Whitney. He parted company with the party only once, when it proposed legalizing the sale of beer in Ontario. Once when his son was driving him about the countryside on a schedule of campaign speeches the lad ventured to suggest that his father was somewhat overstating the Conservative case.

"Come now, Dad, you don't really believe all those things you're saying, do you?" he asked.

"My son," replied Mr. Hilliard, "anything great ever done for this country was done by the Conservatives."

CHAPTER 4

Tuesday's Child

Three days after Mr. and Mrs. Hilliard celebrated their ninth wedding anniversary, on June seventeenth, 1902, a cool and cloudy summer Tuesday, Anna Marion Hilliard was born at Piety Cottage, their quaint two-story-and-an-attic frame house standing almost within earshot of the famous Rapide du Plat.

The new little girl was named Marion by her mother, who had read or heard the name and liked it, and Anna by her father, for his beloved wife. In a double sense she owed her life to her mother. Mrs. Hilliard had not been well after her first two children were born, and the gynecologist who performed a necessary operation, impressed upon Mr. Hilliard her need for protective care. He took the doctor's words very seriously, carrying his wife up and down stairs, seeing to it that she had household help, and making it clear that he did not want her to risk another pregnancy. But Anna Hilliard pointed out to her husband that Canada was underpopulated and said she felt that educated couples with high moral standards were duty bound to have large families.

When he saw that his wife was determined that they should make this contribution to the future of Canada, Mr. Hilliard insisted that there was to be no more amateur midwifery (Mrs. Hilliard's mother had delivered her first two children), and went out to call on his good friend Dr. Charles Hickey.

Tall, handsome, heavily bearded, Dr. Hickey was a graduate of McGill University's School of Medicine. Like Mr. Hilliard, he was a Conservative and a public-spirited man. He had been one of Morrisburg's leading doctors for thirty years and was in his early sixties when he brought Marion Hilliard into the world. Along with the good doctor came Miss Theo Nash, a young woman who had chosen to begin her career as a nurse in her own home town.

Foster, the Hilliards' first child, named for his mother's minister uncle, and Ruth, named by Mrs. Hilliard for one of her favorite books of the Bible, were bundled off to spend the summer with their grandparents and Aunt Luella in Avonmore, a nearby village where the Reverend McAmmond was finishing his last pastorate before retirement.

It was a normal birth and, with Miss Nash's good care, Mrs. Hilliard recovered quickly. When Foster and Ruth returned they were ushered upstairs to their parents' room where the new little sister, rosy, quiet, and peaceable, slept in her old-fashioned cradle. Then, when darkness fell, the baby woke up and began to cry; during her whole first year she cried all night long.

In the fall the Hilliards moved to Oak Hall, Grandfather and Grandmother McAmmond took over Piety Cottage as their retirement home, and Mr. Hilliard's niece Bertha came up from the farm to take care of the new baby and help Mrs. Hilliard in return for her room and board while she studied music in Morrisburg. Cousin Bertha had had some experience with young ones, and quickly decided that the baby cried purely and simply from hunger. She privately thought that her aunt followed the doctor's instructions not to overfeed the baby a bit too much to the letter, and she observed that instead of relaxing as a mother should when breast feeding a baby, Aunt Anna used the time to accomplish something else, such as giving little Ruth her piano lesson.

One night when her aunt and uncle were out, Cousin Bertha tried out her theory by giving little Marion some bread and milk. The baby stopped crying and went right off to sleep.

The splendid constitution of which Marion was to boast in later years and which was at least one-third of the secret of her success did not begin to develop until she matured at age thirteen. As a baby she was healthy but quiet, almost passive, and as a child wiry and a bit on the spindly side. The first sign of what was to be a gourmand's appetite was her passionate fondness for butter. Once when she had been dressed to go calling, in the pastel frock and pale blue hair ribbon her mother chose to set off her great blue eyes and ash-blond hair, she found a bowl of butter in the icebox and, when discovered, was lapping it up like a little puppy. Ribbon, hair, and dress were lathered with yellow smears from her feast.

Marion very early showed a characteristic she retained all her life: she loved to be on the go. In her elegant carriage trimmed with green taffeta she was wheeled by her sister and brother up and down Victoria Street, beside Oak Hall. When winter came they put her in the doll cutter, a snowtime doll carriage made for the children by Grandfather McAmmond, and took her for exciting rides over the snowy roads.

They found her a trustful passenger. Once they accidentally dumped her into a two-foot ditch, and she lay quietly until they ran and got someone to lift her out. Another time the doll cutter hit a bump under the snow and the baby rolled directly into the path of an oncoming horse-drawn sleigh. Frantically her sister dragged little Marion into the snowdrifts beside the road. Then, remembering the pennies she had thoughtfully provided for the outing by jimmying open her missionary "mite box," she took her placid little sister to the candy store for a treat.

Neighbors who had witnessed both the rescue and the trip to the candy store brought the incident to parental attention and Mrs. Hilliard took prompt action. After satisfying herself that Marion was unhurt and unfrightened she asked sternly where the money for the candy had come from. Completely without guile, Marion told of the rifling of the missionary funds, to which she had been an interested witness. It was the beginning of understanding that must come to all younger family members of the code by which one does not tell on brothers and sisters.

Some years later when Marion's younger sister had got away with a forbidden act without having to tell an outright lie Marion knew it but kept silent. Then one night after supper their father called both into his study. The interview was short.

"You did this and didn't tell?" he asked young Helen.

"Yes, Father."

"And you knew and didn't tell?" he asked Marion.

"Yes, Father."

"Then you are both guilty of deception, which is the same as telling a lie," pronounced their lawyer father succinctly. "Hold out your hands."

A couple of good thumps with a ruler ended this lesson, which neither sister ever forgot.

"The home of Mr. Irwin Hilliard, Barrister, brother-in-law of the bride, was the scene of a very pretty house wedding, Wednesday evening, when Rev. James Morgan Warner, B.A., was united in Marriage with Miss Luella E. McAmmond, M.E., youngest daughter of Rev. Thomas McAmmond and sister of the Rev. R. B. McAmmond of West China," reported the *Morrisburg Leader* a week after Marion's fifth birthday in 1907.

Aunt Luella's wedding to her high-school sweetheart was the first Marion ever attended, and it was a real family affair. Grandfather McAmmond not only gave the bride away but also assisted Grandmother's brother, Uncle "J. J." Hare, in performing the ceremony. Aunt Laura sang "O, Perfect Love," and the bride, recounted the *Leader,* "was preceded by her little niece, Miss Marion Hilliard, strewing the ribboned aisle with marguerites."

The bride's dress of cream silk trimmed with chiffon and satin, her real lace veil, which had been worn by Mother and Aunt Laura at their weddings, and her bouquet of white roses and lilies-of-the-valley; the dining room and library decorated with roses from the garden; Father serving as toastmaster; and the trip to the station to see the happy couple off—all added up to the most thrilling day yet in Marion's five years.

For the rest of her life Marion loved weddings—the service, music, and afterward the tears, joy, and family fun—and some of the best letters with which she favored her friends were descriptions of weddings she attended or took part in; but always a home wedding, with the family and close friends gathered together, seemed to her the ideal way for a young couple to start their lives together.

Marion's older sister loved to tell how her mother attempted to convey the facts of life to her by way of two books, *Perfect Girlhood* and *Perfect Womanhood*, the texts of which were somewhat vague. One chapter was particularly puzzling; titled "Hands Off," it left the teen-ager wondering, "Off of what?"

Her own first recollection of her mother's inducting her into the great mystery of life made an unforgettable impression on Marion. It came only a few months after Aunt Luella's wedding, and years later Marion wrote of the incident and how it influenced her in her choice of a profession.

"My mother took me into our guest room—I remember it was chilly because it was unheated unless we had company—and pulled open the bottom bureau drawer. The smell of camphor and cashmere stung my nostrils and I saw the drawer was filled with beautiful baby clothes.

" 'This is our secret,' my mother told me with a sweetness in her face. 'We are going to have a baby.'

" 'Does Daddy know?' I whispered.

"My mother chuckled and closed the drawer. 'You can come here whenever you like and look at the baby's things,' she told me.

"I learned of the tenderness and responsibility of having a baby in those few moments. For many years the thought of babies evoked a smell of camphor and cashmere and the loving tone of my mother's voice. I wish all women could have such an introduction to childbearing. It would settle something that too often is in doubt—that the business of creation is warm and fundamental. Babies are the result of warm love that overflows into physical union. That's my idea of sex education."

The Morrisburg of Marion's early years was a horse-and-buggy town, except for one automobile, owned by the piano and organ dealer and dubbed "Mr. Fetterly's sawmill" by the villagers because it was so red and so noisy.

There were three stretches of cement sidewalk in town; the dusty streets and footpaths were dampened by the town water sprinkler each summer day.

In many homes there were aspidistras in the living rooms and player pianos pumped out "Wait Till the Sun Shines, Nellie," and "After the Ball Is Over." The Hilliard living room was adorned with garden flowers and an upright piano that was constantly in use, since each little Hilliard began music lessons at the age of five. Sometimes one had to practice at the Von Dorans'. Eventually there had to be two pianos.

The ladies sometimes entertained each other for afternoon tea, always with a certain amount of ceremony. Occasionally there were dinner parties, after which some non-Methodists played cards, but more often evenings were spent in conversation. Many of the townspeople had attended institutions of higher learning, were great readers, and had fine personal libraries. Like Mr. and Mrs. Hilliard, most parents were primarily concerned with their children's religious training and the quality of their education.

Except for the winter concerts and entertainments at Merkley Hall, social life centered in the churches. Villagers were objective in their attitude toward differences in religious persuasions, and all denominations supported each other's teas, suppers, and bazaars. The monthly Ladies' Aid suppers were particularly popular, since customers could eat their fill for ten cents' each and still guarantee the "Ladies" a comfortable profit.

The biggest event of the year was the Union Picnic, when all church members ferried themselves and a mountain of food over to Broder's Island, a sizable national park in the middle of the river. After a hearty dinner of roast turkey, leg of lamb, boiled potatoes, and samplings of the long row of cakes and pies baked by the women of the churches, washed down with innumerable cups of tea from a steaming boiler on the outdoor stove, the young fry ran three-legged races and held jumping contests to shake down the food. Then their Sunday-school teachers took them swimming, leaving the elders to their conversation.

In the long snowy winters there were skating and cutter racing on the frozen canal. No good Methodist family would watch the racing, much less take part in it, but all children who were good skaters could have the glorious experience of struggling up the canal against the west wind, then opening their coats and sailing home, being careful to avoid the edge of the snowbanks on either side.

A new season was ushered in by the Queen's Birthday, May twenty-fourth, celebrated much as youngsters across the river in the States celebrated the Fourth of July, with firecrackers by day and rockets and sparklers by night. On the roadway outside Oak Hall the neighborhood children pooled their fireworks under the watchful but benevolent eyes of porch-sitting parents.

Summertime brought the all-day boat excursions up the river on the *Thousand Islander,* a trip across to the States on *The Eloise* or *The Morrisburg,* most famous of the ferryboats, and happy hours playing in the coves that scalloped the river bank and the crisscross of creeks that drained into the river. Morrisburg children learned early to swim, and row a boat.

Soon after school started in the fall came the day when the Citizens Band paraded up the gravel road to announce the opening of the three-day Morrisburg Fair. Everybody went to see the exhibits of fancywork, quilts, home baking, woven rugs, plants, flowers, vegetables, preserves, and pickles. Prizes were given for everything, including the prettiest baby and the best-ironed shirt. Visitors wandered through the poultry building, had a look at the sheep and cattle, and stopped to admire the horses high stepping it up and down before the judges. In those days the most satisfactory sight in the world was a well-fed, well-groomed horse with polished harness, a shining buggy, and a good horsewoman handling the reins. Off to one side children clustered around the steam-driven merry-go-round, for it was well known that the owner could not resist a little one who looked on with awe and longing, whether he had the price of admission or not.

The fall after her little brother's second birthday eleven-year-old Marion came home from school one day, washed his face, combed his hair, dressed him in his best clothes, and, unbeknownst to the rest of the family, took him to the fair grounds to enter him in the baby contest.

A frail, small child, he seemed an unlikely candidate, but Marion sat in the contestants' ring with him on her lap, beaming upon all comers and serene in the conviction that her baby was the most beautiful of all. Strolling through the fair grounds, Vonnie came upon them.

"For heaven's sake, what have you got that little thing here for?" asked Marion's outspoken neighbor. Furiously Marion turned her face away, not deigning to reply. When another baby won the contest she cried all the way home, dragging the baby at her heels. It was almost the end of a beautiful friendship, for Vonnie thought it too good a story to go untold, and it was a long time before Marion could forgive her.

The Hilliard family's day began when Mr. Hilliard arose at seven-thirty and made the breakfast porridge. Before each meal everyone repeated together the family grace that Mrs. Hilliard had composed: "God bless this food to our [sometimes pronounced "twar"] use and make us thankful and good." After each meal Mr. Hilliard led family prayers, each member kneeling on the floor beside his or her chair.

Often his prayers revealed something hitherto unknown to the family about the coming day. If, for example, he said, "And with all the places we have to go today, keep us safe and help us to be careful," this being translated meant that he was probably going to drive the horse and buggy down the river to Cornwall to a court session. Later, when he began to drive a car, he sometimes confessed to the Almighty that he hadn't meant to drive through that stop light.

From office and school the family gathered for a full dinner at noon, usually topped off with apple pie, Mr. Hilliard's favorite. Mrs. Hilliard prepared dinner and the girls washed dishes and got supper.

Piano practice began right after school, so that each would have a chance to get in an hour a day. After family prayers in the evening Mrs. Hilliard played for all to sing hymns together; then the children gathered around the dining table to study. Their mother studied with them, taking the opportunity to relearn French, German, and Latin, and get some understanding of subjects that had not been on the Stanstead curriculum. Lights out came early. Even after the children were grown and earning their own way in life, Mr. Hilliard insisted on an eleven-o'clock curfew when they were staying under his roof.

Not only the days but the weeks and seasons had a definite, predictable form. Until Friday, evenings were for study. Friday night was open house for the children's friends. The parents retired to the study to read and talk, while the youngsters let off steam by sliding down the banisters, tobogganing down the blue carpet runner of the front stairs, and bowling with carpet balls. The evening ended with making candy or a pitcher of lemonade.

Saturday was music-lesson day, after the girls had finished the weekly house cleaning. Although many families strolled along Main Street, shopping and meeting friends, Saturday and Sunday were family days at the Hilliards and everyone stayed home, where they played games, read aloud, and sang together around the piano.

Everyone went to church and Sunday school on Sunday morning. Mrs. Hilliard sang in the choir; the rest sat in a row in the Hilliard pew. Mr. Hilliard took the opportunity to rest his eyes, and when the sermon was overlong he sometimes snored gently. The Hilliards were the only ones of the congregation who knelt with both elbows on the pew seats, facing the back, to say their prayers before seating themselves for the service.

When she reached her teens Marion's young sister was embarrassed. "Why can't we just bow our heads when we first sit down, like other people do?" she asked her mother.

Mrs. Hilliard wouldn't hear of such a thing. "Sometimes it's good to be different," she told her child gently but firmly.

While the distaff side of the family got the Sunday dinner of roast pork and apple pie Mr. Hilliard read aloud from *Pleasant Hours,* the little magazine given out at Sunday school. When the stories dwelt upon touching situations, having to do with children or separated family members, his voice wavered, but he read bravely on. The children observed that their mother was not so touched by imaginary happenings, and was much more likely to cry when praying, for she threw herself into suffering for the sins of the world.

Six days a week the household overflowed with activity and the whole family played tennis and croquet or skated on the rink on the front lawn. On Sunday everyone sat quietly at home, reading the Bible or other religious books, or went for walks together. Marion especially liked the walk to the edge of town and along a lane lined with great old trees to the point of land where the Fairview Cemetery was. It was a drowsy, peaceful spot, and the children liked to sit on the grassy bank, watching the boats and looking across to the American side of the river, which was so near that one could see the houses and the carriages on the river road.

For weeks before Christmas the house took on a special excitement, ringing with carols and redolent with delicious kitchen odors. Mrs. Hilliard baked an excellent Christmas cake, and each of the children made a different kind of candy. Marion's specialty, nougats with fruit, was popular, but the family favorite was a concoction of white sugar cooked to caramel flavor and laced with nutmeats. It was made by Mrs. Hilliard and called "patience" because of the endless amount of beating required to get the proper consistency.

Like many another husband, Mr. Hilliard left the choosing of gifts to his wife, except for his gift to her, but he loved to fill the stockings that the children cut out of tarlatan and sewed together with a blanket stitch. A methodical man, he set up an assembly line, and each year the stockings were filled in exactly the same way, from the apple in the toe to the orange on top, with lots of nuts and raisins in between.

Mrs. Hilliard spent hours behind closed doors in her sewing room, making new doll clothes, and the children found secluded corners where they could work on their own gift projects. As Christmas drew near, there were secrets in every bureau drawer and on every closet shelf, and the children played a teasing game with those who were in the know about their presents.

"Just tell me what color it is," or, "What letter does it begin with?" they would beg. Marion loved the game. Once she told her little brother, "You're getting four things exactly alike." It turned out to be two pairs of boxing gloves. Another time one of the youngsters guessed ten different colors, and Marion, who had bought a pencil box holding ten different colored pencils, said "Yes" to every guess.

Dear to the hearts of Marion's younger sister and brother was her traditional nightly story to them that began six weeks before Christmas—never any later, and, in spite of much pleading, never any earlier. On the general theme of "What is Christmas going to be like this year?" the continued story grew in content and excitement as the great day approached. What aunts, uncles, and cousins would come? What would be the plans for skating parties, tobogganing, neighborhood hockey games? Where would they go in the woods to get ground pine, blue spruce branches, and the tree? Who would make what kind of candy? Each night she reviewed all previous anticipations and added a new one. By the last week before Christmas the story would begin while the girls washed the supper dishes and continue until bedtime.

Christmas day, with its company, present-giving, and enormous dinner, was climaxed by the annual Christmas-night concert at the Methodist church, which was lavishly decorated, and had what seemed to the children the biggest Christmas tree in the world. A procession of children sang or recited to a packed house, and one or another Hilliard was always on the program.

The high point was the bestowing of gifts placed on the tree by parents for their children. Some parents saved the biggest and best present for the occasion. Mrs. Hilliard did not approve of this; in fact, she did not exactly approve of having presents on the church Christmas tree at all. Not wanting her children to be left out, but certainly not wanting them to get anything any better than other children, she compromised by slipping over to the church with packages containing new moccasins, a standard gift received by each young Hilliard each year.

Right after the first of the year came a special day that was purely Hilliard in character. All year family purchases were charged, and on this day Mr. and Mrs. Hilliard retired to the study for one grand financial settling-up session. It was like the crisis that besets North American homes today when income-tax returns are made out. The children were under strict orders to keep the house quiet, and behind the study door voices rose and fell, for Mr. Hilliard was generous but businesslike, and Mrs. Hilliard, as one of her children once put it, "believed in giving everything to the poor and charging the rest."

Mrs. Hilliard led the family through Easter in a true reliving of the religious experience. Good Friday was a silent, sober day. The curtains were drawn, the family fasted except for an orange in the morning and a boiled egg for supper, all members went to church from two to three in the afternoon, and no one touched the piano. Saturday was a quiet day too, with a sorrowful atmosphere.

On Easter morning the mood of the house changed to one of joy, with Mother singing and playing the piano and everyone happy. (Of course the usual Sunday rules held, but it was a relief to get back to normal.) The more pagan aspects of the holiday, such as contests to see who could eat the most hard-boiled eggs, were reserved for Easter Monday. One year when Marion and Marjorie had tied with a score of eight eggs apiece Mrs. Hilliard called a halt and the contest remained undecided.

In fine weather there was often a family drive in the surrey, always a memorable adventure. Mr. Hilliard never drove around to pick up his passengers, preferring to have them come out to the barn and settle in their seats.

"Everybody ready?" he would shout, picking up the reins.

"Yes, Father," would come the answering chorus.

He gave his brisk-stepping horse all the leeway it wanted, and the surrey took off like a skyrocket. The barn door lifted up on a pulley; one morning when it hadn't been shoved up far enough the fast start took off the surrey top, fringe and all.

Once, driving along at a fast clip, looking for a picnic spot, Mrs. Hilliard saw one just as they passed it.

"That's all right," said her husband jovially, "we'll just turn around right here in the lane." The sudden turn in made the horse rear up on his hind legs. One of the younger children who had secretly feared for some time that disaster would strike on one of these drives jumped out of the surrey. Her father was furious that his child had so little faith in his driving.

When, in 1921, he bought his first car, a McLaughlin Buick, family drives became even more adventurous. He couldn't get used to the fact that a car, unlike a horse, took a few feet to come to a stop.

Once he pulled out to pass another car and had to take to the ditch to avoid collision with an oncoming vehicle. He left his wife sitting in the car and went for help. A neighbor drove along and stopped to ask what had happened. Mrs. Hilliard told her, ending proudly, "And do you know, my dear, all Mr. Hilliard said was, 'Whoops!'"

On her way home from a fishing holiday in Quebec in 1957 Marion drove west along what had been the St. Lawrence River. Now the river bed was being dredged and the shore line altered drastically in preparation for the St. Lawrence Seaway, to be opened the following year.

Nine miles west of Morrisburg she paused, and then, on impulse, drove south toward Iroquois Point. After a while she slowed the car and her eyes misted over. Where once the headland had risen majestically above the river with its topping of great pine trees, the earth was gashed to make way for a gigantic lock to accommodate oceangoing vessels, and the grove of trees through which one used to glimpse the summer cottages was gone. A few ragged pines stood out against the sky, forlorn reminders of the former grandeur, and there was no sign of habitation. Twentieth-century machinery dominated the landscape.

Tears coursing down her cheeks, Marion stopped the car and turned to her companion. "I'm sorry," she said, "I just can't go any farther. I can't stand it."

Marion was still the baby of the family when, in 1906, her grandfather proposed that he and Mr. Hilliard build a summer cottage in the pine grove at Iroquois Point. For years it had been the tradition of the McAmmonds to attend the camp meeting held for a week each summer in the grove near the old church that had been Methodism's first stronghold in Dundas County.

Begun in 1823 by the county's Sabbath School Association, the camp meetings had a tinge of evangelism, but were primarily educational, focusing on methods of teaching in Sunday schools and providing an information rallying point for foreign missionary work. Families who came to the meetings lived in tents and went to meetings in a big canvas top or, in fine weather, under the trees.

Anna and Irwin Hilliard, dedicated as they were to missions and Sunday-school work, had become ringleaders of this beloved institution. They looked forward to the week of living out-of-doors and being part of the meeting atmosphere with its "work-study-pray" slogan.

Why not spend the whole summer in this beautiful spot? That was Reverend McAmmond's argument. Mr. Hilliard took a somewhat cautious view at first, but was soon won over by his wife's enthusiasm. She thought it would be good for the children; he thought it would be good for her. Theirs was the second of the twenty-six cottages that eventually sprinkled through the grove, providing a carefree, idyllic summer for families from Morrisburg and nearby towns.

Irwanna was built for outdoor living. Only the small kitchen with its old-fashioned wood stove and one room on each of the two floors were enclosed. Downstairs a wide porch ran around three sides of the cottage, with rocking chairs and a hammock at the front facing over the river; another side was devoted to a long slab of a table where at mealtime children sat on the bench opposite the chairs for their elders; and at the back were a sink and icebox. Upstairs, sleeping porches were fore and aft of the room divided by a curtain to provide dressing quarters for male and female. The front porches overlooked a grass tennis court and were decorated with Japanese lanterns and eight flags hung in pairs from the rafters, a detail that made later generations joke about the possibility of the cottage's becoming air-borne in a high wind. The crowning touch was the white canvas sign on which the cottage's name was proclaimed in eighteen-inch-high letters.

Each year in June a wagon drew up to Oak Hall, and the upright piano was carefully put aboard, followed by furniture, clothing, cooking implements, and smaller treasures dear to the hearts of big and small Hilliards. All family members but one were then tucked away into nooks and crannies for the nine-mile trip. The remaining member—for many years, Marion's brother Foster—reluctantly set off on foot with Daisy the cow in tow.

It was a pleasant—if bumpy—ride, for the road paralleled the canal with its ever-fascinating burden of boat traffic. Pulses quickened when the wagon turned south and crossed the narrow bridge over the canal and the first sight of the noble pines on the headland came in view. All hands set to work quickly to unload the wagon, make up the beds, start a fire in the cook stove, and trim and fill the lamps, so that the family would be settled before dark and supper would be ready when Daisy and her unfortunate escort arrived in a cloud of dust and weariness.

The day at Irwanna began early. Nobody slept much after six-thirty when the iceman clanked up the road to the cottage and someone called out sleepily, "Just one," or, "Two today, please." Every day except Saturday, Sunday, and summer-school week, Father went to his office in Morrisburg, either driving the horse and buggy or walking the two miles to the Iroquois station to catch the train. After breakfast the menus for the day were planned, and lists made up for the bread man, milkman, meat man, and grocery man who called daily for their orders, and the farmer who drove in with fresh vegetables twice weekly. There was no question about dessert—sherbet was always on the dinner menu; but the biggest decision of the day was its flavor: orange, lemon, or banana.

Jobs were parceled out. Even though there was a maid of all work, Mother believed that each child should have a chore. There was great activity while dishes were washed, beds made, lamps trimmed, knives pumiced, and small Hilliards and their guests took turns at the ice-cream freezer handle, cranking away for dear life.

By ten o'clock Mother was ready for her daily fishing expedition. The child assigned to do the rowing had been excused from other tasks—and well he might, for the river was swift and Rapide Du Galop, which lay off Iroquois Point, was as dangerous as Morrisburg's own rapids. Mother took along a volume of Dickens from which she read aloud to her commandeered oarsman (or oarswoman) while she trolled for her fish. Marion, to whom the rowing job fell after her elder brother went to war, used to say that rowing on a lake or paddling a canoe was really quite restful—"A cinch after rowing Mother on the river."

The trick lay in rowing down the river close to shore and crossing below the rapids to the calm waters on the American side of the river. Marion teased her mother about fishing in foreign waters. Mrs. Hilliard stoutly maintained that they had been in residence on Iroquois Point long before there was a rule forbidding crossing of the invisible international line.

"And besides," she would add triumphantly, "how do we know those weren't Canadian fish that just happened to swim across to the other side?"

After a full-scale dinner there were afternoon naps, then swimming and games of tennis, horseshoes, and "duck on the rock." Each child had to prove that he or she was a good, strong swimmer before being allowed to clamber down the rocks to swim on the side of the point where the river was thrillingly swift. When they had mastered the technique of negotiating two miles of turbulent water the young swimmers dared to go farther to ride the majestic swells from the *Rapids Queen* and the *Rapids Prince* that steamed up and down the river between Cornwall and Kingston every summer day with their loads of tourists.

Soon it would be suppertime and Father would return from Morrisburg. After family prayers it might be light enough for one more tennis game. Then while their elders sat on the porch, enjoying the summer twilight and the sweet smell of the pines, the youngsters played "run-sheep-run," or sat under the trees to plan tomorrow's fun. Bedtime came early, just as it did at home.

Irwanna became a summer mecca for Hilliard and McAmmond relatives and friends, and was crowded to the rafters nearly all during the season. When summer-school week came, the family circle expanded to include missionaries on furlough and other guest speakers and musical performers. Chores, swims, and naps had to be crowded into shorter time; meetings were held morning, afternoon, and evening, and every Hilliard was expected to attend every meeting. The final session of the week ended with a call to "stand up and be counted." Mrs. Hilliard was always first on her feet, gathering up her brood and shepherding them in front of her; later, when the children were old enough to sit with friends instead of family, they would come from all directions to join her—knowing that if they didn't a lecture was in store for them later!

Products of a Puritan background and a Victorian upbringing themselves, both parents were strict with the Hilliard children. The Methodist prohibitions were scrupulously observed: playing cards, dancing, and attending the theater were definitely out. Keeping the Sabbath was an implacable rule; even when the minister's children were allowed to go swimming on a summer Sunday, no Hilliard could go near the water.

Marion was eleven when her older brother entered the university. One day a letter came from him and that night Mrs.

Hilliard was missing from the supper table. It was explained that Foster had written about going to see a Shakespearean play. Mother was in her room, praying, and Foster was to be brought home immediately.

No sooner had this crisis passed than another was precipitated by a letter in which Foster described enthusiastically how he was learning to dance.

"For heaven's sake," Marion's sister Ruth, the next one slated to go away to school, wrote frantically to her brother, "confine your letters to news about your marks and the weather."

Marion was an affectionate, obedient child with little of the rebel in her, but once when she was about twelve she appeared at Whittaker's studio, which the Hilliards visited annually to have a family picture taken, wearing, instead of the usual hair ribbon, a circular comb that gave her a sort of Alice in Wonderland look. When her mother pressed for it, Marion pulled a hair ribbon out of her pocket but showed clearly that she set great store by the comb and felt that she looked very well in it. Time was on her side, for in those days even a studio picture had to be taken at high noon, when the light was best. She was allowed to carry the day, but her mother had the last word.

"Now let's have a special picture of the little mother and the baby," said Mrs. Hilliard, knowing that posing alone with her little brother would have great appeal for Marion, "and this time wear your ribbon so you can see how much better you look."

Although Marion respected her parents' wishes and was well into her university years before she learned to dance and play bridge, she was not above abetting others in such pursuits. When her older sister brought a boy friend to the summer cottage to visit, Marion played hymns in three-quarter time for them to dance to, while the adults were at evening prayer meeting. And she hugely enjoyed the time when the Methodist choir was practicing at the Hilliard home, and, while Mrs. Hilliard was preparing refreshments, the pianist, on a dare, played "Too Much Mustard" while somebody put out the lights so no one could see who danced and who didn't.

Marion appreciated deeply the love her parents had for each other and for their children, and willingly learned the lessons of duty and discipline set for her. While she was still in her early teens she assumed a major share of responsibility for running the household. She enjoyed her own domestic skills, and was elated when, at the Ladies' Aid tea the year she was thirteen, she won the apple-peeling contest—the object was to peel an apple and have an unbroken peeling at the end—although she was the only young girl in a group of women.

That same year she began to exercise her talent as a leader by taking over the Mission Band, the children's missionary group her mother had organized. Later she taught a Sunday-school class of younger girls, whom she organized into one of the first groups of Canadian-Girls-In-Training. Each week the youngsters met to work on projects related to the next Sunday's lesson and to have games and refreshments, and every summer she took them camping at Iroquois Point for a full week of sports, crafts, discussions, and evening sings.

One Sunday when she was fifteen the church organist did not arrive for the service. Mrs. Hilliard nudged Marion and told her to go up and play for the singing. Marion, who was an accomplished pianist but had never touched an organ, walked to the front of the church, experimented a bit with stops and pedals, and before the service was over, was doing a creditable job.

Mrs. Hilliard's feeling was that every community needed leaders, that having a good education carried with it the responsibility to use and develop one's talent for leadership—and, indeed, not using such talents was something to be ashamed of. Her daughter absorbed her philosophy and was always willing to try.

In spite of their great love and loyalty to their parents, sometimes Marion and her younger sister chafed against the restrictive side of their home life. One of their great bonds was an unspoken agreement that it was best not to argue but just to look forward to the freedom of the university years and the time afterward when they would make their own lives.

"Marion had a native smartness, as well as intelligence," a

blunt and perceptive friend who knew Marion all her life once said of her. "She instinctively knew better than to let her family know too much of what was going on in her mind. Another child might have fought openly against the restrictions. She made up her own mind about things early in life, but lived according to the family rules until she was on her own."

Before they left home the Hilliard young people had been given a clear picture of how their parents wanted to see them in the future—willing and able to give service, well disciplined, not to be pushed around by customs and conventions, but having their own standards to which they adhered. Marion took unto herself the basic principles, so that, although in her adult years she adopted most of the social customs that had been forbidden in her youth, she became "wisely worldly," and was able to retain and build on the essentials taught her by her parents.

CHAPTER 5

Wartime Teen-Ager

The beginning of World War I in August, 1914, came as a shock to the Canadian people. The Canadian–United States border had remained peaceful for a century, and the country had been busy assimilating the population that had poured in during the nineteenth century, developing its far-flung provinces, and building the nation that had come into being forty-seven years before, with the adoption of Confederation. The men and women of Canada's quiet villages and towns believed that they had built a safe way of life for themselves and their descendants.

Unprepared as they were—there were three thousand men in the Canadian Army and no Reserves—the Ottawa government offered an expeditionary force to Britain, and early in 1915 the first of nearly three-quarters of a million volunteers were shipped across the Atlantic. Of these, sixty-seven thousand were to die and three times that many were to be wounded in action. In the four years one in every eight Canadians of military age became a casualty. Few families remained untouched.

As Marion moved into her teens in these war years the closely woven, quiet-hued pattern of Hilliard family life took on a different texture, a different look. Her older sister Ruth entered Ontario Ladies' College for two years of preparatory work before going to the university. Her brother returned for his second year at the University of Toronto. Very soon he wrote that he intended to volunteer for the Army. Mr. Hilliard's old friend Sir James Whitney, who had served for some time as both premier

of Ontario and member of the provincial parliament for Dundas
County died suddenly, and in the by-election held in December,
1914, Mr. Hilliard ran for County representative on the Conservative ticket and was elected. The following spring Foster was
sent overseas with one of the first Army contingents, and Mr.
Hilliard went up to Toronto to be seated in the fourteenth session
of the legislature.

Now there were four places instead of seven at the big dining
table, except on weekends, when Marion's father came home
from Toronto. Often he arrived on the Grand Trunk's slow
train, the Moccasin, but occasionally he exercised the prerogative of an MPP and asked that the crack train to Montreal make a
special stop at Morrisburg. Mrs. Hilliard's civic life was busier
than ever, and the whole family co-operated to see that Foster
was followed across the battlefields of Belgium and France by
long, loving letters, bulkily knit sweaters and socks, and candy
whipped up in the Hilliard kitchen.

A victory-garden project was launched at school, and it was
announced that students could do farm work during the summer
in lieu of certain school requirements. Marion and two teen-age
friends signed up to work on a neighbor's farm, and for three
hot months, wearing cotton print dresses and large straw hats,
they labored all day and came home with enormous appetites.
That summer marked the end of Marion's days as a lightweight.
By the next year she had attained her full growth and embarked
on a lifelong struggle—sometimes a losing battle—against overweight.

Perhaps because of the burden of worry shared by the family
in these anxious years, perhaps because of the turmoil of growing
up so fast, Marion was for a time a sleepwalker. Mrs. Hilliard
took the position that she would grow out of the habit, and cau-
tioned Helen, who shared a room with Marion, not to frighten
her by waking her suddenly. Marion didn't believe the tales
they told her about her nocturnal wanderings. Once Helen hid
and watched as Marion walked downstairs, got a pitcher from
the kitchen shelf, set it on the sewing machine, and went back to

bed. The next day she laughed at Helen's story and said it was impossible.

Marion loved school and had easily been among the two or three at the top of her class in grade school. As she dug into the more difficult courses at the Collegiate Institute she worked hard to maintain her standing, and did especially well in the sciences. Occasionally she slipped below the class average in composition; nevertheless, she placed first or second, and once tied for first place, in the average for all term examinations. Her name was always on the honor roll that it was the *Morrisburg Leader*'s custom to publish. She never won praise at home for her good record. Her parents made it plain to their children that they were expected to do well.

Encouraged by her piano teacher, Marion began to work toward the examinations given by the Royal Conservatory of Music. After school she came home promptly, made preparations for supper, and practiced for two hours, leaving evenings for study.

Around town she was known as a vivacious, good-looking, happy teen-ager who spoke to everyone, young and old, in a friendly way. She was one of the strongest swimmers—boy or girl—in the village, and one of the few girls who could, or even wanted to, play hockey. The distinction had not been won easily; in an effort to get her to quit, the boys had tried putting her in as goalie and aiming for her, but even without guards she always stayed in the game.

At home she alternated between being the fun-loving child and the high-minded idealist, serious about working for good school marks, caring for her little brother, and running the Mission Band. Her sister Ruth took to calling her "Aunty" when she got in one of her solemn, literal-minded moods; but when Marion and Helen swiped their sister's sweaters and read her love letters, they became her "bratty kid sisters." Above all things, Marion detested being called "sturdy" or "reliable," although she was developing into a young woman of a somewhat stocky build and was the soul of responsibility.

Her friend Vonnie had grown to be her trusted confidante, the one to whom she took the questions and problems teen-agers are happier to discuss with someone outside the family circle. Miss Von Doran's vivid personality, her sense of humor, and her manner of speaking her mind freely and frankly made a great impression on Marion. For her own part, the young woman watched with love and pride the youngster's development, observing how genuinely appreciative she was of others' thought for her, how well and cheerfully she shouldered responsibility at home, how naturally she took to leadership. She liked the child's independence of mind. Once they disagreed in their estimate of a boy in the village, Vonnie believing he was a weak character and perhaps not quite bright.

"Oh, no, Vonnie." Marion spoke up earnestly in behalf of her friend. "You've no idea how really brilliant he is. Someday you'll see."

Years later they laughed together to see that they had both been right. The young man in question turned out to be both intelligent and unstable.

For many years Vonnie had played audience for Marion when a piano number had been practiced to perfection. Now Marion confided to her the hope that if she worked hard and did well in the conservatory examinations she might become a pianist. Vonnie encouraged her, while watching for signs of other developing interests and abilities. She was keen to see what direction the youngster would take.

One evening when Marion was fourteen she dropped in to see Vonnie. "I had the most wonderful fun today," she bubbled. "I skinned two rabbits for supper."

Vonnie looked at the strong, square young hands, and an idea came to her. "Did you ever think of studying to be a doctor?" she asked casually.

"Oh, yes," replied Marion readily, "but I don't think my folks would stand for it."

"If you really want to be a doctor, you'll do it," prophesied Vonnie.

She went on to tell Marion about the new hospital in Toronto that was staffed entirely by women doctors, and about her great friend Dr. Edna Guest, who was one of them. It was Marion's introduction to Women's College Hospital.

After that they talked often about the possibility of a future in medicine for Marion. Sometime later, when Mr. Hilliard got wind of it, he told Miss Von Doran bluntly that he didn't approve of the idea. Although the two were a constant challenge to each other politically, and sometimes had differences of opinion about the business matters on which she consulted him, she had always tactfully avoided disagreement with him on any matter having to do with his children, even when he asked her opinion, which he sometimes did. This time, however, she went to bat.

"You're being shortsighted," she told him firmly. "Marion is physically strong, and is both gifted and competent. She would be a success at anything she wanted to tackle. I believe it's wrong to put obstacles in her way."

It was summer-school week, 1916. Most of the young men of the families that gathered at Iroquois Point were fighting in Flanders with the Canadian Corps. At Irwanna there were special prayers each day for Foster, and the Hilliards had welcomed his fiancée, the beautiful Leila Robinson, who had come to spend the summer. From Montreal, Mrs. Hilliard's friend Mrs. Nichol, a prominent churchwoman and missionary worker, had come as a guest speaker, bringing her seventeen-year-old daughter, Helen.

For the tall, slim, dark Montrealer and the fourteen-year-old Marion, who had reached her full height of five feet, four inches, and already had the sturdy build of the athlete who would win plaudits on the university playing fields, it was the beginning of a lifelong friendship. Helen's black pigtail was looped up and tied with a taffeta ribbon; Marion's thick masses of straw-gold hair were in one huge pigtail, fastened with an elastic band, with the ends brushed out. Both wore the standard teen-age "uniform"; pleated skirts and blouses.

"We were both mad about sports," wrote Miss Nichol many years later, reminiscing about that wartime summer, "and we admired our mothers and their great enthusiasm for good causes. But, more important, we were both middle children, who had learned to cope, to pitch in, to solve problems. One middle child recognizes another!"

Mrs. Hilliard, then in her early forties, was "trim, feminine, graceful, with curly dark hair, lovely blue eyes, great animation and charm, and a swift, eager, loving manner of speech." Because she was assuming more than her usual responsibility for the meetings, she had turned over the running of the household to Marion.

"We got up with the sun and made breakfast for the fourteen people at Irwanna that week, on the old-fashioned kitchen range. After a good 'tuck-in,' Mrs. Hilliard led morning prayers, that delightful, family kind we all used to have that were a boon in getting through exams and keeping naughtiness down to a minimum.

"Marion and I washed the dishes, our tongues wagging madly, then up to the loft we went, to whisk up the beds. After a few quick preparations for the lunch hour, we ran off to our class.

"The leader was Frank Outerbridge, a teacher at the University of Tokyo. He was an attractive man—bright, brownish hair, grey eyes, nice features, ruddy cheeks. And he was our ideal. We cajoled Mrs. Hilliard into inviting him for dinner, followed him around, cooked up big questions for him to answer while we sat at his feet.

" 'What should we do to prepare to be missionaries?' we would ask. We made him promise to write us, which he did for years. To each other, we swore we would be missionaries so that we could be near him in farthest Japan for ever and ever. We vaguely knew he was married, but this did not lessen our devotion to him. He showed great sense in dealing with us for he elevated our glorious crush to a charming, genuine friendship which lasted many years."

Each afternoon the two mothers gave talks about missionary

work and the two daughters went to hear them before going down to the rapids for their swim.

"It was an experience of wild, daring swimming I never knew elsewhere. We walked up the river, undressed in the bushes and donned our complete Annette Kellerman bathing costumes, then plunged into the river to be carried into the rapids and swept downstream. The rule was that as one's knees were banging on the rocks in the foaming water, to swim like mad for shore where there were big boulders and overhanging apple trees. Missing the signal could mean being swept away in those wild waters. To race down the rapids in a canoe is one thing, but this was more challenging and more rewarding.

"Our mothers came to see us just once. I dare say that their prayers in the meetings after that were rather a muddle, what with their offspring in daily danger of being lost forever in the foaming rapids of the St. Lawrence."

At suppertime Marion produced great casseroles of scalloped potatoes, baked ham, berry and apple pies, and her new-found friend marveled at the way she whipped up cakes and homemade bread and rolls with such energy and speed.

"There was great chatter as we did the dishes for the fourteen, while the twilight came on and we had the good feeling of cementing a friendship. We talked about skating, about school—so different in Ontario from what it was in Quebec—and a lot about our families—Foster and his romance, the glamorous Leila, their separation, and how he would go into the mission field when he came home from war. I felt Marion had an advantage over me, for if Foster went to Japan, she would be closer to Frank than I would. But jealousy does not exist for us middle children!

"In the evenings we went to 'sings' at some of the cottages, or lay in hammocks under the trees and went right on talking. In the big, open attic where the children slept—Marion's young sister and little brother and others who were there that summer —we whispered from one cot to another after lights out until we fell asleep.

"That chuckle of Marion's! Her laugh that rolled out appreciatively and lovingly on one note! We had time to laugh and play, but we were serious, too. There was that war on our minds, and all the boys away in France, the cause of Christ and his great command, 'Go ye into all the world,' laid upon us by our mothers and by our crush on Frank. College life was just ahead for me, and not much further for Marion. We were typical teen-agers of the First World War, for whom life was real and life was earnest!"

One day in the late winter of 1918 Mr. Hilliard heard that a Main Street house he had long admired was to be put up for sale. A fine red brick, built in the Georgian style that had come from England to Colonial United States and brought to Canada by the Loyalists, it had simple conservative lines and beautiful proportions. It pleased Mr. Hilliard to know that it had been built nearly fifty years before by his mother's brother, James Gillespie.

Marion had been left at home to keep house for her father, when her mother had taken the two youngest children to California to avoid the rigors of the Canadian winter and to pay a visit to her beloved Aunt Barbara and Uncle Foster, now living in retirement. Together Marion and her father went over the beautiful house, admiring the fine wood of its floors and paneling; the massive front door, flanked by insets of colored glass, and the lion's-head knocker; the two large front rooms, each with a fireplace, whose triple-paned windows looked down the sloping street to the canal and river. It was just the right size for the family, they agreed, and quickly they decided to surprise the returning Hilliards with a new home.

While Mr. Hilliard had the veranda stripped from three sides of the house and replaced by a wide front porch more suitable to the lines of the new home, Marion supervised the cleaning, packing, and moving. One April day Mrs. Hilliard and the two rosy-cheeked youngsters were brought home from the Grand Trunk station to a completely settled house. Aunt Luella's picture hung over the mantelpiece and the dishes were arranged in the dining room's built-in china closet. The surprise that crowned them all stood in one of the living rooms: the grand piano Mrs. Hilliard had long coveted.

"It was typical of the kind of family we were," wrote Marion once, "that the only possession of value in our home was a magnificent grand piano. I don't understand yet how my father managed to pay for it, but I do follow his reasoning. He had respect for the mystical value of music to enrich and strengthen, and he felt so great a force deserved proper mounting."

The whole family loved the new house from the start. There was space for a tennis court-skating rink, and Mrs. Hilliard saw at once where she could put her flower beds, and how the porch could be set off with a white spirea bush at one corner and Dorothy Perkins rose vines and clematis to decorate the archways between veranda pillars.

The children were enchanted with the sleeping porch, a room over the kitchen that had dark wainscoting to window height and rows of windows on the two outside walls. In its heyday the porch held two bunks and several cots, and it was a cold night indeed that didn't find the Hilliard youngsters and their guests lined up for the lark of "sleeping out." The porch became a kind of sanctuary to Marion; she often took her books and letter writing there in the sunny hours, and slept there all year long, professing to find it invigorating even in the bitterest weather.

That fall an influenza epidemic swept through Morrisburg, felling whole families at once and causing the deaths of many of the village people. Mr. Hilliard was the only member of his household to escape the illness. His knowledge of cooking was confined to making tea and baking apples; in consequence, the kettle was always steaming and the oven full of apples that he fed his ailing family three times a day. Once, overburdened with his responsibilities, he got angry at the teakettle because it boiled dry before he could get to it, and hit it a mighty wallop with his fist, imprinting upon it a dent that remained there ever after.

When Marion got over her bout of flu she went out to help neighboring families where illness still lingered. The experience made a great impression on her, and she told her family and

Vonnie that she liked taking care of sick people and hoped someday her job would be to "help relieve suffering people."

The Armistice came, and the rejoicing in the Hilliard family
that Foster had come safely through three years of war was tempered with sorrow for other families who had not been so
fortunate. The day the great news was confirmed Mr. Hilliard
started out to canvass the town for contributions to a memorial to
the Morrisburg boys among the casualties. Some people favored
building a town library; Mr. Hilliard headed a group who
wanted a statue that would "be here forever." Today the memorial
still stands—a great bronze figure of a Canadian soldier, cradling
the flag in his left arm, his right hand raised in a victory salute.

Soon after the Armistice bad news came to Mrs. Hilliard.
Laura, the friendly, gay contralto of the McAmmond sisters'
trio, had died from the flu during her convalescence from a
serious operation. Laura, who had remarried, left a three-year-old
son, Fletcher, whom Mrs. Hilliard brought home with her. The
two youngest Hilliards, as Marion had done for them when they
were small, took special care of the motherless little boy, who remained with the family for ten years, until his father's remarriage.

The men of the Canadian Army began to return home. Foster
wrote that he would like to do some studying at the University
of Edinburgh; it was the summer of 1919 before he returned to
his family and fiancée and resumed study at the university.

That fall a provincial election was called for the first time
since 1914. Mr. Hilliard stood for re-election, although it was a
trial for the devoted family man to spend three months each year
in Toronto at the legislative sessions. It was an exciting campaign,
ending in an upset when a new party, the United Farmers' Organization, swept all of Ontario. Although he polled more votes
than he had in 1914, Mr. Hilliard was roundly beaten by
William H. Casselman, the UFO candidate in Dundas County.

On election night the young Hilliards watched from the
windows while a crowd rounded up by the victors gathered near
the house on Main Street, strung up an effigy of Mr. Hilliard,
and burned it. Mr. Hilliard looked upon the demonstration

more in sorrow than in anger, explaining to the children that it was against the Conservative Party rather than himself personally; but he was hurt to learn that his relatives in the farm areas had voted against him, and disappointed that his gesture of plowing up his front lawn and planting it with potatoes to show that he was a farmer at heart had not been effective.

He himself never ran again for office, but loyally worked for his party, except for the time in 1927 when the Conservatives of Ontario introduced a plank in their platform to liberalize the sale of beer. Hard as it was for him—when Miss Von Doran, the staunch Liberal, tried to tease him about his dilemma, his eyes filled with tears—his belief in the importance of temperance sent him stumping the county in behalf of the "dry" Liberal candidate, and the latter won the election.

Marion began her last year at the Collegiate Institute, a stiff academic year required of Ontario youngsters following twelfth grade, in which the work is the equivalent of the first year at a university. She was determined to—and did—keep her standing as an honor-roll student, while she made final preparations for the conservatory examination. As she polished up her performance of Beethoven's "Moonlight Sonata," and Rubenstein's "Kamennoi-Ostrov," she was confident that she would score the seventy-eight points needed to pass the examination, perhaps even the eighty points that would give her honors standing. She went to the examination letter perfect in five numbers, and was completely deflated when her final score was sixty-eight points. For a short time she clung to the idea that she might continue her lessons, take the examination again, and work toward being a concert pianist. She confided as much to her father.

"That's out, Marion," he said firmly. "Unless you're good enough to be one of the best there's no point in doing it at all."

That settled it, and there was no more mourning for Marion; after all, her university years, long looked forward to, were just around the corner.

CHAPTER 6

The Clear Winds of Freedom

During the 1950s Marion Hilliard was a panelist on a television program devoted to a discussion of the values of higher education. The moderator's first question, as the program began, was directed to her. What had she felt was the greatest value of going to the university? She started to answer truthfully, "Getting away from home and being on my own."

Suddenly she remembered that her kind and loving mother was out there in the audience somewhere, and thought better of it. She stuttered an answer and got off entirely on the wrong foot. Later she told her sister (only another Hilliard would understand), "I was completely befuddled because I couldn't tell the truth."

"My daughters will take English and history and be teachers," Mr. Hilliard was fond of saying. His oldest daughter wanted to study political science. He forbade it. When it was Marion's turn to go to college it was agreed that she should go to Victoria College, a Methodist coeducational institution affiliated with the University of Toronto, but there was something less than agreement about the goal she would pursue.

For several years her secret determination to study medicine had been growing. Finally, in her last high-school year, she confronted her father.

"I want to be a doctor and I think I'd like to be a pediatrician," she declared. In her dreams she always saw herself bringing health and happiness to undernourished, hopeless little children in some foreign land, something Mother would certainly approve of, so she added, "In India."

Mr. Hilliard replied flatly that she would be a teacher; it was a much more sensible occupation for a woman.

"We glared at one another," she wrote many years later. "My father and I were much alike and our wills locked solidly."

When he gave permission for her to enroll in college as a science student Mr. Hilliard was convinced that after four years she would forget about wanting to study medicine and would gladly settle for teaching science. Marion kept her own counsel. This was the opening wedge to the medical career upon which she had decided. And at last she was free to try her wings.

"And so I went to university," she wrote much later. "I covet for every girl entering her adult life such an experience—the clear winds of freedom blowing through a waiting spirit and open heart. Every door stood open."

At the end of September, 1920, she registered at "Vic" for the course in the natural and physical sciences. It was a tough course, calling for long lab sessions nearly every day and physics problems that took most of every weekend. Examinations were given in May. That first year she established a pattern of concentrated study—"submerging," she called it—during the six weeks before, so that she could enjoy the sports and other extracurricular activities that beckoned her on.

In the large room at Oaklawn, a tranquil old private residence converted into a women's dormitory, Marion and her three roommates, Izzy, Betty and Maryon, each had a bookshelf, bed, and chest of drawers, and very little space to move around in. Marion's shelf always held a row of Morrisburg apples, a reassuringly wholesome sight to one of the mothers who, on her first visit, was appalled at the situation of four youngsters being crowded into one room.

Maryon Moody, a Winnipeg girl, was very pretty and had an impish twinkle in her brown eyes and a great flair for choosing and wearing the modified flapper styles of the day. She and

Marion took to each other at first sight. Because their Christian names were so similar, they became "Moody" and "Hilliard" to each other and their classmates. Perhaps because they felt unsophisticated in comparison with their more intellectual and worldly-wise roommates, Hilliard and Moody became bosom friends, although some of their interests were widely divergent, Hilliard being an essentially athletic type and Moody a social one. For one thing, Moody was a very good dancer, and Hilliard, of course, had never been permitted to learn to dance.

To her classmates and teachers Marion looked like the healthy, rollicking small-town girl she was. Her homemade clothes, particularly a heavy gray cloth coat with military cape lines and an outsize sailor hat that fitted down almost to her eyebrows—a product of Aunt Sue's millinery shop—did nothing to conceal her inclination to chunkiness. She wore her long hair in a big bun low on the back of her neck. It was always coming down in wisps, probably because she was in constant, dashing motion.

She joined the glee club, the literary society, and decided to take an honors course in English, with Dr. E. J. Pratt as instructor. "Ned," as he was known to his admiring students, was even then one of the foremost Canadian poets, and Marion was deeply devoted to him. Along with scientific German and the sciences of her major course she was required to take French, mathematics, and "religious knowledge," the latter taught by Dr. S. H. Hooke, another of her favorites. The impression he made on her would do much to direct the course of her life in the next ten years. A brilliant, warm, and inspiring teacher, Professor Hooke had won students' interest by his fresh and compelling presentation of the gospels and his interpretation of the meaning of Christianity.

Life on the university campus in a city offered parties, receptions, concerts, and plays galore, and Marion wanted to go to everything. She was as excited over a costume party in the dormitory—to which she wore an old granny gown and appeared with her long hair streaming down her back—as she was at the freshman reception, at which she was introduced to the custom of promenades, the Methodist substitute for dances; the program listed eight or ten musical numbers to which the couples would promenade, and suggested topics of conversation for promenade partners, whose names were filled in just as on a dance program.

Typical freshmen, the roommates thought and talked of little else but food, basketball and hockey scores, and parties. The college fed them three times a day at Annesley Hall, but at least once daily they gravitated to the Diet Kitchen, a small tea-room just off campus. They were proud of Marion when she was asked to give a piano solo at a college function that fall, but were much more impressed at her being chosen for the basket-ball team that journeyed to Montreal to play McGill, and her popularity soared when she returned, having stopped at Morris-burg, laden down with goodies from Mrs. Hilliard's kitchen. When Moody had to go to the infirmary each of the other three wrote her cheering notes. After listing the important news, such as what happened at basketball practice, Marion wrote her new-found friend, "Gee, I wish I could come to the infirmary too. I hear you have chocolate cake there."

After Christmas, Moody's father came to town and took the girls to the theater to see Drinkwater's "Abraham Lincoln." Other parental visitors took them to "Babs," with Helen Hayes in the leading role, and "Mary Rose," in which Ruth Chatterton starred.

Marion's brother Foster, a student at the university's theologi-cal seminary that year, undertook to extend her musical educa-tion. With him she heard Toronto's famous Mendelssohn Choir, an experience of pure bliss for her; except for her year in England, she went to one of the choir's concerts each year for the next thirty-seven years. At Eastertime he took her to hear Bach's "St. Matthew Passion," which also became a not-to-be-missed annual event for her.

The most fun of all for Marion that year, though, was ice skating on her college's Little Vic Rink. Right after dinner each evening the Little Vic band tuned up and the girls tumbled over the fence on to the rink, skates in hand.

"It was my great avocation," reminisced Marion in later years.

"There with the music and the cold night air, skating had a curious effect on me. I lost myself in it, and knew an exultation so real I have remembered it all my life. It was beyond knowledge and description. I seemed lost in the rhythm and flight with the beat of the music and the cold air rushing by."

Four years hence the yearbook, *The Torontonensis,* would refer to Marion as "a lady of letters" because of the Varsity Ts she won in ice hockey and tennis, and the Vic Vs for performance on the college volleyball, basketball, and hockey teams. Of them all, hockey was her first and best love. For six years she was a star player for the all-university women's team, but it would be her second year before her name would go up in the equivalent of neon lights on the campus as the pride of "2T4" (the designation of class year, a University custom) and her fame begin to spread among Canadian sports lovers. This year she would acquit herself well, but have some skating energy left for Little Vic Rink.

With the coming of spring, tennis took the place of hockey. Marion, in a middy, wide tie, and long white skirt, was a familiar figure on the campus tennis courts. The years of playing against tough opponents on the Hilliard court at home had given her a stroke that she herself described in later years as "part cannonball." Now she started on the road that would lead her in two more years to the women's championship.

Good Friday fell on a lovely spring day and there were no classes. Mindful of weeks of examinations ahead and a long summer of separation, the roommates escaped the campus with a picnic lunch and took a ten-mile hike. It was a day to be remembered and duly recorded in all memory books.

Then suddenly it was May twenty-first and freshman year was over. The roommates parted with fervent promises to write often about everything, and Marion took the train to Morrisburg.

The train passed through the east end of Toronto with its row houses, its factories, its children playing in the streets. This was Marion's first real homecoming and she was full of the exciting college year that lay behind her, yet glad to be going home to another summer at Irwanna. It would be wonderful—but sad too. Foster and Leila were to be married on July twelfth and leave almost immediately for Japan, where he would be a missionary. She wouldn't see him again for seven years.

The route curved south to the lake edge, where gulls clustered along the shore. Then suddenly they were in open country with fields of white flowers and stands of cedars. There was French-man's Bay, a delicate arm of land curved around the small harbor like an illustration for a fairy-tale book. Inland again, and Marion, after eight months in the city, reveled in the sight of the trees—ancient elms, birches, maples, rows of Lombardy poplars, and the graceful sweep of weeping willows.

With the beginning of the apple orchards she began to count the stations. Some were small frame buildings with weathered red paint; others were good solid gray stone like the ones at Morrisburg and Iroquois. But the real milestone was past Kingston where the lake ended and the river began. All her life, whether she went by train or drove the highway that links Toronto with Montreal, her first glimpse of the St. Lawrence was where the excitement of homecoming really began.

Early in June the Toronto newspapers, as is their custom, published the results of the "recent examinations of the First Year and Senior Matriculation in the Faculty of Arts at the University." Among the successful candidates was Miss A. M. Hilliard, who had tied for seventh place in first-class honors in the natural and physical sciences course.

One of the two most exciting medical events in Marion's lifetime, by her own account, took place in the winter of 1921–22, her second year at Victoria. Working in a shabby little laboratory on the university campus, Dr. Frederic Banting and Dr. Charles Best discovered the effect of insulin on diabetes.

"Many people today owe their lives to this discovery," Marion wrote in her second book. "I will never forget the excitement.

It put a whole new dimension on my experience as a medical student."

For a few weeks the eyes of the medical world of six continents were upon this campus of a North American city. No one enjoyed the reflected glow and the feeling of being in the midst of great medical progress more than the nineteen-year-old sophomore at Vic, who made up her mind more strongly than ever that a medical career was for her.

(The second event in this "most-exciting" category for her was the first time she heard Dr. Hans Selye speak on his theories about "the stress of life." It was in the 1950s and late in her career, but, as she wrote in *Women and Fatigue,* "I felt at last we had the key to unlock the secret of nature's power to revive—and also of the lassitude that defies arousal.")

Marion had come back to register as a biological and medical sciences student. During the summer she had decided to steer her educational course closer to the shores of the medical profession. Her father, still clinging to the idea that she would become a science teacher, did not resist.

Again it was a year of long afternoons in the laboratories, punctuated by exciting musical "firsts" for Marion: she heard Madame Louise Homer sing, went to her first opera, a performance of "Faust" by the San Carlo Opera Company, was up in the clouds for days after a concert in Massey Hall given by the New York Symphony Orchestra, then conducted by Walter Damrosch. Then too, she began to center on the two activities that meant the most to her in her university years: hockey and the Student Christian Movement.

> *Someone, anyone, everybody roar,*
> *2T, 2T, 2T4,*
> *Rima, rama, chicka, wah,*
> *Zis, boom, bah,*
> *2T4 Victoria,*
> *Rah, rah, rah!*

From the moment there was "first ice" in the arena Marion, in her ballooning serge bloomers, white V-neck sweater, great ribbed stockings with their horizontal stripes, high-laced shoe skates, and huge padded gloves was out practicing. Her most frequent companion was her classmate Marjorie Fenwick. A Maritimer, Marge was pretty, charming ("She charmed us with smiles and soap," read the legend under her picture in the year-book), and a topnotch hockey player; in their senior year she was captain of the women's varsity hockey team. She and Marion were roommates one year and close friends for life.

As soon as afternoon classes were out, hockey practice began, often running into the dinner hour, but such tender care did Vic take of its players that dinner was kept hot for them and they ate at a special table when they came in late. In February the undergraduate newspaper *Varsity* headlined a four-to-one victory: "Varsity Girls Defeat McGill."

"The women's hockey teams of McGill and Varsity battled it out on Friday afternoon," read the account, "and all the world and his wife turned out to see the struggle. They were amply repaid. . . . Marion Hilliard was Varsity's star on the forward line. She is a strong, easy skater with more speed than anyone else on the ice. It was a treat to see her come up behind a McGill rush and check back. She stick handles well and her shot was the envy of many a mere male looking on. Her first score was the result of a beautiful rush and her second was whipped in from a scramble."

From then on, Marion was a "big name" on the campus. Her fierce concentration, strong skating, and expert stick handling won her plaudits season after season in *Varsity* and in the Toronto newspapers, articles from which were, of course, copied by the *Morrisburg Leader*. At the end of the season in her third year she won, by student vote for the outstanding woman athlete of the year, the coveted Athletic Stick, a hockey stick bound in silver with the names of sucessive winners inscribed on the handle.

When they went on to their graduate years—Marion at the

medical school and Marge at the college of education—the girls continued as members of the women's varsity team, and in the spring of 1925 met with the greatest triumph of all. The team won both city and intercollegiate championships and, in a game still remembered by Ontario sports enthusiasts, defeated the Ottawa Alerts (final score: 5 to 2), thereby winning the Ontario ladies hockey championship. For this feat team members were presented with gold little-finger rings imprinted with the seal of the province of Ontario.

After that, Marge left hockey to the new generation, but Marion couldn't bear to give it up. Once a patient looked up from the operating table at Marion and said drowsily, "I remember you. We wondered if you would ever stop playing hockey and give somebody else a chance."

The most far-reaching influence of Marion Hilliard's university years arose from her devotion to the United Student Christian Movement of Canada, which was organized at an assembly of Canadian students in Guelph, Ontario, during the Christmas-holiday week of 1920. Compounded of disillusion after World War I and the normal rebellion of youth and its idealistic yearning to have a hand in blueprinting a better world, it took the form of a revolt against denominationalism and fundamentalist teaching, and a "seeking after the pure heart of Christianity," as one young leader wrote in the SCM publication, *The Canadian Student*.

Earnestly these young people sought to apply the morals of religion to the forces creating war and the universal social problems, and to "bring the Kingdom of God on earth," not in the future, but *now*. With sympathetic adult leaders they formed a close-knit group that shared an exciting religious and educational experience; and from that group emerged many of the great names in Canadian life during the next three decades, including the nucleus of the League for Social Reconstruction, a great force for social progress in Canada in the 1930s.

The movement was worldwide, national organizations merging into the World Federation of Students. It drew upon the teachings of such men as Mahatma Ghandi; William Temple, who was later to become Archbishop of Canterbury; and John R. Mott, the American missionary and evangelist; found expression for its spirit in the writings of the war poets—Rupert Brooke, Joyce Kilmer, John McCrae, and Alan Seeger.

In Marion's second year at Victoria College, SCM groups sprang up on many Canadian campuses, and in a year or two had eclipsed the religious youth programs conducted under traditional auspices. The shocking experience of servicemen who were lucky enough to survive and return to complete their education induced a ferment of thought and feeling among students who were ripe for examining the conventions under which they had been brought up. The mood was one of searching, of need for something more than the religion that had satisfied their parents. It offered answers to the questioning of Marion's "waiting spirit and open heart," and she threw herself into the movement with characteristic enthusiasm.

Enlightened scholars such as Professor Hooke and Dr. Henry B. Sharman emerged as the true, accepted leaders of the young people. A lean, sensitive-faced, friendly man, Professor Hooke taught the parables as human stories with symbolic meaning, and presented the life of Jesus as a dramatic study of a religious genius. Students who gathered at his home for Sunday-evening study groups were introduced to Chekhov's plays, and the writings of John Middleton Murry, Katherine Mansfield, Bertrand Russell, and the Huxleys.

Dr. Sharman, then in his mid-fifties, had retired from a successful business career to devote himself to religious teaching. A disciplined, meticulous scholar, he directed his students in a slow, struggling effort to rediscover Jesus the teacher by "examining the records" in the Bible. The conviction that denominational interpretations had overlain the true record of the life and teachings of Jesus excited the young students. One wrote, "The world has never given Jesus a fighting chance"; another, that Christianity had become "loaded down with denominationalism, doctrines, dogmas, and superstitions," and been handed on to the present generation in "a thoroughly handicapped condition."

Some of Marion's friends became very snobbish about going to church. They felt that their religious experience was superior to that of ordinary church members. Marion, though she would not for the world miss the study group at the Hookes, continued faithful attendance at the Methodist church on Sunday mornings.

Loyalty to her parents and appreciation of the way of life in which she had been brought up was strong in her; and the gap between the generations was not so great for her as for some other students. Both Mr. and Mrs. Hilliard were staunch "unionists"—those who favored unification of the Protestant churches. (This was a seriously discussed issue of postwar days, and in 1925 an Act of Union was signed, creating the United Church of Canada; Methodist, Congregational, and some Presbyterian churches were thus joined together.) In a report of a World Missionary Convention in the early 1920s that Mrs. Hilliard attended as one of the Canadian delegates she declared that she felt that denominationalism was obsolete, and that she herself no longer took pride in it.

"The Kingdom of God with its wealth and power is not contained within any bounds of 'ism,'" she declared. "I hope all churches will join together in making the world 'His Kingdom.'"

For the most part SCM credos were couched in conventional religious language, but some of its ideas alarmed adult church leaders. An editorial in a church publication entitled "Poisoning the Student Mind" expressed horror that students were being exposed to "doubt" at just the time their faith needed strengthening. The title was seized upon for a hilarious song, written by the late J. Davidson Ketchum, a gifted musician and one of Marion's best friends.

"Dave," a piano student in Germany when war broke out, had spent the war years in an internment camp. A moving spirit of Toronto's SCM, he collected folksongs and hymns set to good music for an SCM songbook. Under his leadership, music and group singing became a popular part of the program. Blake's "Jerusalem" seemed the most satisfactory statement of the feelings of the young searchers after truth. It was sung often and with great fervor.

It was at an SCM songfest that Marion first heard the Christmas carol "Mid-Winter," written fifty years before by Christina Rossetti and set to music by Gustav Holst, the English composer. To Marion, Christmas was the happiest season of the year, and she loved all the carols, but this became her all-time favorite. The exquisite lyric, with its irregular, almost medieval rhythm and its simple wholeness, expressed her feeling about the true meaning of Christmas—and of life itself.

The high point of the SCM year was the fall meeting at Elgin House, a resort hotel in Ontario's lake district. Held in September before the universities opened, the meeting attracted many foreign visitors and two to three hundred Canadian students from a dozen or more campuses.

Daily Bible study, lectures by scholars of many countries, discussion groups, and plenty of time for sports and socializing constituted the program.

For a half dozen years Marion was a dynamic figure at Elgin House meetings. She knew everyone, loved everyone, and was in her element, taking part in impromptu entertainment, playing tennis and canoeing with Moody and other Vic friends, and cementing friendships with men and women from other universities. For two years her constant companion was a McGill man, for whom she felt enough romantic stirring to be worried when she heard that he was engaged—and relieved to find that the rumor was unfounded.

She was an inspiring speaker. After nearly forty years Elgin House goers remember vividly one vigorous and moving speech, at the end of which she turned to Dave at his piano and said, "Play 'Jerusalem,' Dave, and we'll all sing it together and we won't go back on each other."

These friendships paved the way for others. Once, after a

speech, a Nova Scotia girl came up to congratulate her and added shyly, "I have a sister who's just like you."

In time Marion would meet the sister, Eva Mader, who would become one of her most valued friends and medical colleagues.

In discussions Marion was vocal. Her contributions were, one adult leader wrote, "marked with forthrightness, a devastating capacity for pricking the bubble of pretentiousness, and a strong sense of vocation, all tempered with spontaneous and warmhearted friendliness." It was in discussion groups led by an English religious educator and pioneer in modern sex education that Marion learned how to talk about sex openly and without self-consciousness. The experience was to stand her in good stead. It would help shape the personality who, thirty years later, would, as one of her patients put it, "put a fast, clean breeze through subjects that had been kept under wraps for years."

In the autumn of their second year Marion and Marge were initiated into Kappa Kappa Gamma, a women's fraternity to which Moody and other friends belonged. Pre-initiation torments were on the hilarious side: the girls were required to appear in the dining room with pails from which they must eat their soup with a shovel, and to "eat all other courses with knife only." The initiation itself was a solemn affair, with the pledges in white dress, carrying candles and repeating extravagant vows.

The next spring Marion went to the Kappa annual dance. It was the first she had ever gone to. It may have been loyalty to the sisterhood that overcame her Methodist scruples, but it may also have been her gradual change of values, which was described once by a classmate and close friend.

"Marion hung onto a fundamental core of faith, but she was very open-minded about new ideas. She grew to feel that some of the things that were terribly big issues to our parents' generation—dancing, taking a drink, smoking a cigarette—had nothing to do with a person's basic faith and ideas."

When examinations were over in May it was the Kappa custom to hold an all-female house party, usually at Grimsby Beach on Lake Ontario. Marion won recognition as the only hardy soul to brave the cold water, freely exercised her prowess on the tennis courts, and organized daily baseball games. While some played bridge, others strummed on ukuleles or roamed the nearby fields, returning with arms full of daisies. Enjoying the relaxation from the college year, they sat in the sun in rocking chairs in field grass as high as the chair seats, and clowned it up for snapshots with skirts hitched up, showing hose rolled below the knees and held up by satin rosette garters, in the fashion of the day.

Marion spent all four summers of her undergraduate years at Iroquois Point, where the cottage was filled to the rafters with Hilliards and their relatives and friends—plus, during the summer-school session, visiting missionaries and other lecturers. One year Marion presided over the ménage while her parents attended a Sunday-school convention in Scotland and did some traveling in Europe.

She kept up a regular correspondence with her college friends, reporting on all her summer activities.

"We've been having a gorgeous time," she wrote Marge, when a favorite aunt and cousin were visiting. "They motored from Ottawa. Their machine is a Case and a perfect bird. Yesterday being Sunday, Mother wouldn't let us go driving, so we went to church in Morrisburg and didn't get home until ten P.M. My, we had a glorious ride, and I have a wonderful T.L. for you. I showed our pictures to my cousin and he said, 'Jove, that girl with the fair hair is a peach!'"

"Yours till the third time down," she signed herself gaily.

Once on a windy day she wrote a friend about swimming around the point when no one else could make it—and, "I haven't got over it yet!" Gossip about college friends and plans for the coming year alternated with descriptions of corn roasts, fishing on the river, and knitting a sweater, "to go with my knife-pleated crepe de Chine skirt."

The biggest event of the summer of 1923 was her twenty-first birthday, which was celebrated in Morrisburg with a tea party on the veranda.

Of a college friend she wrote, "Well, he has come and gone and both events were much appreciated. I have never known things to go quite so wrong. It poured rain and thundered incessantly. Father came home sick and I myself was feeling none too energetic." The big news of the moment was that "in a round-about way" she had found that the McGill boy was "Not engaged after all."

Shortly after her twenty-first birthday she attended an international student conference at Silver Bay, a mountain lake resort in the Adirondacks. From there she wrote Marge that she was enjoying herself to the full, but "have had a strenuous time though." As a result of the conference she was invited to speak to American student groups at Smith College and in New York City.

Later the same summer she was a delegate to the national convention of the Kappas. There she began to learn golf, impatient with herself because, "I am so frightfully awkward with right clubs and they insist on my shooting right." (When her hockey days were over, she turned to golf, and learned to play what she called "a fair game.") There was not much to report from the convention, she said, except a masquerade which was "not very dignified but a glorious romp."

At the end of her second year Marion stood third on the first-class honors list in the biological and medical sciences course. It was the best record of her years at the university. True to form, her mother and father said that they were not in the least surprised—they *expected* their children to do well.

In the last two years she slipped down to second-class honors, although she was second on that list. She confessed freely that the drop was because of her extracurricular interests. When she wasn't on the hockey rink or the tennis court she was planning an SCM meeting—or at the Diet Kitchen with her

friends, having her favorite snack of tea, toast, and sliced tomatoes, which she preferred to the house specialty, muffins and
marmalade.

The sturdy, golden-haired, laughing young woman, whose blue
eyes were "so heavily lidded, it almost seemed her long, thick
eyelashes were weighing them down," as one friend said, was a
well-known figure about the campus. Besides being a hockey star,
she was president of the SCM and a member of 2T4's executive
committee. Her best friends were prominent also, Marge being
president of the athletic society and Moody president of the
women's undergraduate association, which was made up of the
presidents of all undergraduate societies.

When not in hockey or tennis costumes Marion wore suits
and sweaters and skirts—usually blue, of course—and brogues. In
dormitory gossip sessions over ten-o'clock cups of cocoa she and
her friends discussed, in time-honored tradition, clothes, men,
and marriage, and Marion listened interestedly to others' wardrobe plans and admired new purchases with genuine enthusiasm.
But she knew that her father still had two more children to
educate, and she cheerfully wore the clothes she or "Aunty Gale"
made, topped off with hats from Aunt Sue's shop.

When men and marriage were on the gossip agenda she
shared her romantic dreams with her friends, but it was clear
that these were set in a more distant future than theirs. Even as
an undergraduate she was realistic about the fact that the price
for the medical career she wanted so much was to rule out romantic entanglements for the present. She had companionable
dates with the boys she met, but "played the field," as she
wrote later, and avoided getting involved.

Only one of her friends really understood her situation, since
she had had to make the same decision. Midway in her Vic years
Marion was delighted when her friend Helen Nichol came to
the Toronto campus, having graduated from McGill and been
appointed education secretary for the SCM of Canada. Helen
had wanted to go on to medical school, although she had fallen

in love and was engaged. Her father, a Montreal doctor, had put his foot down.

"If medicine is what you want to do," he had told her, "it must come first. Marriage, if it comes, has to be second. If you complete your training you must be prepared to devote yourself to the profession. This is a profession that cannot be treated as a sideline."

Helen had decided for marriage and against medicine, and accepted an interim job that would allow her to do some graduate work. Over tea and toast (and tomatoes) at the Diet Kitchen and on walks around Elgin House she and Marion confided their feelings about the hard choice each had made, and their plans and hopes for the future. Both still clung to the idea of going eventually into the mission field. The years since Helen's summer visit to the Hilliards at Iroquois Point had not diminished in them the exhilarating combination of the desire to serve the Lord and to live an adventurous life while doing so.

Senior year Hilliard, Moody, and Marge drew single rooms near each other on the second floor at Annesley Hall. Marion's room was popular; it overlooked the dormitory entrance and was an excellent point of vantage from which to accumulate firsthand information about the general appearance of new dates and to assess the effects of a classmate's costume.

This was the year when new romances began or old ones blossomed. The most exciting one to Marion began that fall.

"We're going to try the new man," Moody and a classmate had announced on their way to register for classes. The "new man," Professor Lester Pearson, was all of twenty-six years old, good-looking, an enthusiastic hockey player, and had a slight lisp that the girls found charming. Just back from Oxford, he was giving tutorials in history. The course was interesting, but the professor more so. Soon he was joining the crowd of students and young faculty members that met for Dutch treats at the Diet Kitchen, and very shortly Moody's confidential talks with her former roommate, Hilliard, held scant mention of any matter less exciting than her dates with "Mike" Pearson.

Marion and Mike became good friends. On occasion he and the two girls made a congenial threesome at tea or in the bleachers at varsity games. Marion abetted the courtship, listening happily to its ups and helpfully to its downs; being on hand when Moody was dressing for important occasions and waiting up to make cocoa and hear about the evening; and once gleefully helping her friend crawl out of the window to go to a forbidden dance, then waiting up to help her in again.

Before graduation Maryon and Mike were engaged. Marion's excitement and happiness knew no bounds.

Marion's own last year was an exhilarating round of classes and labs, whose difficulties seemed well worth while since they were laying the groundwork for medical school; hours on the hockey rink where she had risen to stardom, and on the tennis courts where she had won the women's varsity championship; and, of course, SCM meetings.

Each week she joined the small group that sat at the feet of Professor Hooke for two hours of study, and enjoyed the tea and toasted buns supplied by Mrs. Hooke. Questioning, sifting, engaging in free-for-all discussions, coming back to the Bible again and again to try to settle their conflicts of opinion, the young people were now coming to the end of a study process that, as Marion said, looking back on it, "awakened, matured, and developed our young minds as no study had before."

Gratitude for these lively sessions was not all on the students' side. After Marion's death nearly forty years later Professor Hooke wrote, "I still have a vivid memory of this bright, fair-haired girl, full of zest for life, pursuing the study of the gospels with enthusiasm and tenacity. She was a brilliant, warm-hearted student with an immense gift for friendship."

At the nightly ten-o'clock cocoa party the girls fell into the habit of reading poetry to each other. Marion formed a lasting admiration for John Masefield's verse, her favorite being the poem "Good Friday." Moody made her a present of a small leather-bound volume of Masefield, which she kept among her most cherished volumes.

The days began to race toward graduation. Victoria's president, Sir Robert Falconer, and Lady Falconer gave a dinner party for the seniors. At the senior reception Marion handed on the honored Athletic Stick to its new winner. The Kappas gave a farewell banquet at which Marion performed as toastmistress. The student body held the annual election of the best all-around student, the winner of which would receive the Moss Scholarship, a three-hundred-dollar award for postgraduate study, and Marion was runner up to one of the men of 2T4.

The *Torontonensis* for 1924 came out, with surprisingly good pictures of Marion and her best friends. The legend under her innocent and appealing profile read: "Something will come of this. I hope it mayn't be human gore."

The list of her activities and honors concluded: "Though a scientist in name, she is pre-eminently a lady of letters [there followed the list of letters she had won in sports] and now having captured a B.A. is in hot pursuit of an M.D."

In a clairvoyant moment the yearbook editor had chosen the legend "Future anything but dull" for the picture of Maryon Moody, the future Mrs. Lester B. Pearson.

The university's war memorial, a carillon in a great Norman graystone arch, was dedicated and christened the Soldier's Tower. President Falconer bade the graduating class "with high purpose to hand your inheritance to the next generation enriched by your own effort [and] go forth resolved to strengthen all that is best in our national life."

Before the huge audience packed into Convocation Hall, Marion took her turn in the long line of candidates and knelt to receive the hood of the Bachelor of Arts.

After the ceremonies she and Marge posed for a typical graduation picture, complete with background of vine-covered stone wall, academic gown over white dress, and armful of garden flowers. Then they hastily discarded the gowns and raced downtown to have their hair cut short, fulfilling a pact made the week before.

Marion prepared to spend her last summer at Iroquois Point,

full of excitement to think that another few months would see her back on the campus to begin medical school.

The clear winds of freedom were still blowing; she was on course and getting closer to her goal.

CHAPTER 7

Medette, 1927

When Mr. Hilliard came to the full realization that Marion was more than ever determined on a medical career he was, as Marion later recalled, "stunned at the failure of his strategy." Nevertheless, he rallied gamely and prepared to subsidize her three years in medical school. Both he and Marion were gratified to learn that the winner of the Moss Scholarship had changed his plans and Marion had fallen heir to it after all.

The autumn of 1924 found her back on the campus she had come to love so dearly, her sphere of activities transferred to the medical building on the curve of Taddle Creek Road opposite the rotundly majestic Convocation Hall.

The medical faculty, established in 1887, was then presided over by Dr. Alexander Primrose, and enjoyed excellent standing. Not many years before, the Rockefeller Foundation had recognized its quality by a gift of a million dollars to its capital funds, and in the spring of Marion's first year it was among four Canadian medical schools given top rating by the *Journal* of the American Medical Association.

Dean Primrose was a dignified man with an objective, well-ordered mind, a rectangular face, cool gray eyes, and a brush mustache. He particularly admired Sir William Osler, and at a dinner meeting held soon after Marion entered the school quoted a passage from Osler's writing that so impressed Marion that she wrote it down and kept it among her papers.

"Work is the open sesame to every portal, the great equalizer of the world, the true philosopher's stone that transmutes all the base metal of humanity into gold. The stupid man among you it makes bright; the bright man brilliant and the brilliant . . . steady. The miracles of life are in it. The blind see by touch, the dumb speak with fingers. To the youth it brings hope, to the middle-aged confidence, to the aged repose. True balm of hurt minds, in its presence the heart of the sorrowful is lightened and consoled."

In the beginning "Meds '27" was a class of a hundred and forty-three members; of the one hundred and thirteen who stayed the course, Marion was one of seven women.

Later, when she was interning at Women's College Hospital, a senior staff member loved to tell Marion and her generation about her own days in the medical school shortly after 1906 when the school had first opened its doors to women students.

"Blushing is a dilation of the peripheral blood vessels," an instructor had once remarked during a lecture, adding sarcastically, "Of course, these—we call them young ladies—in the class won't know what blushing is."

No such embarrassing experience befell Marion and the other Medettes, as female Meds were then called. As Marion once wrote: "The pioneer work had been done by the time I went to medical school. There was no difficulty about our being allowed to attend all classes and clinics. Of course, the girls had to sit in the front row and you could hardly say we were welcomed —but we certainly were not outcasts."

In time Marion learned about the pioneers who had paved the way for the Medettes: Dr. Emily Howard Stowe, the gentle Ontario Quaker who, refused entrance to the University of Toronto, won her medical degree at Women's New York Medical School in 1868 and returned to Toronto to practice; her daughter, Dr. Augusta Stowe-Gullen, who succeeded in entering Victoria University's Toronto School of Medicine and graduating in 1883; the group of progressive-minded men and women who joined with Dr. Stowe-Gullen and Toronto's courageous professor of physiology, Dr. Michael Barrett, to establish the Ontario Medical College for Women that same year; the women doctors and their husbands and unprejudiced male colleagues who had worked for the next two decades for the cause of women in medicine. Then, with the admission of women students to the University of Toronto Medical School, the women's medical college had evolved into the Women's College Hospital and Dispensary, where women doctors could find hospital beds for their patients and women medical students could be accepted as interns.

Lectures and laboratory sessions were scheduled for students in groups of twelve to fifteen. In a few weeks the members of Meds '27 knew one another and their professors very well, and were quite at home, clattering through the wide hallways, with wainscoting of dark wood, and rushing up and down the stone steps whose risings were fluted by the footsteps of the twenty-five Meds classes that had preceded them.

In the lecture rooms, with their semicircular tiers of seats rising from the demonstration tables, the students spread out notebooks on the chair arms, grumbled about the lighting and ventilation, and laughed at the late-coming student tiptoeing up the creaking rear steps to the top row of seats.

In long lab sessions they dissected cats and rabbits, worked over chemistry experiments, examined stained slides where imprisoned bacteria were to be identified. In the anatomy laboratory they began to learn, by the slow—and at first grim—process of dissection, the intricacies of the human body. In the immortal tradition of medical students they spoke affectionately of "my cadaver," to which they gave names such as "Dead Ernest," and about which they made jokes ("I call him Frank because he's so open"), to relieve the tension.

In this year of 1924 campus life was a yeasty mixture of sports, jazz, and advanced intellectual ideas. Along with its play-by-play accounts of football, basketball, and hockey games *Varsity* was printing articles by Arnold Bennett and William Allen White, and sprinkling its pages with long quotes from the writings of Dean Inge and H. L. Mencken. Students whistled, "Yes, Sir, That's My Baby," and "The Varsity Drag," and learned to do the shimmy and the toddle. An indignant mother wrote to the *Varsity* editor protesting these dances that had been "borrowed from the seamier side of life," and he replied patiently that "the past is always a golden age" to any generation, and it was entirely unnecessary for parents to be alarmed about students on the Toronto campus.

Marion Hilliard was one of the university's prized athletes, and she looked the part, with her short, straight hair, sports skirt and blouses, and her blue blazer with the big white T. Some girls wore make-up and high heels; Marion occasionally remembered to powder her nose, and wore sturdy brogues. When she clomped into classes the young Meds teased her by stamping their feet in time to her step.

Her best friend among the Meds was Bill Keith, a wiry, energetic, rapid-fire talker, who held top standing in Meds '27 throughout the three years. The son of a Presbyterian minister, Bill had been brought up in much the same kind of home as the Hilliards'. He couldn't abide giggling girls; Marion's wholehearted laughter and sense of fun appealed to him. He admired her skill as an athlete, and she admired his excellent performance as a student.

They were both great organizers and became the moving spirits of the Honor Science Club, which was a great force for knitting together the medical-school students. Like Marion, Bill had come to medical school convinced that getting established as a doctor took precedence over everything else, including romantic attachments. They understood each other completely, and a companionable friendship grew up between them, one that was to last all Marion's lifetime.

Marion lived in a boardinghouse just off campus, and quickly made friends with another Medette who boarded in the same place. Gwendolyn Mulock, daughter of a St. Catharine's, Ontario, doctor, was a tall, lanky brunette and a brilliant student. Although she too was somewhat of an athlete, winning distinction as a swimmer and basketball center, her main interest was in writing for Daffydil Night, which had begun as a Punch and

Judy performance to spoof the medical faculty and now had grown into a full-scale amateur musical show, produced by the Meds classes each spring.

Gwen's particular brand of irreverent, sardonic humor and iconoclastic view of all tradition endeared her to Marion as well as the rest of the class. Marion's cheerful conservatism and unshakable idealism challenged Gwen, and her happy humor, energy, and forthrightness enlisted Gwen's admiration. Theirs was a deep and lasting bond of affection and congeniality.

To her classmates Marion's enthusiasm and friendliness were attractive; as time went on, she was also respected for the intelligence, hard work, and steady performance that kept her in the middle or upper third of her class. Making some adjustments for the longer lab periods and additional reading, Marion lived by the formula that had served her so well in her undergraduate years, reserving her concentrated study for the two months before examinations.

The inter-faculty basketball play-offs began, and she and Gwen plunged in to bring honor to the Medette team. One of the games was with the Ontario School of Education, where Marge was studying to be a teacher, and for the first time the two teammates were pitted against each other. When the hockey season began they were joyfully reunited on the women's varsity team.

In the spring Marion applied for a summer job as camp doctor. It would be her first summer away from Irwanna, but she was eager to earn part of her expenses for the next year. As soon as classes were over, she rushed to Morrisburg to help with the annual move to Iroquois Point, and went happily off to the thrilling experience of beginning to be a doctor.

There hadn't been a wedding to liven things up since Foster and Leila had been married four years before. Now the most exciting one yet was on the horizon, for Maryon and Mike were to be married on August twenty-second in Winnipeg, and Marion was to be a bridesmaid.

Stowing away her camp clothes, she hastily assembled a wardrobe, including two dresses borrowed from Marge, dashed down to Irwanna to say good-by to her family, and set off on the long train journey to Winnipeg.

The round of gay pre-wedding parties, for which she was paired off with the personable best man, and the fun of being in the midst of that particular excitement that is the prerogative of the bride and her family, satisfied Marion's heart. The wedding itself satisfied her soul.

On September first, back in Morrisburg, she wrote Marge the second of a three-installment description:

"I left off with the arrival of the best man, and there the interest really begins. He was absolutely wonderful to me. The wedding atmosphere is quite fatal for the bridesmaid and best man. Nevertheless, I kept my head.

"I hardly know where to begin. The last week was so full—three evening parties in a row, and one night a dinner party as well. Then Mrs. Moody had a dinner party for the family. It was great, a wonderful dinner. I enjoyed the social whirl but it was nice to be at home.

"The day before the wedding we slept late. There was no hustle or bustle about the house at all. After breakfast I went down to have my hair waved, did some shopping, got my berth home etc. After lunch my dress arrived and I immediately got dressed in all my finery. Marge, you wouldn't know me. I really looked nice.

"The shoes are grey kid. The dress was delphinium blue, just the right shade, and the purple taffeta scarf suited also. But the hat was best of all, and I can wear it all winter for the brim is felt, bound with georgette. The crown is georgette and has lovely velvety leaves on it of all shades from blue to purple. The most important thing about it is it's very becoming. The bridesmaids' presents were chokers of cut amethyst which matched the purple scarf. Mike and Maryon gave me something special —I guess I told you—a beautiful bracelet. Well, enough of me!

"That night was the rehearsal. Maryon was much more excited than at the wedding. We practiced going in, going to the vestry, going out again; it was quite tricky. When we went to sleep the wind was howling, there wasn't a star and there was lightning in the south. But in the morning the sun was shining, and there wasn't a cloud in the sky. I have no idea what we would have done if it had rained.

"All morning we fussed around getting the baggage off, looking over wedding presents. Then the photographer came and took pictures of the family without wedding trappings. I had great fun watching. We had a huge steak lunch and ate heartily, realizing we wouldn't get food again for some time.

"We got dressed leisurely. Mrs. Moody and I left the house at 4:20, arrived at the church to find gangs of people on the steps—six-deep at the sides of carpet—and the church packed. We just got there when the bride came.

"Then the ushers shut the door—a signal to the organist, who pressed a buzzer letting the men in the vestry know we had arrived. We formed in line, the ushers opened the doors, the organist pressed the buzzer again and the men issued forth. Then the wedding march began. I get so thrilled just to think of it again. Maryon was the most beautiful thing you can imagine. The veil on her black hair, and that wonderful complexion, just like roses as usual—well, it couldn't be excelled.

"The service was very fine. Guests, spectators, wedding party and all, sang 'O Perfect Love' as an opening hymn. It changed the whole thing from being a show to a religious ceremony. When the service was over, Maryon turned to me and I put back her chapel veil. All salutations were left for the vestry. It was very exciting signing as witnesses.

"Back at the house, the wedding pictures were taken and the reception began. I was on the end of the line, and not knowing many people was often left out, much to my joy. And my goodness, there certainly was a lot of kissing! After that was over, there was the cake-cutting, the bride's health was proposed by Sir James Aikins. Mike nobly responded. We had had no food as yet, but all the guests guzzled merrily.

"There were no tears at the station. Mrs. Moody was a brick.

Then the bridal party returned to the house where the best man and I entertained. We ate heartily. After the guests had gone, we went for a little spin just to end off a perfect day. Will continue in my next . . . "

Shortly before she began her second year in medical school Marion went off to the annual SCM meetings at Elgin House. There she had one of the most memorable experiences of her life.

One night, after a session during which, as she wrote, "a Biblical scholar had taken us over the well-worn hurdles of fundamental theology," she went out into the autumn evening, feeling that her orthodox upbringing was at stake, confronted with her scientific education, and now a theological struggle.

"Body, mind and spirit were caught up beyond all knowledge," she wrote thirty years later, "and the memory of this is still a living thing." Under a starlit sky, "quietly, irrevocably, I came through to the greatest decision of my life: I believe in God. This is my Father's world. I was born to love.

"It is a faith that has never failed me and I would be a poor person without it."

After a year boardinghouse life had palled on Marion and Gwen. When they were invited to join three Vic seniors, Kappa sisters all, in taking an apartment for which the fraternity would pay part of the rent in return for meeting space, they were tempted to accept.

Marion had some misgivings. As she wrote Marge, who was now on her first teaching job, "The idea of the frat being ever present gets my goat, especially with all those rushing parties."

The economic factor prevailed, however, and the five students moved into the third-floor apartment of a large Victorian house at the corner of Bay and Bloor Streets, where the growing city was encroaching on what had been a fine residential section. Wearied of dormitory and boardinghouse fare, they wangled weekly rates for their meals from the Mulberry Tea Room, which occupied the first floor of the old house. (No more lemon snow with custard sauce, no more thin-sliced meat, no more Welsh rarebit, they chanted. Marion was the object of great scorn when she said that she went along with them except that she still loved poached egg on spinach.)

The new roommates' life was centered in the thirty-foot living room with its fireplace and built-in window seats. Once a week the sisterhood crowded in for its regular meeting, and there was continuous open house for Kappa students, alumnae and their friends. Two tiny bedrooms were completely filled by the five narrow cots, so the students, using tables for desks, had to call upon all their powers of concentration to rise above the distractions of the record player in one corner and the frequent bridge foursomes in another. A piano that stood in the center of the room alternately gave off Marion's rendition of the classics and the jazz at which one of the Vic students was adept.

Once a week Marion, with some assortment of other Kappas, went to the apartment where Maryon and Mike had settled down, to sample the bride's cooking. Except for the infrequent occasions when a man friend had the money for a movie, the girls and their dates played bridge, sang around the piano, or danced to the music obligingly provided by one of the two pianists.

Marion was a Rock of Gibraltar in the small household. She tutored one of the Vic students who was having trouble with chemistry, and acted as mother confessor to the younger girls when they wanted to talk about romances, family difficulties, or academic dilemmas. Since she had so many irons in the fire she did her listening and counseling over meals.

"Come on and tell me about it while I eat my lunch," grew to be a familiar response, when one of the girls mentioned something that troubled her.

In later years they came to her as patients because they had so appreciated her common sense, steadiness ("One thing about Hilliard: she never panics," they agreed), and her directness. Occasionally these friends who had treasured their hilarious year together would come to Toronto just to have lunch with her. After her article on fatigue of women appeared one of them said to her over the lunch table, "You said there were three times in life when a woman is bound to feel fatigue. You left one out."

"What was that?" asked Marion.

"Well, take me," said her friend. "I was born tired."

Delighted, Marion picked up the idea and used it in her subsequent speeches and writings on the subject.

Having thoroughly digested the *Outline for History Taking and Physical Examination,* Marion and her classmates began their clinical work. Like the generations before them, they were soon using the familiar nicknames for Toronto General Hospital, St. Michael's Hospital, and the Hospital for Sick Children —"The General," "St. Mike's," and "Sick Kids."

Most of them eagerly discussed their experiences. For Marion, these experiences were very nearly her Waterloo. She was appalled at the suffering; the sick and afflicted people for whom little could be done haunted her even when she was on the hockey rink. The disadvantaged life of children in low-income families shocked her. The clinic odors made her sick. She felt completely inadequate to cope.

The crowning blow was her first surgical case, that of a woman who had fallen out of bed when making love with her husband and broken her arm. To the patient her mishap seemed the height of comedy; her attitude and the joking remarks of the clinician before whom Marion presented the case were too much for her youth and inexperience.

Shocked, she fled for the telephone and told her father that it was too expensive for her to stay in medical school and she was going to leave.

"You'll do nothing of the kind," said her father firmly. "You'll finish what you've started, Marion, and be a doctor. We'll manage."

Marion was eternally grateful to her father for his bracing words in this moment of crisis. It was only a few months later that she had the experience which settled the direction her life would take. Many years later, she described it.

"I was in the delivery room for the first time, watching a baby being born. I saw the mother's face, wet with tears, felt the tense concentration of the doctor and nurses riveted on the moment of birth, heard the baby howl with his first breath. I had a flash of insight that has never betrayed me: 'This is what life is all about.'

"I decided then to be an obstetrician and it is a decision I have never regretted. Even when I am saddled with exhaustion, I never fail to be moved to my soul at the drama of birth."

The professor of obstetrics, Dr. William B. Hendry, now became Marion's closest advisor. A genial, kindly man, he was a good teacher, whose presentation of his subject had great appeal for students. Marion sought his counsel until she was well started on her career.

At the apartment she and Gwen, to the great amusement of their roommates, practiced deliveries, using a dummy made of a buttoned-up raincoat for a patient and old tennis balls for the baby's head. Carefully outlining the baby's position, they would work out, obstetrics textbook in hand, how to go about the delivery. For the benefit of the audience it often became a riotous performance, accompanied by the irrepressible Gwen's clever nonsense.

In January, 1926, the medical advisory board of the Women's College Hospital received an application for a junior internship from Miss Anna Marion Hilliard who was midway in her second year at medical school.

The board voted to appoint her, then rescinded its vote in favor of another applicant from McGill. When that candidate changed her plans a month later, the board pulled Student Hilliard's application from the "rejected" files and notified her that she had been appointed junior intern for six months, beginning the following June.

Such was the somewhat haphazard introduction of two Canadian institutions that were slated to make a great impression on each other.

Fifteen years before, the hospital had been established in an old house on Seaton Street, with seven beds, a converted kitchen table for the delivery table, and three bureau drawers for bassinets. The efforts of the strong-minded and determined Dr. Stowe-Gullen and the medical women who followed her (the medical college she had helped to found graduated well over a hundred women doctors before it closed) won support from Toronto men and women, and in a few years the little hospital moved to a larger converted residence on Rusholme Road. Soon this too was outgrown; for a time the nursing staff, for lack of other space, slept in tents in the back yard. In 1918, seven years after its founding, the hospital added a new wing, bringing its complement up to fifty-two beds and twenty-five infant cots. When Marion began her internship, plans were already afoot for a hospital to be built near the university campus.

The battle of equal opportunity for medical education had been won, but the low budget, cramped quarters, and lack of equipment testified to the fact that a women's hospital staffed by women had not yet been accepted.

Into this hard-working atmosphere came twenty-four-year-old Marion, bubbling with enthusiasm, brimming with ideas.

"Raring to go all the time. Needs to be held down," summed up Dr. Elizabeth Stewart, chairman of the medical staff, who, along with Vonnie's friend Dr. Guest, and the hospital's superintendent, Clara Dixon, were Marion's first three friends in her new home.

She was an eager learner, willing to take on extra clinic duties, always on hand to watch operations and deliveries, easy to waken when she was on night call. Obstetrics and gynecology were the hospital's main business, which suited her purpose well. However, the women under whose tutelage she worked were general practitioners who were developing specialties out of natural bent and experience, and her training was a generalized one.

Marion was horrified at the nurses' schedules which were a matter of twelve-hour duty, after which they attended lectures and studied. Appearing to have neither time nor energy for recreation, they looked exhausted and acted years older than they were.

Marion shocked the whole staff by getting into basketball bloomers and sweater and sitting in the living room, strumming her ukulele and singing.

"Come on down, let's have some fun!" she would call upstairs to the nurses, and, after a little persuasion, they began to join her. Under her prodding, they began to sew and knit, making articles for a bazaar, the proceeds of which would buy tennis and badminton equipment. She arranged for them to swim in the YWCA pool, and organized Sunday-evening sings in the hospital parlor.

After a few months Miss Dixon noticed that her nurses were brightening up and seemed to be enjoying their jobs. It did not seem logical that an hour of tennis or badminton on the courts rigged up on the lawn should revive these fatigued youngsters, but young Dr. Hilliard had demonstrated that this was so.

As time went on, a more reasonable schedule was established for nurses. As long as she was associated with the hospital Marion kept her eye on the nursing staff and interns and tried to make their lot a happier one.

She loved the hospital from the start and listened intently to stories about its beginnings. She was deeply impressed that the founders had raised the money to buy the Seaton Street house, dollar by dollar, and that one had even mortgaged her own home for her contribution. From the doctors, she learned how they had kept their clinic fees to ten cents a visit, worked cheerfully in the face of appalling shortages of equipment, and accepted the obstacles posed by husbands who would not allow clinic patients to return when they found that they were being treated by women doctors, and druggists who refused to fill their prescriptions. The friendly help of those male colleagues who contributed to their funds, gave free consultations, and took a personal interest in the growth of the hospital had helped to balance out the discouraging experiences, they said.

One story from the hospital lore that delighted Marion was Miss Dixon's account of the birth of the hospital's first baby on Christmas Day of 1911. She had planned to have Christmas dinner with her family, leaving their one patient in the care of the housekeeper, but before she could get away a young woman arrived on the doorstep, accompanied by her husband and obviously well advanced in labor.

Miss Dixon telephoned the doctor on call, Dr. Isobel Wood, who sped to the hospital, driving her horse and buggy, and the two improvised from moment to moment to make up for the equipment they lacked. A little girl was born and placed in a clothes basket, which Miss Dixon had hastily emptied and lined with sheet, blanket, and hot-water bottle. A piece of string from an old hospital shirt was used to tie the cord.

The grateful young mother proposed to name the baby for the nurse and doctor.

"I couldn't saddle an innocent, newborn baby with a name like Clara," her story ended. "I asked if she wouldn't give the baby my favorite girl's name, so she ended up as Helen Isobel."

Before Marion's appointment as intern expired in December she was invited to extend it to the end of the spring term.

Now it was the final medical-school year. In the small room at the hospital where she lived, laboratory and lecture notes piled up beside textbooks on pathology, pharmacology, obstetrics, pediatrics. She raced from lecture to lab to clinic.

Much as she had loathed her early clinical experience, now, as she wrote once, "I realized it was all necessary in order to learn the art and practice of medicine." Looking back on those crowded years, she added, "How a woman can undertake such an arduous, time-consuming course without a definite sense of mission and the beginning of a career, I do not know. And we take it for granted she must also have a strong body and a stable nervous system."

She could not resist a last crack at hockey, especially since a brand-new arena was opened by the university in November. As captain and left defense player she led the varsity coeds through one smashing victory after another. After the final game of the season with the women of Queens University, which gave the coeds the intercollegiate championship, her picture appeared for the last time as "Star Player of Varsity Team" in the Toronto newspapers. When the yearbook came out the victorious coeds were immortalized for all time in print and picture, and on another page a demure Marion appeared as the only woman in a group of eight T holders in the class.

The Toronto *Globe* printed a picture of the seven graduating Medettes, and, with classes and intern duties finished, Marion rushed out of town to visit one of her last year's roommates who helped make her graduation dress from a length of brocaded white crepe sent from Japan by Leila and Foster.

The university celebrated the one hundredth anniversary of the granting of a royal charter to its predecessor, King's College, and nearly all the five thousand students on campus that year stayed to witness the ceremonies. Then once more Marion knelt before the chancellor in Convocation Hall, this time to receive the hood of the Bachelor of Medicine.

All during the winter and spring the crucial topic of conversation for the Medettes, as well as the Meds, was: "What about next year?" Very early, Gwen had decided to return to St. Catharine's and go into practice with her father, who was elderly and ailing. The men who intended to specialize were angling for good internships, some in the States but many in Toronto, where an appointment to "The General" was especially coveted; general practice seemed to be the answer for the majority of Marion's classmates.

More than anything else in the world Marion wanted to be an obstetrician, but she had been a drain on the family purse long enough, and an internship was not for her. She still dreamed, perhaps a bit vaguely, of going to India as a medical missionary;

but even so, she believed she should have at least a year's internship. A talk with an official of the women's missionary society of a United Church in Toronto strengthened this feeling; they could send her to India but agreed that she should have some postgraduate work first.

Talking with Professor Hendry and some of her clinical instructors, Marion hit upon an idea. Even a year's postgraduate work in England, at that time, carried great prestige in Canada, especially if one could pass the British qualifying examinations. Several London hospitals offered postgraduate courses for reasonable fees. Marion wrote to a friend in the British SCM for help in finding inexpensive living arrangements, and went to see her "fairy godmother," a Kappa *soror in urbe,* a well-to-do older woman who had taken a special interest in Marion's career and who now agreed to lend her a modest amount to subsidize the year.

When her plans became known, the SCM asked her to represent Canada at an international student meeting in Switzerland in August, and at the annual meeting of the British SCM in July.

In great glee and excitement Marion booked passage for early July, and as soon as graduation was over rushed back to the wedding of her last year's roommate to a Toronto Meds graduate of 1926. It was a joyous reunion for the Kappas, who gathered early to decorate the house for the wedding. Maryon and Mike Pearson arrived with the glad news that, come Christmas, there was to be the first little Pearson, and Marion was torn to realize that she would be on the other side of the Atlantic.

After seeing the newlyweds off she caught a sleeper back to Morrisburg, her mind already busy with the next great event in Hilliard family history. Her sister Ruth, who had joined Foster in Japan and spent three years there teaching, had met Wentworth Myers, the son of an American missionary, and they were to be married in Morrisburg on July fourth and go to New York City to live.

Morrisburg
Monday July 4, 1927

Dearest Gwen,

I just have to write to you tonight, though my eyes are heavy and I ache in limb and branch.

All the guests have departed, the house is deserted and the flowers are drooping. But *everything* was lovely, even me in my immense hat.

Things have been happening so fast. Friday morning I did the baking and Saturday cooked the chickens. I don't mention such details as borrowing dishes and buying supplies. The foresight one must have! I'm thinking of going into the catering business.

Yesterday morning—it seems years ago, Irwin, Ruth and I went down to Cornwall to meet Wentworth. Oh, Gwennie, I was *so* glad when I saw him. He is *fine,* and just the one for Ruth. He has quite a southern accent, being a Virginian, and is tall and dark with stunning brown eyes. Helen and I quite welcomed him with open arms.

In the afternoon, the best man and his wife appeared. He is good looking and his wife is quite flapperish—wears lipstick—and very friendly. We had twelve for Sunday dinner and fourteen for supper. We had our rehearsal after church. Irwin was a scream, galloping down the aisle. We finally got him into line properly.

All during the church service I had been planning how we'd decorate. The day before, Helen and Irwin and Fletcher with three friends took the car and their suppers and went picking daisies—three washtubs full. I had the male part of the family bring the dining table into the living room and move all the wedding presents into the dining room and put moveable chairs on the veranda or into the den. It gave a much greater feeling of space to the house. This all took until about 12:30.

We've passed through decades today. It's positively tons of years since I opened my eyes. Helen and I rose at six and gazed anxiously at the weather first. The day couldn't have been better, cool and shiny. By 8:30 I had baked and iced a cake and had the house decorated—syringa on the mantles, large bouquets of white and pale pink peonies with a few daisies in front of the fireplace and on the piano, white peonies on the bride's table, and white roses on the wedding cake. It was a dream. I wish you could have seen it. Then we went to the church and decorated, using ferns, bracken and asparagus with the daisies. Oh, it was so graceful!

I wish you could have been here to have watched and laughed and worried with me. I spent the awful hour from 10 to 11 running from the kitchen to our room, dressing. Ruth was simply beautiful. Her veil was banded over her forehead and the ornaments were over each ear. It was exactly right for her. It looks well on me, too. I know because I tried it on last night when no one was looking. Her bouquet was very pale pink roses and lily of the valley, very lovely. Helen and I wanted mauve sweet peas and ophelia roses but we got two bunches of American beauty roses, which were great with Helen's outfit but not so good with mine.

When it came time, we walked across to the church, Helen carrying my flowers and I carrying the train. There were only about ten looking on. Fletcher was the "buzzer system." He told us when Wentworth got to the church and gave the signal when we arrived. Then Helen poked her head in the door and the ministers were up and before we could get properly arranged, the wedding march began. Irwin was just taking Aunt Sue down, so he dumped her into the first vacant seat and came dashing back. Aunt Sue was the only one disgruntled over his ushering. He explained he was afraid the people might think she was the bride!

The procession was uneventful except I could see Helen's knees shaking and Father got tangled up in Ruth's train. Von insists that before I get married he must learn a two-step so he can negotiate it better. The organ began to play "O Perfect Love" and at the same moment came "Dearly beloved brethren," so we were done out of our hymn. Wentworth was wonderful looking in his morning clothes, quite the talk of Morrisburg, and he smiled so beautifully as Ruth came down the aisle. I wish you could have seen us gallop back across the road, everyone laughing and talking.

I was like a hen on a hot griddle all during the food. It was very good but the ice cream *didn't come*. I was very distressed, but the punch took its place. It was rare punch, I never tasted better. The wedding cake *tasted* good—I was relieved over that. I told the family to send you some.

Von motored the bride and groom and Helen and me to take the train to Toronto. Such happiness! When we got home the house was in order. Kind friends had done it. So I got supper, and just to show that a wedding was nothing in our young lives, we had a steak dinner with new potatoes and all the trimmings!

Wish me luck on my wedding cake. I will write you on the boat.

Heaps of Love,
MARION

CHAPTER 8

Year of Decision

Twenty-four hours after the bride and groom climbed on the train going west to Toronto the Hilliard clan again gathered at the Morrisburg station, this time to see Marion off on the east-bound train. At the last minute she hated to leave, especially when she saw how touched her father was.

"It was the first time I'd ever seen tears on Father's face," she wrote Gwen. "That old verse about 'Men must work and women must weep' seems to be turning round."

The S.S. *Empress of Australia* sailed from Quebec July sixth, loaded with students and tourists bound for Europe. Marion was stowed away in an outside stateroom on upper deck with "a sweet little English woman, a brusque schoolteacher, and a nonde-script." With four friends from "Vic" also sailing on the *Empress* she had driven around Quebec City in a victoria and toured the ship immediately after going aboard.

"We examined the Prince of Wales suite," she reported, "and decided ours weren't so bad. But there is a faintly cadaverous odor such as Osler alludes to in typhoid fever."

Lulled by the ship's slow progress along the St. Lawrence, Marion spent an hour in a deck chair, "which revived me years and years," ate chicken and sweetbreads at her dining place by the window, then settled down on deck to watch the sun set over the Laurentians, leaving the sky "lit with pink and blue mauve." Now came a time for reflection, after the excitement of Meds graduation, the Morrisburg wedding, and the leave-taking from the family. She peered into the new year coming toward her and resolved, "One thing I shall learn from this trip—poise. I'm not used to being absolutely on my own."

It was an eight-day voyage, an interlude of peace although for two blowy, rainy days she and the rest of the passengers had trouble keeping their feet. ("It's the funniest feeling. I think it must be the same thing the tabetic feels—the ship sometimes comes up to meet you, but unfortunately is just as apt to fade away.") A McGill student at her table turned visibly green when the ship began to roll, but was determined to finish her dinner.

"Finally I told her I thought she'd feel better in bed. She left, and just in time. After dinner, I walked frantically." By the second day of heavy weather Marion was spending full time on deck, wrapped in two sweaters, her blazer, winter coat, and steamer rug. "My hands are nearly frozen, and my feet are numb, but I'm not seasick. I just have a queer feeling in the pit of my stomach. Heaps of people are sick. I almost didn't go in for lunch but couldn't bear to miss a meal. . . . I hope by tomorrow to enjoy life normally. I'm enjoying it now but *not* normally."

The weather cleared, leaving plenty of time to "enjoy normally." The *Empress* passed the "pitchin' Minnie" (*The Minnedosa*) and "it was a wonderful experience to pass a big ship at sea." A whale appeared, and she wondered, "Why is it that whales are always on the other side of the boat?" It was a great thrill when the baggage man came to put the London label on her trunk. She and her friends crashed the first-class promenade and "had a gorgeous walk before we were sent down again." What with shuffleboard and a hilarious game of hide-and-seek one evening on the now steady deck with Vic and McGill students she began to feel "spry as a kitten."

The sunshine, the blue ocean now white-capped and again "calm as an inland lake," the moon shining behind a bank of clouds, the gentle patter of summer rain on an early-to-bed night —all heightened Marion's feeling of pleasure at being suspended between one chapter of living and another. Watching for Land's End, with gulls wheeling overhead, she wrote, "As the waves come from the bow they splash and the sun makes little rainbows out of them. Then I look back over the stern and the sun has turned the water into a veritable silver sea. I don't want to leave the quiet and beauty of the sea, and honestly, Gwen, I'm scared of London. It's so peaceful here."

But she had enjoyed her first two adventures into sophistication. One was an initiation into the mysteries of betting on the horses. With visions of the entire congregation of the Morrisburg United Church peering reproachfully over her shoulder she bet twenty-five cents on a white horse, which won and paid four dollars and ten cents. She settled her conscience by playing until she lost her winnings.

"Nondescript," her third cabin mate, provided the second venture into hitherto forbidden territory. After the farewell dinner of roast beef, plum pudding, and ice cream, Marion went for a last turn around the deck and back to her stateroom to pack and go to bed early. She found her "quiet-looking" cabin mate playing hostess to a small champagne party.

"It was a big black bottle," she reported to Gwen, "quite enormous. It's a wonder that I can still write. I enjoyed it very much as a matter of fact. We really had a great time. And you will cheer! cheer! cheer! for my downfall, won't you?"

The *Empress* docked at Southampton on July thirteenth, and soon Marion found herself in Waterloo Station, searching in vain for both her trunk and the SCM friend who was to meet her.

"We waited, we stewed and fussed, but no luggage. Woe's me, this being a woman of the world has its worries." Eventually the trunk appeared, but the friend didn't. Marion spent her first night in London at Bailey's Hotel, where Mrs. M———, a shipboard acquaintance, had found her a room. Although Mrs. M——— had a room on the same floor, Marion wrote, with a mixture of apprehension and thrill, "Here I am, all alone in London. But there's nothing like being on your way even if you're not sure where you're going. And right now I'm going to have a hot bath and go to bed. Love from funny old London."

Getting her bearings in the big city had to be delayed a week while Marion represented Canada at the annual meeting of the British SCM in Swanwick, Derbyshire. There she met others who would be delegates to the international meeting in Switzerland, remet Bishop and Mrs. F. A. Cockin, with whom she had become great friends during their visit the year before to the Canadian SCM, and made her first acquaintance of Margaret Read, SCM's international secretary. (The Cockins had arranged for Marion to live in the home Miss Read shared with Margaret Wrong for the first half of her year of study.)

Back in London, Marion made the most of the ten days remaining before she would set off for the Continent. First on her list was to go window shopping. The clothes were "gorgeous," especially the kind she liked best: woolen suits and ensembles. She decided that her big purchase of the year would be a suit from Burberry's, but it wasn't until she was on the home stretch the following spring that she actually parted with the money to buy it. There were many temptations, but the greatest was a real ruby in Liberty's window.

"I was almost overwhelmed with the desire to buy it," she confessed in her weekly report to Gwen. "Of course I couldn't have got it even with all my travelers cheques, but I loved looking at it."

After locating 32 Russell Square, the SCM's international student club, and Canada House, Marion began to feel at home. Canada House was a great place; she couldn't wait to sign her name in the register. On this first visit she found that the way to meet visiting Canadians was to be seen reading the Toronto papers, a formula she used regularly from then on. With two students she met she went to see the changing of the guard and to watch the king and queen drive by "in an immense wine-colored Rolls-Royce."

Another day, after finding the Bank of Montreal on Threadneedle Street and establishing herself as a depositor, she took a bus to Kensington Gardens, which she loved on sight.

"It is so remarkable to step off a busy street into the heart of woods absolutely apart from noise," she wrote ecstatically. The ponds, children feeding swans and sailing boats, the beautifully kept grass, the spreading elms and oaks made the gardens a place of sanctuary to Marion who returned again and again in times of fatigue and upheaval during this important year in her life. But her best friend was the statue of Peter Pan. "He is perfectly beautiful. I carefully examined each little bird and mouse."

Between sightseeing jaunts to St. Paul's, Cheapside, Bow Church, and Highgate, "to see the stone marking the place where Dick Whittington turned back," and a theater trip, where she learned how to get three-shilling seats by standing in the queue, Marion visited the College of Physicians and Surgeons to get information about postgraduate courses in obstetrics. It was time to make plans for the main business of the year.

One of the precious documents she had carried across the Atlantic was a letter of introduction from one of her clinical instructors, a surgeon at "St. Mike's." In a note to her he had advised not being shy about asking for appointments, as "good students are soon recognized, and it is easy to meet the best men and women and every one of them ready to discuss cases and give information." He added personal good wishes from himself and his wife, saying that they hoped Marion would "continue to be as rich in friendship" as she had in her university years.

Armed with this helpful and friendly greeting, Marion made her way to Gray's Inn Road and the Royal Free Hospital, where she turned over her letter of introduction to Miss Gertrude Dearnley, a gynecological surgeon and lecturer and at that time medical officer in charge of the hospital's antenatal department. From her first meeting with this petite red-haired surgeon, who was already well started on a brilliant career, Marion had a guide and mentor for this year of study, and the gifted doctor had a protégée—and they both had a friend for life.

"I had a gorgeous time with Dr. Dearnley [she had not yet learned the British custom of using "Miss" or "Mister" to refer to surgeons] at her flat for dinner," Marion reported in a letter to her parents. "We had a great talk and got my work planned for the winter."

Miss Dearnley had encouraged her to try two examinations, one given by the Royal College of Physicians to test general medical knowledge, which would allow her to become a licentiate of the college (an LRCP); the other, given by the Royal College of Surgeons to test proficiency in surgery, would make her a member of the latter college (an MRCS).

The surgeon's other suggestions brought out an array of possibilities for clinical assistantships, internships, and special courses in midwifery in London, which offered practical experience under expert medical supervision. Finally, Miss Dearnley said, she should not leave without taking the special work that she would be eligible for at Dublin's famous hospital, the Rotunda.

"I quite agree with Dr. Dearnley, it is better to travel around than to stay cooped up in one hospital writing innumerable histories. She will give me letters of introduction to all the surgeons and I can follow them around and assist so I am *very* happy about it all," she wound up breathlessly.

On the Thursday of the August first Bank Holiday weekend, Marion, with a group of delegates bound for the Switzerland conference, left London for Paris on the Newhaven–Dieppe route because it was a little cheaper; after the first half hour on the English Channel they had definitely decided to go back by the short Calais–Dover run. The wind was high, the boat rolled about, and everyone was sick. Marion wrote home that she had managed to keep her sickness down to an hour and then was able to stay on deck "as long as I kept my head down." Describing the generally dispirited scene about her on deck, she added, "I am glad I was sick for I can appreciate the feelings of others better."

In Paris they were met by Roy, a young Australian and an Anglican theological student who had been appointed to shepherd them about Paris and bring them safely to the conference site. They stayed in the Foyer Internationale des Étudiants, where their room and breakfast cost thirteen francs a day. "So," she wrote her parents, "we hope to do very well as far as money is concerned."

For the first time in her life Marion was kept awake by noise. The horns of the Paris taxis were so varied and different that they sounded like a circus to her, and the fact that they kept on all night long and people kept walking by and talking was a continual source of wonder to her. "What it is like on the main thoroughfares, I can't imagine," she wrote home, "for our room is on a remote street down in the Latin Quarter." She noted that a Paris crowd "certainly is jovial and not at all weary even at midnight" and soon was enjoying coming home late herself and seeing the men bringing in their produce to market.

With Roy they walked miles along the river to Nôtre Dame to see it in the twilight just as the lights were coming on. Marion loved the Tower St. Jacques and paid two or three return visits to the Louvre to see the *Mona Lisa,* the Venus de Milo, the Winged Victory of Samothrace, and the Gobelin tapestries.

One evening the tourists took a bus to the Place de la Concorde and walked along the Champs Élysées to the Étoile where they visited the Unknown Soldier's grave.

To Gwen she wrote, "It was a wonderful experience to sit under the arch and watch the stars come out and all the time the fire burned over the grave."

They visited the place "where student fast life holds out," and "there we drank lemonade at a cafe sitting out on the sidewalk with about two hundred others. A couple of people got into a fight so it was all rather exciting."

On the rue de la Paix she saw a glorious sapphire, the most wonderful she'd ever seen, and went back twice just to look at it, although it fell in the same costly category as the ruby at Liberty's. Later she found an old silver shop whose prices were more reasonable, and took two happy hours to choose rings for Gwen and for her sister Helen.

Versailles was, to Marion, "the height of artificial art." When she saw the fountains she wished they had come to see the gardens by moonlight, but the Hall of Mirrors was a disappointment to her because "the only thing I could imagine in it would be a masquerade." One night she and Roy climbed to the top of Montmartre Hill and sat on a pile of stones in front of the Church of the Sacred Heart, watching the lights of Paris come on, and her last evening in Paris, the best of all, they went to the opera. She was so excited when she got home that she couldn't sleep.

"This city simply intoxicates me," she summed up to Gwen, "and it isn't the wine either for I can't drink it—it screws my mouth all up." London, she thought, was "steady," and there was "something about it that makes you admire and love it" —but Paris!

The Schiers meeting, sponsored by the International Student Service, was attended that year by three hundred young people from all over the world. Its general purpose was to foster international understanding, its specific purpose to draw up a program of assistance according to the postwar needs of students in various countries and to secure financial pledges from each delegation. The eight-day meeting had been planned to allow for daily discussion sessions and a good deal of free time for the young people to sing, dance, talk, and get acquainted.

Although this was Marion's first experience at a large international meeting, she had met so many missionaries as well as nationals of other countries at the Iroquois Point summer schools and in her SCM activities on the university campus that she was quite at home. She believed deeply in the Canadian SCM's fervent wish to help restore order in Europe and promote international understanding, and was proud to be a member of a highly respected delegation, for the Canadian SCM had won the name of being a dependable, mature, and reliable contributor to the cause of international student service. Partly because she was exuberant, enthusiastic, and friendly, and partly because she was one of those unique creatures, a woman doctor, she quickly emerged as one of the outstanding people at the conference, vocal in discussion groups and able to make friends easily.

1. "Piety Cottage," the village house in Morrisburg, Ontario, where Marion Hilliard was born.

3. Oak Hall, the Hilliard home during Marion's "glorious childhood years."

2. When Anna Marion was still the baby of the family. Ruth and Foster pose with her.

4. At Iroquois Point, the summer of 1908. Marion (center) cuddles her doll, surrounded by family: (left to right) a McAmmond cousin, Aunt Laura, Uncle Fletcher, Grandma and Grandpa McAmmond, Mrs. Hilliard holding baby sister Helen Barbara (Barby).

5. The family at Oak Hall (1906). With Mr. and Mrs. Hilliard are Ruth and Marion in front, and Foster in back.

6. Marion, the serious teen-ager.

7. The "new house" on Main Street, Morrisburg—"a surprise for Mother and the youngest Hilliards." Note the sleeping porch, which the children loved.

8. Women's College Hospital on Toronto's Rusholme Road, where Marion began as junior intern. (*Canada Pictures, Ltd., photo*)

9. Following Ruth Hilliard's wedding to Wentworth Myers, July, 1927: (left to right) Irwin, Helen (Barby), Marion, the bride and groom, Mrs. Hilliard, Mr. Hilliard.

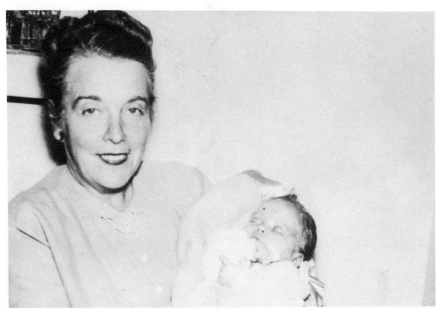

10. A proud father took this picture of his new offspring with Dr. Hilliard.

11. Dr. Marion and her friend Ethel Barter of the nursing staff pose with a "Hilliard baby." *(Toronto Star photo)*

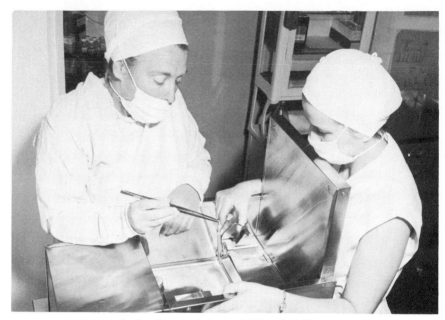

12. With a hospital colleague, Marion Hilliard (left) prepares to give a radium treatment. *(Canada Pictures, Ltd., photo)*

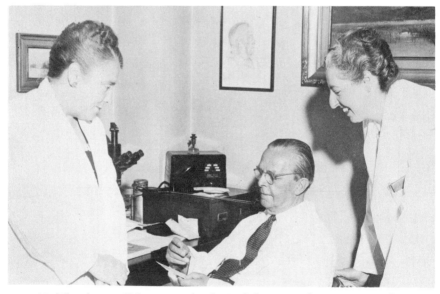

13. The three collaborators who devised the cervical scrapings test for early cancer detection in 1947: (left to right) Dr. Marion Hilliard, Dr. W. L. Robinson, Dr. Eva Mader Macdonald. *(Toronto Globe and Mail photo)*

She willingly took on the job of being conference doctor. She could be nonchalant about minor digestive upsets and colds, but one night, called to see one of the boys whose temperature was 103, she had no clue for a diagnosis except a clammy fear that it might be diphtheria.

"I really didn't know what it was," she wrote Gwen. "I was frantic, but then he suddenly recovered. A severe case of flu, I guess. Oh, well, that's the way it goes."

Troubled by the postwar antagonism between French and German students, Marion made a special effort to make friends with both. A young Austrian student won her particular interest because he was struggling toward a career in science without the aid or approval of his parents, who wanted him to go into the Army. For the next year they corresponded, as she encouraged him toward his chosen goal and he poured out his hopes, fears, and frustrations to her.

On the last night of the conference the people of Schiers reproduced their annual national celebration for the delegates. Marion described it in a letter to her mother and father.

"We were all in a Conference meeting when we heard the cannon go off and we dashed off to the top of a nearby hill. We were hurrying along a goat path when I raised my head and bang, the cannon went off again and I thought I was shot. So we climbed above the gun and above the fires. I do wish you could have seen it—fires blazing on all the hills and the moon shining on the snow-capped mountains. As we stood there, all the children from the village came along, each carrying a lighted lantern, and they wound along the road singing. I never hope to see anything more wonderful in such white moonlight. It was a crime to have to go back to the Conference and discuss some more."

On Sunday morning, the last day of the conference, an international service was held, with Roy taking the service and Russian refugees singing the chants. Talks were given by a Frenchman and an Austrian, and a Chinese doctor read the lesson. This was a marvelous experience for Marion. "If only our politicians could get to such a meeting and see a true League of Nations," she wrote home.

The day after the conference closed, the delegates were treated to a day's trip to St. Moritz, courtesy of the Swiss Railways and the municipalities along the way. Starting out at six o'clock in the morning, they had morning coffee at Davos, the noted winter sporting place, and went on to St. Moritz, where they had dinner at the Grand Palace Hotel and heard a concert. On a long walk over the mountains they were impressed with the "frail, frilly carnations and mountain roses."

"The French interpreter insisted on coming with me," Marion wrote home, "and he is a scream. I've never seen such bright eyes and such wit. I came back to the hotel reduced to a pulp from laughing and walking so far." After supper at another hotel they rode back to Schiers. Everyone was so tired and overfed that the doctor's services were in demand.

"Halfway home, someone came dashing for me," wrote Marion, "and the rest of the way home was just like one long ward rounds."

One of the other Canadian delegates was Chuck, a boy who had, like Marion, come to the conference before a year's postgraduate study in England. Chuck and Marion decided that this was an ideal time to take a tour of the Continent—goodness knew when they would ever have the chance to do such a thing again. Making inquiries, they found that if they could sell the idea to ten other people so as to travel in a group of twelve, the cost could be brought down to their level.

They settled on an itinerary that included Innsbruck, Munich, a sail down the Danube River to Vienna, an overnight train trip to Budapest, and then a fast trip north to Dresden, Berlin, and back into France by the way of Cologne—a fifteen-day trip for the magnificent sum of seventy-five dollars each.

The conference furnished a built-in travel agency in the form of student groups who advised the excited "tour leaders" on the best places to go, and wrote back home to their student houses to wangle extra-cheap rates for them. The only thing that remained was to find the other ten people. Chuck and Marion joined forces and for three days orated to anyone who would listen to them about the delights of travel on the Continent, and by the final day had cajoled the required number of people into taking the trip.

Eight countries were represented in the group of a dozen who started out from Schiers on August sixteenth, with Chuck as leader and an Irish boy as treasurer. Marion was especially delighted that an Indian couple with whom she had made friends at the conference had agreed to chaperone the tourists; Mr. M———, a magistrate, was studying juvenile-court systems of European countries, and his wife, whose fascinating, brilliant-hued saris had been the envy of every girl at the conference, was "breaking hearts wherever she trod," according to Marion. One of a pair of sisters from Finland and a Spaniard spoke no English. The non-English-speaking Finn was unanimously elected interpreter because of her proficient German, and her sister, who had learned English at Bryn Mawr College in the United States, agreed to be a "relay" interpreter. These complications did not really matter, Marion explained to her parents, "as we are all adept at smiling in any language."

In the first two hours of the journey to reach the border station between Switzerland and Austria there were four train changes, accompanied by great stress because of the mountain of luggage. At one of them there was thought to be time for lunch, but only part of the group made the train. The carefree students were overcome with mirth until they suddenly realized that Chuck, the only one who knew where they were to stay the night, and the interpreters were among those left behind.

"There we sat, plunged in silence and gloom during which time we passed through twenty-one tunnels," wrote Marion. "We imagined ourselves changing trains every half hour and losing at least one at each junction. Soon our party would be completely dissolved. I made a mental note that I'd stick close to the treasurer."

As the afternoon journey wore on, "I leaned far out of the window and watched the mountains on either side. In the distance at intervals we saw those capped with snow and on them the sun was shining. Often, as we came out of a tunnel, the first thing to meet our eyes was a gay little waterfall tumbling down the side of the mountain. Clear and white and slender, they leaped from ledge to ledge sending up their spray. In contrast to these were the sandy troughs running irregularly down the side.

"There was one church high up on a precipice all white and shining in the setting sun and on this steeple there was a cross. I shall never forget that little church with verdant green all around it and, below, the harvest fields with families working in them, mother, father, and little children."

The end of the first day found the travelers finally reunited at Innsbruck, where the Austrian delegation to the conference had arranged accommodations at a student house. But the student house proved to be for men only. While Mr. M—— went off looking for a place for the female contingent, the girls huddled tiredly together, deciding that if there was no place for them to stay they'd sit under the windows of the men's rooms and sing so they'd have to stay awake too. Finally rooms were found, and the tourists had dinner with their Austrian and Hungarian friends, who were leaving the group at this point to return home. Marion hated to say good-by to them. She and the Austrian boy who had made her a close confidante slipped off together before his train time to see Innsbruck's war memorial —a great bronze eagle—and to have a last walk and talk together. Although they corresponded for sometime, this would be the last time she would see him. Years later, after World War II, when she was traveling in Germany, she was greatly saddened to learn from mutual friends that he had been killed early in the war.

The room she and Mrs. M—— shared in a village house

looked out on the river and toward the mountains. It was all very beautiful, she wrote home—"But I'd hate to live so shut in by mountains."

Before starting for Munich next day, the entire group trouped to the market place, where their highly visible international character attracted a great jam of local people. Marion decided that this was something to capitalize on; perhaps later on, they could take up a collection! On the train they enjoyed the fruits of their marketing: buttered rolls, cucumbers, tomatoes, apples, and chocolate—and arrived in Munich in time for tea at the student house and a tour of the city.

Marion was impressed with the lack of crowding, the "clean just-washed look" of Munich, and the distinctive architecture, and the fountain she thought the most beautiful in the world.

The war memorial "is very difficult to describe, but it is the finest I ever hope to see and the saddest," wrote Marion. "The whole thing is in an immense basin. There is a marble slab at least thirty feet high supported at the four corners by tall pillars. You go down steps and under this enormous stone is a carved image of a soldier life size. As we stood there, mothers came with flowers. On the outside of the slab was written, 'They Shall Rise Again.' The weight of that stone is still on my shoulders. It was the greatest argument for peace I've ever seen."

In the Munich art galleries she was thrilled with the works of Rembrandt, Van Dyke, and *The Crucifixion* by Rubens; and the Mozart opera they heard was "one of the most perfect experiences" she had ever had. It was in Munich too that she found the gift for Gwen that she had been looking for ever since leaving London—a brilliant red shawl.

On their way again, they had a wait changing trains and settled down in the station to play games and sing and were shortly joined by three stray Americans who liked to sing too. That night at Passau, which quaint village delighted Marion with its "streets so narrow that a car could hardly go down them," they stayed at a little inn, Two Green Trees, overlooking the Danube River. Marion reported in awe that both window curtains and sheets were hand embroidered, yet the fee for the night was the equivalent of only fifty cents.

The fifth day the tourists took a boat at five o'clock in the morning and sailed down the Danube to Vienna, still talking about the pipe organ they had seen in Passau. "It is the largest pipe organ in the world, and has 1400 pipes," she reported to her father. "It was very beautiful as well as immense. The organist wasn't at home or I'm sure he would have played for us."

Walking along the boulevard one of their two evenings in Vienna, Marion and Mrs. M——— became engrossed in animated conversation and got separated from the group. Before Chuck found them, a man had approached the lovely Indian woman. Marion stoutly protected her, but confessed later that she was "a little miffed" that the man hadn't at least glanced at her too!

On the long train rides Marion pondered again and again about the war memorial she had seen in Munich and its carved inscription "They Shall Rise Again." Was it revenge they wanted? she asked herself. Would they "try to rise again to smite us and regain their power and turn the tables and retrieve their lost possessions?" Or did the inscription signify "a spiritual awakening, a new world where men would live in peace and try to live their own lives to the full, to give of their best to each other?" She finally decided that, yes, there was a hope here, a braver spirit, because it had faith. She thought of "the enormous burden of peoples' prejudice, the lust for power, the insidious treachery of international politics," and decided that in that stone was the realization that it was "a weary way we must struggle through before the new world could be built and those inspiring words come true." She asked herself the sad question, "Must some country always suffer?" and wished a tour could be evolved for "all the leading statesmen of the world to visit together the various war memorials in each country," for, "peace would certainly come that much more rapidly."

Dresden to Marion was the greatest thrill of all because she felt that it was a truly beautiful city—like Paris, only not so artificial. In a letter to Gwen she told about her most exciting evening there.

"I wore your red shawl. I knew you wouldn't mind it going to the opera in Dresden. We were guests of the State and sat in the King's box directly back from the stage, set apart by itself. Everyone stared at us through opera glasses. I restrained a desire to get up and bow. Chuck blew out his cheeks and put his pencil in his mouth at a rakish angle and pretended to be the picture of the American millionaire. I've never had more fun. People looked at us for fully ten minutes but then the curtain went up and oh! it was beautiful beyond description. I never expect to see such settings again. I was very thrilled and *didn't* weep. However, I was pretty well up in the sky.

"We went to a fashionable cafe afterwards and joked and played just to get back to normal. When we started to leave and the treasurer went to pay the bill, the orchestra began to play 'Tea for Two.' It was too much for me. With my hands on my hips, I began to prance about, much to the amusement of the rest. The headwaiter came up and said to me politely, 'You may go now please.' It's the red shawl, Gwen. It goes to my head, so what in the world will it do to you?"

By the time they got to Berlin the travelers were pretty tired. Even Marion found the city "ordinary, new, smelly and hot" and complained that there were "nothing but huge eiderdowns to put over you at night."

From Berlin they traveled for twenty-four hours straight to London, with a glimpse of the Cologne cathedral between trains, as a last bit of sightseeing. It had been a glorious trip, and probably the most exciting, in its way, of the half dozen European trips Marion would take in her lifetime. She was not a "memory-book" type of person, but she made up a small book of photographs and postcards as a memento of the journey and kept it always.

A white stucco, gabled house, standing cheek-by-jowl with others of its kind on Temple Fortune Lane in Golder's Green, became Marion's home for the six months beginning September first. Its owners, "the two Margarets," both employed by the British SCM, had welcomed the arrangement suggested by the Cockins, of providing a home for the Canadian graduate student in return for part-time housekeeping services. Thanks to her training at home, Marion was eminently qualified to undertake such a bargain.

She liked the little house with its sloping roof just visible from the street over the high hawthorn hedge and laburnum tree. At the front the dining room looked out over a flower garden. The living room faced on the back garden, as did Marion's own small room upstairs, where there were—oh, happy reminder of Morrisburg's orchards—two apple trees. She was intrigued with the stone-floored, stone-walled larder and soon became accustomed to the absence of an icebox. After she had unpacked she looked around her neat little room with its single bed pushed up against the wall in a corner, her desk and chair, the casement windows with their gay curtains, and the gas fireplace all her own, and pronounced herself "settled at last."

Margaret Wrong, daughter of a distinguished Canadian historian, had begun her career as a lecturer on the University of Toronto campus, where she became interested in the Canadian SCM. She had spent four years in Geneva, working on the European student relief program and then had come to the British SCM to develop its missionary program. In connection with this, she had spent the previous year in Africa and was full of her experience. Margaret Read, an English girl who has since become a well-known anthropologist, also had had traveling assignments, so that during the winter and spring many interesting visitors from all parts of the world were entertained at the little house, and there were long evenings of conversation around the coal grate in the sitting room. As a member of the family, Marion brought her friends home too—visiting Canadians, and others she had traveled with in Europe. To her great joy one of the Australian girls who had been on the tour, another Margaret, settled in an apartment nearby, and she and Marion became concert-and-theater companions as well as neighbors.

An early-to-bed, early-to-rise regime was quickly established. Marion got up first and got breakfast for the two Margarets and herself, leaving at 8:30 for clinics or lectures. Twice a week she marketed on the way home, arriving before six and, with true Hilliard speed and efficiency, serving dinner promptly at seven. On weekends the shopping, cooking, and domestic chores were shared by all three. Mrs. B, the charwoman, came every day to clean and "clear up."

Marion slipped into the routine easily. Sociable and friendly, she enjoyed meeting the new people who visited frequently. The two Margarets liked her unconcern about the impression she was making, and her interest in what people said and thought. "Their" student was bustling, gay, enthusiastic, full of energy, and the little house was full of fun and laughter; yet on occasion, they observed, Marion could be very serious, especially when she was trying hard to grasp another's idea or thought.

On Monday, September fifth, Marion began what was to be a six-months' clinical assistantship in the Hospital for Women in Soho Square.

"I arrived at 1:25, was told to put on a white gown and given a table and told to interview the old patients. All I did was put down their complaints and repeat medicines I knew about. It was pretty awful. Dr. R—— came in, beautiful in navy blue serge and white spats. He took the new patients, about fifty in all, and then the fun began. We examined about ten each, there were three of us clinical assistants. We examined our patient first, then he examined them, then we discussed it. I was alright in my diagnosis except once. Joy! It's great experience. There must have been over a hundred cases in today and the doctor is so kind but firm! We had a carcinoma and I felt sorry for the poor little lady, she was so sweet. At 4:15 the doctor said, 'I must break off now for a moment,' so I thought we'd all have tea but instead we just sat and waited for him to come back."

Her second day was better because she "didn't miss a single diagnosis."

Marion started a series of ten surgical pathology tutorials with the head of surgery at the Royal Free the same week, and stayed to watch her friend Miss Dearnley operate.

Overawed, she wrote to Gwen, "Jove, is she fast! In an hour and a half she did three operations. She operates like Dr. Manson. In fact, she reminds me of her all the time. She is little and very well dressed with red hair with a permanent, only it's long. I did ward rounds with her as well. She really is a pet. She has invited me to go motoring with her some Sunday down to see her family."

Marion took a lively interest in all the new people she was meeting. One of the other clinical assistants, an active member of the British Labour Party, made an especially interesting companion at teatime. Her Australian friend went with her to a promenade and concert at Queen's Hall, and to the National Art Gallery, where she was delighted with Sir Joshua Reynolds' *The Holy Family* and *Angel Heads*.

She was a little homesick at first.

"It gives me such a thrill when people are friendly and so this week has been quite filled but when I think of college beginning and rugby and Elgin House, oh how I want to go back. Canada is such a splendid country. I don't know how I'd ever leave it again. Even India is a bit far off to me now," she wrote mournfully.

Then the Canadian mail arrived, and she heard from everyone at home and received some copies of *Varsity*. One of the letters she treasured was a joint epistle from ten of her SCM friends written from Elgin House. Full of loving good wishes and news of her old friends, it contained affectionate notes from her teacher and friend "Hookie," her sister Helen, and Roy, the Australian who had shown her Paris and was now en route home.

The early afternoon of Tuesday, October fourth, found candidate number 140, Dr. A. M. Hilliard of Canada, turning up at

Examination Hall with the pink card that entitled her to take the examinations for LRCP and MRCS. Four days of written examinations covered medicine, midwifery, and surgery.

A week later her oral examination on midwifery came in the early afternoon, and she was to return at six o'clock "to be personally informed of the result." The next day the clinical and viva voce parts of the examination in medicine were given in the afternoon, and at six-fifteen she was to get the results.

She passed the licensing examination but failed in surgery, a blow to her pride that sent her scurrying to find out where she could do extra surgical work before January, when the examination would be given again.

From this setback, Marion bounced back quickly, in the excitement of her new experiences at Soho. She enjoyed her work in the antenatal clinic, observed carefully the handling of septic abortions, and was so admiring of the work on sterility that she wrote enthusiastically that she was thinking of doing an article on the subject. Later this was to become one of her major interests.

At the same time the SCM fall program began and she was in demand as a speaker, and as a guest at foreign student parties. She heard the London Symphony Orchestra give a Bach concert, went for a long country walk in Windsor with some of her Canadian and Australian friends, and with them began to plan a Christmas party.

On the evening of the ninth annual observance of Armistice Day for World War I Marion was pleased to have a reunion with Mr. and Mrs. M———, her Indian traveling companions. Earlier in the day she had one of the outstanding experiences of her entire year in England, about which she wrote to Gwen in great detail.

"Today was one of the greatest sights of my life. I dashed thro' my work and got down to Trafalgar Square by 10:15 and even then the crowds had gathered. I got a good place at the corner of Whitehall and Downing St. just about 20 yds. from the Cenotaph. The various detachments of soldiers marched past—

the Grenadiers were marvellous examples of military deportment, but I fell for those guards—long red capes, brass helmets with a long cream tassel on top which waved back and forth as they swung along. The 'Old Contemptibles' were a sight to behold—poor broken-down men. The music was very patriotic, altho' at times they lapsed into 'Keep the Home Fires Burning,' 'It's a Long Way to Tipperary,' etc. At about ten to eleven I decided I was going to see what was going on right at the Cenotaph, so I shinnied up the wall of a building and clung by my finger tips.

"From this precarious position I saw the King walk up and lay the wreath on the stone steps. The Prince in the blue grey uniform of the Air Force looked very well. Chamberlain, Winston Churchill, Baldwin all were in the charmed circle arranged around the Cenotaph. I never hope to see such a crowd again.

"As Big Ben struck the last note of 11, the big cannon went off, then there was utter silence. You simply can't realize the silence of such an enormous gathering. Across the street from me were a few trees with just a small number of leaves left. The rustle of those leaves sounded like a mighty forest in the stillness. It gave me a very eerie feeling to hear those dead leaves trying their best to give utterance.

"After the 2 minutes silence, there was the Last Post done by the King's buglers. Then the Bishop of London conducted a short service and everyone sang 'O, God, Our Help in Ages Past' to the accompaniment of massed bands.

"After the service all the contingents passed by the Cenotaph, laid down their flowers and went on to Westminster Abbey where they passed by the Unknown Warrior's grave. By this time I had found my friends and we went to the Abbey too.

"Then I had lunch for twenty-two cents," she finished, returning rapidly to everyday matters, "and went for my first clinic with Mr. R———. He is very good and I like him."

Usually the mail from Canada was the high point of any day, but Marion was "chilled to the core" by a letter from Dr. Guest suggesting that Women's College Hospital wanted her "to be able to *do* good work as well as to have *seen* good work." Was she going to be expected to "do a Caesarian the day [she got] back?" Marion wondered. Though briefly depressed by the letter, she was, on the whole, very cheered at how much she was learning. In the clinic work with Mr. R———, the teaching surgeon at Charing Cross Hospital, she was gaining "an enormous amount, particularly in prognosis." Whenever she could she returned to watch Miss Dearnley at work in the operating rooms at the Royal Free. In a letter to Gwen she listed six gynecological operations Miss Dearnley had done one afternoon.

"All of this in less than three hours and taking time off for tea," wrote Marion incredulously.

Chuck and the Irish treasurer of the European trip invited Marion and her neighbor Margaret to a weekend at Oxford late in November. Marion wrote a six-page letter to Gwen, excitedly describing the high points—the sightseeing ("Magdalen's tower was my favorite because Hart House tower on our campus is so much like it. The architect must have had it in mind when he built ours"), the conferring of degrees ("If I were getting one, I'd certainly get it in absentia"), the formal theater party ("We were astonished to see how handsome the boys were in their dinner jackets"), and lunch at the erstwhile treasurer's rooms.

"Those Oxford youths certainly are surrounded by comfort. There were six of us and we were served by a Scout. We had white bait, veal cutlet, potatoes, peas and cauliflower, coffee ice cream with whipped cream, and coffee. Mac's living room is about twice the size of our old room, with piano, books, table and fireplace. And my, we had a good time."

On Mac's piano Marion discovered a book of Canadian and American college songs. After lunch they played and sang so lustily that they attracted visits by other students who joined in. It was a gay afternoon, and "Never did I think I would be singing 'Lydia Pinkham' from an Oxford sitting room," she wrote.

The Sunday began with a service at Christ Church Cathedral,

where the girls were entranced with the choir boys' singing, and ended with high tea in rooms overlooking Magdalen's beautiful gardens, where their host was another "alumnus" of the European tour, and finally a supper party given by a Canadian girl who had just come to Oxford following her graduation from the University of Toronto.

"A triumphant weekend," Marion wound up her letter. "They are such nice boys. I feel like their aunt sometimes—and their sister the rest of the time. And listen to this—I'm invited to the Commencement Ball at Worcester. Joy! I was thrilled! Can you imagine me dancing *all* night?"

Christmas was bound to be difficult; it was Marion's first one away from home and family. She and her two Margarets of Temple Fortune Lane always laughed when they got together in future years to remember how she "rode home on a London bus, hugging a bunch of holly and crying all the way."

Christmas day turned out to be cold and wet. Marion went off to the morning service at Southwark Cathedral, which she found "curiously interesting" but "lacking in the spirit," and returned to get dinner for six at Temple Fortune Lane. Reporting her menu to Gwen—turkey, potatoes, creamed artichokes, cranberry sauce, fruit salad, plum pudding and hard sauce, and salted almonds—she said that it was "excellent—even if I do say it as shouldn't." The best part of the day for her was the end. In late afternoon it began to snow hard and kept on for hours.

The next day, Boxing Day, she struggled through the snow ("They never heard of such a thing as a snow plow here," she grumbled) to the Royal Free, where she had promised to help Miss Dearnley give a small party for the patients.

"They asked me, little Prohibition Anna, to pass the port, so it was through me that all the patients had a merry afternoon, but you might keep that a secret, please."

This December twenty-sixth was topped off in great style by a cable Marion had been waiting for. "Boy. Both well," read the welcome message from Mike Pearson.

Marion's Christmas presents and mail from home were delayed until early January, so New Year's Eve was "a bit lonely and sad." Then Bishop and Mrs. Cockin invited her for the holiday dinner and she started the new year as cheerfully as was possible, considering what lay ahead for her.

On December twenty-ninth Marion began two grueling weeks' study to get ready for her surgery examination. It proved to be fifteen days of nervous apprehension.

"I may fail again and, oh Gwen, the humiliation. I could never live it down." Her days were "the regular old Maytime grind," with four hours in the library or the hospital doing anatomy in the mornings, a quick sandwich and coffee, then back to the clinic, then tea, then more surgery, then dinner, then still more surgery, and so on.

One day, to shake the cobwebs out of her brain, she had a good long sleep, then a two-mile walk to see the charwoman's new baby. It was her eighth, and, as Marion wrote home, "What do you think they're going to name it? 'Dawn!' I advised 'Sunset.'"

A packet of letters came from her family; thrilled, she sat right down to write back to them, noting in her diary that she was "sorry to have written to the family when I was in this mood, but then they'll probably enjoy the lonesomeness."

Finally, the first examination was over and except for a slight difficulty with "that old oesophagus," she found to her surprise that it was easy for her. She was very relieved to have it over with but a little worried because it had seemed easy. Yet this was no time to let up, for there were three more examinations to come—her orals and the clinical examinations.

By Sunday, January twenty-second, they were all over but one, and she went for a long walk through Kensington Gardens, which was particularly beautiful, with "blue-grey mist in the trees," a deep blue sky above, and "one lone star." The peacefulness was balm to Marion's sick nerves. She hadn't been able to sleep for several nights and indeed, on Saturday night, had noted in her diary, "Will this worry ever end? Sure I've failed again—

so hard to be a failure—my family will love me but won't understand."

It was one of the few times in her life, either as a young person or as an older person, that she had a tinge of self-pity. She decided that she had had too many examinations in the last year: twenty last June, ten in October, and now these four. She was afraid she had been "all dithery and stammery" at the oral examination, and seesawed between being glad that they were over and fearing that she really was "a dithery person" after all. She assured herself that she had worked hard and steadily, doing surgery five days a week for two and a half months—and that should have taught her something. She thought of Dr. Guest who would be so frightfully disappointed and decided that if she had failed she wouldn't try again because it just wasn't worth it. Gloomily she thought that probably the Women's College Hospital wouldn't take her on, but then brightened to remember that at least she did have her LRCP.

She wrote all of these sad thoughts to Gwen and then added a P.S.: "Do you think my failing in my exams is a judgment on me for not being a missionary?"

The next morning she wrote in her diary, "One of the worst nights of my life, couldn't sleep, tossed and tumbled, re-did the exams all the time. Can't get away from the idea of failure, but oh the beautiful park and the lone star, the world is beautiful and is a good place to live in after all, but I still am sure I failed."

As she was going into her surgical-pathological examination that Monday afternoon she found that the reports had come in on two microscopic slides which she had had to examine in connection with her Saturday examination. One was a myeloma of bone that she recognized easily, but the other had her puzzled. She knew it was a glandular carcinoma and finally had put down "carcinoma of prostate," only to learn when she got outside that the other students agreed that it was thyroid. Since she had done considerable work on the thyroid at medical school, she was very upset to think that she had missed it. But now she found that she had been right, and the examiner said to her, "I congratulate you. You are the first one who has diagnosed that correctly."

Briefly comforted, she went to her examination.

At four o'clock she returned to hear the results of the final examination, so sure she had failed that when the man told her she had made it she just stood looking at him, openmouthed, then tore home to write a new installment on her letter to Gwen.

"Oh Gwennie, I hate to write it but I *passed,* and very well too! I couldn't believe it. I knew I knew my work but that hound of an examiner simply took all my nerve. He bawled at me so! You've no idea how I've worked and the anatomy I've done! From now on, I do obstetrics and gynaecology alone. . . . I can never again feel as much of a failure as I did on Saturday night, but after I had thought of that P.S. about being a missionary, my sense of humor returned and I was perfectly tranquil at the thought of failing. There were five of us up from Charing Cross Hospital and only two of us got through. The usual rate is twenty-five percent. The exams are awful and, just think, I'll never have to take another. If you were only here to celebrate with me."

For a week Marion did no more work than was absolutely necessary. After debating about cabling the family, she decided that she couldn't afford it and wrote them the good news instead. Half asleep but happy, she went to her clinics at Soho and South London, and came home to lie in front of the fire, thinking about the "nice parts" of the examinations, but by the end of the week she was admonishing herself in her diary, "I must brace up now and collect my wits."

Back in Toronto, where she was having a winter holiday, Vonnie received a note from proud Father Hilliard, telling of Marion's success. By return mail Von wrote him that she had "promptly called Dr. Guest, and she said she would announce it at the board meeting of the Women's College Hospital." Dr. Guest had told her that Marion was the third Canadian woman to win the MRCS.

"Please accept my congratulations to you and Mrs. Hilliard," she wrote, "in having such a brilliantly clever daughter and best of all, a dear good one. What a gorgeous inheritance you both have given your children!"

There was just a month now before Marion would enter Queen Charlotte Lying-In Hospital to do a four-week internship in midwifery, and only three weeks until she would leave Temple Fortune Lane. The two Margarets were expecting a new student to take her place, and Marion had arranged to spend a vacation week, except for her last clinics, with her Australian friend, the other Margaret, before starting her new venture.

It was a happy and eventful four weeks. The so-admired Mr. R——— at Soho recognized the new MRCS by paying particular attention to her performance and allowing her to give more responsible assistance. At South London she chafed at the slowness of the surgeon but stuck it out for three weeks, possibly because she was "neat and thorough." Twice a week she dropped in at the Royal Free to watch Miss Dearnley operate, noting her observations carefully in her diary.

A Christmas gift from a friend, the diary had had rather cryptic entries up to now, but this month it came into its own. Marion fell into a nightly ritual of having a hot bath, then sitting on the floor in front of her bedroom fireplace and writing up her day and her plans for the future.

Relieved of the strenuous studies, she picked up on some social life, going to see *The Student Prince*; to lunch at the Cafe Russe, where she met "a real honest-to-goodness countess, still very beautiful"; to the Cheshire Cheese with two Canadian doctors she ran across at Canada House; and, reciprocating, had the two young men to supper at Temple Fortune Lane. She went on a book-buying spree on Charing Cross Road, and at long last bought her suit at Burberry's, a gray and blue tweed that was destined to see her through her first ten years of practice. The suit was proudly initiated when she attended a medical meeting as Miss Dearnley's guest.

At home in the evenings she wrote letters, listened to the

radio, and read Rupert Brooke and Havelock Ellis. Three of the letters she wrote showed the plans slowly evolving in her mind: one to a friend she had known in medical school, a woman doctor who was in her second year of practice in Toronto, asking how she was getting on and what her experience had been; another to the Faculty of Medicine at the University of Toronto, to ask if there was a possibility that she might be employed part time to demonstrate anatomy; and the third to the Women's College Hospital, applying for an appointment to the obstetrics and gynecology staff.

The picture of herself as a medical missionary in India was receding, although it was to be brought sharply to the fore in another two weeks. Her first half year in England had given her much more than the LRCP, the MRCS, and some sharpening of professional skill. Association with Miss Dearnley and other instructors and experience in the everyday life of the clinics had shown her that there could be such a thing as equality for women in the field of medicine. It might be lacking in Canada now, but this would not always be so, especially if Canadian women doctors turned out topnotch performances in the next years. Perhaps it was now that Professor Hendry's words came back to her. She had asked his advice about trying for a spot at Toronto General Hospital.

"Even if you could get it, don't." The good professor was forthright as well as gentle. "You'd be the last flick of the dog's tail there. Go to the Women's College and help build the department. You can achieve something there. And get into the hurly-burly of practice and prove yourself!"

Now the congratulatory mail from home began to arrive and Marion reveled in every sentence of a "wonderful letter from Von" and letters from her family. "Mother and Father are so pleased and seem to think that that MRCS is so important," she wrote in her diary, "that it makes me want to hang my head and steal away. I'm glad they're getting such a kick out of it."

The highest spot in the entire beautiful month was Marion's visit to the Dearnleys' cottage in Surrey.

"It was perfect in every way," she wrote to Gwen. "The sun shone all day for the first time in two weeks and the air was springy. Miss Dearnley and her sister met me at the train and at the house Mrs. Dearnley welcomed me as though I were a long lost child. She's very sweet to me. We went for a long walk through the woods and gathered pussy willows and catkins. Then I sat in the garden in a shaded nook and listened to the birds.

"We had an enormous dinner after which I had a sleep while the others read. Then I helped with the dishes and made fudge for them. After tea, some company dropped in. I escaped and went out and watched the sunset. It was so wonderful to be at home in such a lovely English home and to be able to see the sun and the sunset. I may not have learned much surgery, but I have made some good friends. When I was leaving, Mrs. Dearnley whispered to me, 'I wish you were never going back to Canada.'"

Before she knew it February twenty-fifth came, her last day at Temple Fortune Lane. "My last night here, a sad thought," she wrote in her diary. "I've loved it so." Then she added a typically Hilliard comment. "Yet the housekeeping has had a funny mental bias on me. I didn't realize it until tonight." Many times in her life Marion plunged head on into the thing at hand, the thing to be done, reserving the "mental bias" until such time as it would not clutter up her life and interfere with her performance.

After moving her belongings to the residential college of the Queen Charlotte, on Cosby Street, Marion returned for her vacation week at the apartment of her Australian friend. Margaret invited people in for bridge, arranged a theater party to see Noel Coward and Raymond Massey in *The Second Man* ("both these men write, produce *and* act," an impressed Marion wrote Gwen). The Oxford boys came down and took the girls riding. It was the first time Marion had seen London from a private car, and she was intrigued with the little Austin that "fairly skimmed over the city."

Among Marion's regular correspondents that year were two Toronto men whom she had allowed herself, in spite of her single-mindedness about a career in medicine, to take at least half seriously. Of one, she had written in her diary on a lonesome night, "I do wish that scamp would stay out of my dreams. It's worse than ever when I don't see him, because seeing him always brings me down to earth! If he'd only get engaged, I could quite easily settle him, but instead, he does insinuate himself in front of my future plans."

Now, in a cozy tea conversation with Margaret, she told all about him. Margaret's instant reaction was that she ought to marry him. Recording the little talk in her diary, Marion added, "And sometimes I think so myself."

The week brought her two batches of Canadian mail. Maryon Pearson sent the first pictures of the new baby, and asked if she would be little Geoffrey's godmother. From one of the Toronto swains came some light reading, a "congratulations gift," and the news that he had a new job and would be in Toronto to greet her in the fall. A friend in the office of the Faculty of Medicine at Toronto wrote, along with news of jobs and engagements among Marion's classmates, and an account of a fire in the medical building on February sixth, that appointments for demonstrators of anatomy would be made in September and she would probably have a good chance for one.

Her young woman doctor friend chronicled her experiences in practice, advising Marion to look for teaching, examining, and consulting jobs, since the financial rewards for straight medical practice were slim at first. In her own case, monthly receipts in the first year had begun with eight dollars and fifty cents and ended with fifty-nine dollars. Other women doctors in town were "just great" about helping new ones, she said, and suggested that Marion team up with one or two other doctors to cut overhead expenses. The cost of announcement cards were "just fierce, and not worth it," and she listed the amounts of fees for professional affiliations, such as the College of Physicians and Surgeons, which then stood at twenty-five dollars a year.

"Please don't get discouraged," she concluded, "because with your nerve and personality, you can get anywhere. When you

come home, I will help any way I can and don't worry, you are
bound to be a success, as you always have been."

All such pleasant and helpful news was swept from Marion's
mind, however, by a note from an acquaintance, congratulating
her on her appointment as a medical missionary in behalf of the
society whose representative Marion had interviewed a year ago.
The president of the society had said, her informant added, that
Marion had not yet been definitely assigned but they were listing
her in the church calendar as "missionary in the field."

Marion was furious, perhaps partly at being confronted with
a loose end she had not quite yet decided how to tie up. "I was
simply dumb with rage," she burned to Gwen, "and tramped up
and down Margaret's flat like a madman. Imagine the insolence
of putting my name on their calendar without my permission."

After twenty-four hours of fuming she cabled the society's
president, "CANNOT UNDERSTAND RUMOR CONCERNING MISSION-
ARY SOCIETY. PLEASE CONTRADICT. SETTLING TORONTO SEPTEM-
BER."

Although the dream of her girlhood seemed to have exploded,
the next episode in this eventful week showed that it was still
there in the "someday" category.

It was only a day later that she came home from a diverting
evening at dinner and the opera to find an astounding letter
from a well-known Toronto surgeon, then a consultant to the
staff of the Women's College Hospital.

"I have formed a rather high idea of your ability and merit," he
wrote, "and now that we are campaigning for a million-dollar
hospital, we propose that those in charge of our departments be
as well trained as those in any other hospital, and will be content
with nothing less."

He had seen her application for appointment to the obstetrics
staff, but he now proposed that she do two more years of postgraduate work in England and Vienna and return to Women's
College Hospital as chief of obstetrics.

"My eyes are popping out!" wrote Marion in her diary. "What
shall I *do?*" The fact that this professional proposal had arrived

at almost the same time as the letter and gift from one of her two favorite men friends seemed symbolic to her. "Thank fortune for his sending me the book right now—it's a good antidote to wealth and fame." Then, as if to steady herself in a rocking world, she added, "Every good gift cometh from the Father."

For several days she went around in a state of concentrated excitement and once again went sleepless. Margaret, who had lived through the prolonged gloom of the January examination days, did not hide her amusement. Marion came down to earth enough to start drafting her reply. Then, at her last clinic at Soho, she asked Mr. R——'s advice. His reply was brief and to the point: "Go home. You need practice now."

To the Women's College Hospital consultant she wrote that she had decided to come home and practice for five years, hoping to keep up her surgery, and after that, if she were "making good," would return for study in Europe. She thought that the hospital was quite right in demanding the very best and she was honored at his thought of her but believed she would be too young even in another two years to undertake such a responsible job.

But to Gwen she unburdened her heart. "It would take all of my youth from this moment, and somehow or other I must have my life first and my profession second. It also bans marriage and I can't turn my back on that possibility now." Telling her confidante about the text of her letter to the hospital, she said, "I said 'if I were making good' in five years—what I really meant was if I have given up my hopes for marriage and my ideas about someday being a missionary." Her thoughts and feelings turned in several directions at once. "If only I were a man, it would be so easy. . . . I can't face a $4000 debt on top of the $1750 I'll have when this year is finished. . . . Life is frightfully thrilling, isn't it? How will I ever sleep tonight? . . . I guess I haven't enough ambition for worldly success. And the idea of women for a women's hospital doesn't fire my imagination."

The last day of this turbulent week was a beautiful early spring Sunday. "The winters here are worse than at home," she wrote to her family, "but we never had a day like this in March." The girls opened the windows wide to the gentle breezes and went for a four-hour walk in Kensington Gardens. It was "sheer paradise" with, again, the blue-gray mist over the trees, crocuses and daffodils coming up, the willows a pale green, and the children playing at the feet of her friend Peter Pan.

The next morning Marion began her four-week course at the Queen Charlotte in a group of ten interns—"Four qualified and six still undergraduates." Marion and Miss L—— were the only women. The fee for this course in midwifery was eight pounds, eight shillings. Students signed an agreement to spend full time in the hospital, working under the direction of obstetrics surgeons, and to wear "overalls provided" while on duty in the labor wards, where they were always to sign in and out.

The way of life was quite different from Temple Fortune Lane. Each intern had a small room and shared a common living room that had a fireplace, Gramophone, and Ping-pong table. A maid turned on her bath and awakened her at ten minutes of nine. After breakfast there were clinics until twelve-thirty. Afternoons were free. Tea was served "if you ring for it" at four, in the sitting room, and after a seven-o'clock dinner interns were on call all night. Tea and toast were to be had whenever they came in after a call.

The minute she entered the labor ward Marion felt the "old lure." She observed a "rather messy job of rotating [turning the baby around in the uterus to the proper position for birth]," done on the patient's bed instead of on the delivery table ("Every time I see someone else do a job like this, it encourages me a little"), and assisted with a forceps delivery the first evening. For the next four weeks she was on the run from night till morning and soon found out that those free afternoons were for making up on lost sleep.

"But oh, Gwen," she wrote, "I love this life! It certainly is the life for me. The irregular hours, the labor room, making tea at 2:30 in the morning, it all simply thrills me to the wick."

One morning at two o'clock she and Miss L—— returned

from a long session in the delivery room. They had forgotten their keys and had to prowl around the still unfamiliar house until they found their rooms. Searching vigorously, they finally found a teakettle, milk, sugar, tea, and cake, and, after opening every cupboard door they could find, a gas ring. With great joy they put the kettle on, but in a few minutes the fire went out and neither of them could find a shilling for the meter.

Marion thought that this was hilarious; in fact, everything was either immensely exciting, extremely funny, or sometimes both, in this four weeks.

One night the first week there were seven deliveries, including one pair of twins and one breech birth. Another night she slept only two hours and there were so many deliveries that every intern had a chance at one. ("Very good night's huntings," said Marion's diary, jauntily.) She learned how to induce labor with injections of pituitary extract, how to deliver a hydrocephalus, and what a Mongoloid baby looked like. One day after the obstetrician had done two "Caesars" and a forceps delivery he asked her to take the next forceps case, which made her very proud. At six o'clock one morning she had a chance to do a delivery because none of the men answered the call—and, "I'm on the spot all the time," she wrote.

After two weeks she was saying in her diary, "If only these four weeks would go slowly for I *must* learn a lot." But by the end of the four weeks she was noting confidently that she was handling cases she "wouldn't have believed possible a month ago." The surgeon, who called her "Miss Canada," she summed up briefly to Gwen: "He's very good to me. I like him. He operates very quickly."

Toward the end of the course, the exuberant Scotch interns rigged a false call to the labor ward, getting Marion and Miss L——— out at three A.M. The girls thought it was very funny and briefly plotted for the men's comeuppance, but by this time were too busy and too tired to carry out their plan.

Although she had little time, Marion was determined to see *The Desert Song*, which she did, standing through the entire performance. She and her Australian friend Margaret spent another afternoon rowing on the Serpentine, having tea and seeing the cinema *The King of Kings*. She recorded that "everything was very reverent and I couldn't help but weep over Peter." Then there was an interesting medical meeting to which she went with Miss Dearnley, who was "looking very smart in a blue evening coat"; and a hurried weekend at the Dearnleys' Surrey cottage where Marion had "a heavenly sleep, then breakfast in bed and heaps of it, a long walk in the woods, a large dinner and then more sleep until teatime."

A "wonderful letter" came from Dr. Guest from the Women's College Hospital.

"Congratulations, my dear, you cannot imagine how thrilled we all were to get your good news and yesterday I got a letter from Miss Dearnley also sounding your praises. Isn't it nice to feel you have a disposition which can adapt itself to different people—it is the greatest asset a physician can have—far greater than degrees or money or influence.

"I thought your application was good and timely. Your judgment is good, Marion. There is no use going off and doing a lot of good work under a bushel in this funny world.

"There are always a disappointingly large number of our profession ready to crush if they can—it just does still amaze me despite my determination to listen to none of it but just go steadily on to the positive goal and carry everyone with me I can. You see I would bring all my lovely medical children up with a silver spoon if it were possible."

She gave some news of the hospital and Marion's friends and enclosed "a little present to be used for how you wish, for clothes, music, or for school."

Immediately from the Queen Charlotte, Marion went to the Mothers' Hospital on Lower Clapton Road, a hospital maintained by the Salvation Army, where she was to take another postgraduate course in midwifery, lasting three weeks and costing nine pounds, nine shillings.

A few days after she arrived at her new post she received a certificate from the Queen Charlotte testifying that she had "attended ninety-two cases of labor" in four weeks and assisted at "various obstetrical operations."

"The Mothers'" was quite a comedown from the luxury of the Queen Charlotte. Marion had one bleak little room with a single light, but, as she wrote to Gwen, "I love the atmosphere of this hospital. Everyone seems so happy as well as efficient. It sounds funny to hear people calling each other 'Captain' and 'Adjutant' and you'd roar with laughter if you could see where I eat—all by myself, screened in from the main dining room. At the Queen Charlotte I was likely to be the only woman at the table with nine men! It's such a change from the man's world there to the woman's world here."

The other interns were not very friendly to Marion at first. No one so much as spoke to her about the weather—"which was appalling at the time," wrote Marion—until they discovered that she was not an American.

"The English seem to picture these carefree Americans as deliberately rushing their barriers of reserve and finding the hidden places where they carefully lock up all extraneous emotions. It can be understood, but personally, I think they miss a lot of fun!" Marion wrote.

During the period of coolness Marion stoutly recorded in her diary that she was now "used to coming into new places," and did not think she would "ever be really lonesome again." "Maybe I'm cured by being on my own so much," she added hopefully.

She got right into the thick of things, with a delivery at eight o'clock the evening of her first day.

"It was perfectly straightforward, no tears or anything. Here they make you bathe the baby as well, so I did and had great fun. Just as I was going to put the baby in the tub with the Adjutant helping, the nurse came in and said she was taking the mother back to the ward, at which the Adjutant fled saying 'I must pray with her first' and I continued and was just finishing drying the baby when she returned. They are such nice friendly souls. I like them and their religion. There's very little intolerance among them."

The first week of this course brought Marion a never-to-be-forgotten lesson in obstetrics that she described to Gwen.

"I am chagrined. I delivered another baby all okay without tearing, but alas, face to pubes [to the front of the mother rather than the normal position of face to the side]. When I examined the mother before delivery, I felt a foot, but didn't go high enough to feel an ear. As the sister said, it's the result that counts—but next time I'll find that ear!"

Before long she was recording two "Caesars" that came while she was on duty, for one of which she gave the anesthetic, and, for the other, assisted with the operation. After that she sailed through the course happily.

For weeks Marion had seethed with anticipation at the prospect of a reunion with her brother Foster, who, with Leila and Marion's first nephew and niece, Joseph and Anna Miriam, would come to England on the way home for their first furlough from the mission field in Japan. She had found an apartment for them, and made a long list of things they could do together.

When they finally arrived, midway in her course at "The Mothers'," she wrote happily in her diary that Foster and Leila were "just the same," and that "Sonny," aged five, and "Mimi," aged three, were "very good and unspoiled."

Her first performance as an aunt was not a success, however. She took the children to the park, got her prized new suit soaked in the rain, and was shockingly late getting back to the hospital. Moreover, she had to confess, she got a little impatient, "Because the children go so slowly and interfere with conversation." When, after a few days, her brother asked her to look after the children for a week while he and Leila went to Scotland for a holiday, she was really downcast. After all, she felt, they had come to see *her*.

"All my plans gone west," she mourned in her diary. "What shall I do?"

However, she took over, with Madge, a 1928 counterpart of the baby sitter, committed to aid her. It was a worrisome week. She couldn't wait to get back from clinics and lectures to make sure the children were all right. Mimi developed a cough. One day at lunch the children were noisy and she was cross.

"I must be better for they are really so sweet," she reproached herself in her diary.

In spite of being able to assist with Caesarians, she found life on the gloomy side for other reasons too. She was running out of money, and a reply to an appeal to her Kappa fairy godmother in Toronto brought the news that her friend had had stock-market losses and could send only the token amount she enclosed.

But by the end of the week life was rosy again. She took the children to call on a friend for tea and they "loved it and behaved beautifully," she recorded proudly. Foster and Leila returned, bringing presents for everyone, and remarked about how healthy the children looked. Marion's Australian friend Margaret offered to lend her the money she needed.

Relieved of her auntly responsibilities and financial anxieties, Marion spent a restful Sunday at the Dearnley cottage. Her last week in London before going to Dublin for her final tour of duty at the Rotunda was the whirl of family fun she had looked forward to. She and Foster took the children to the zoo, then the whole family had a picnic at Hampton Court, and an outing to Kew Gardens, now in full spring bloom. The three adults called in Madge to baby sit, and went to the theater. One day an enormous letter arrived for them from the family in Morrisburg.

Irwin, now a lad of seventeen, wrote that while Mother was away at a missionary convention he and Aunt Sue were "running the house, or rather, letting it creep." He had tried to make a starch pudding, but "the result was hunks," which he put through a sieve. The old McLaughlin Buick was "running like a bird—that is with hops and jumps and a lot of chirps."

Father Hilliard wrote that he had made suggestions to R. B. Bennett (Conservative, then leader of the opposition in the Canadian Parliament) about getting more support for the party from "our young voters." He had gone up to Parliament, but did not wait to hear all the speeches, as, "I am like some of your doctors and leave too soon." There had been a revival meeting at the Iroquois church and one of the schoolteachers "came forward and knelt at the altar." The roads along the Rapide du Plat were "just awful." Mother had just arrived "to gladden four hearts," in a snowstorm, and they had celebrated with a juicy T-bone steak for dinner. It was wonderful, he said, "to be a big toad in the home puddle."

"We are a happy family tonight," Father wound up. "My, won't it be great when we are all at home this summer? We must just thoroughly enjoy it, just have a ripping good hilarious time. I sometimes think if I lived over again I would try to soak in much more enjoyment."

Mother assured Marion that she was always remembered in the family's morning prayers.

"I think of the women you are helping through their confinement," she said, "and pray you may be an inspiration to them. A wonderful life, dear, reproducing the life of Jesus."

She had enjoyed the convention, she said, but had been alarmed for fear she might be dropped from the executive committee, when it was found that there were seven more members than the constitution called for. However, others had been eliminated.

"Of course they have to have some women on the Board and it might as well be myself, that is how I can be happy," said Mother.

One of their dear, close neighbors had died, and his widow hesitated about going to live with her daughter in the city.

"I told her," wrote Mrs. Hilliard, "that I wouldn't hesitate if I were in her place. I wonder if I ever shall live to be queer and my children think me a burden. I hope not," she added wistfully.

"Now, my dear one, good night," she concluded. "We have a lovely happy home. I am glad I am here. Dad seems so *satisfied* when I return. We love your letters, and are so glad your doctors can appreciate a real genuine good girl as our Marion is."

The Dearnleys had invited Marion to come to Cornwall, where they would be on holiday, after she finished her work in Dublin. Marion was thrilled at the prospect of finishing off her wonderful year in such a pleasant way. At the same time Miss Dearnley suggested that it would be much nicer if she and Marion called each other by their Christian names, and at this Marion was shaken.

"How will I ever call her Gertrude?" she wrote in her diary, and to Gwen: "Can you fathom that? I haven't worked up the courage yet. Imagine me calling London's finest woman surgeon by her first name! Please don't tell a soul—not one!"

On one of her last evenings Gertrude gave a party for her. Marion ironed her old white evening dress, met Gertrude and two of her colleagues for dinner and a performance of *This Year of Grace,* for which Noel Coward had written music and book. The whole evening was "a hilarious party," she reported to Gwen, "and I didn't want to go home and end the day. But I did."

In reply to Marion's note of thanks, Gertrude said that she and her friends had enjoyed the evening too.

"It is so nice to meet someone with enthusiasm," she went on. "It has been a real pleasure to know you and we want you to come to Cornwall most awfully. I think you have worked very hard and it is important to get some play in too, in this world. I don't think really English people have as little sentiment as you think. Anyway, *these* English people are very fond of you."

In one of the short essays Marion wrote in the early years of her practice she described her experience with English people.

"I had a funny idea when I went to England," she said, "that I was just 'one of those Colonials,' to be regarded with indifference and hauteur. But I was quite mistaken. Never have I met such real friendliness or hospitality. It isn't the potluck variety, of which we at home are sometimes too proud, but a more gracious thing. You feel you have been chosen from among hundreds to come and grace their table and you shall have the best.

Perhaps it is just that they have more and better manners, but it is certainly something to be cherished."

Marion's first impression of Dublin was "old, dirty, untidy," but she loved the handsome Irish people and their accent right from the start. The little maid who cleaned her room had blue eyes and black hair, which Marion thought "a perfect combination."

Her weekly schedule included three morning clinics in gynecology, two lectures in midwifery, and daily observation of major operations. Again she was on call all night. Carrying a pink card identifying her as an intern of Rotunda Hospital, she went out to do home deliveries, in partnership with a male intern, an Australian, who was "the steady, plodding type and very interested in his work."

She took a lot of joshing from the other women students about running off at night with Dr. X——. One morning she missed her favorite sweater and was searching for it when she ran into him in the common room. Blushing and gulping, he said that the maid had found her "jumper" on his bed that morning. It struck Marion as being very funny.

"His face was priceless," she wrote Gwen, "and every time I think of Elisa holding that sweater at him, I just shake with mirth."

She was amazed at the hardy constitutions she found among the patients. Having a family of twelve children was nothing to them and they got up the eighth day after delivery and resumed all their duties.

"I guess it must be my Irish ancestry that makes me so hardy," she wrote home.

When she had been there a week a patient came in for delivery and Marion diagnosed the case as twins. She was afraid to say so because she could see that no one else thought so. It was.

Midway through her month she was sent out on an ambulance call. The patient was a young girl who had had an epileptic seizure.

"I cleaned her up, brought her in in an ambulance. Great sport," she wrote blithely. Another day she had what started out to be an abnormal delivery and then changed into a Caesarian—followed by a slight accident.

"Baby fell on floor," was the terse diary entry.

She made it known that she wanted to be called every time there was going to be an abnormal so that a day's diary was likely to read: "Good day. Up for operations 8:45. Letters from home. Out in the district with Dr. X., back for operations, and got a dilatation [a minor diagnostic operation] for myself. Lunch. An abnormal, tea with Dr. Y., another abnormal, long drive to beautiful golf course, violets and a heavenly sunset."

One of the male interns fancied himself an expert at tennis. Marion took him on, and beat him 6–1, 6–1, and 6–0.

"I don't know whether he thought he could beat me or not," she noted smugly. Then she found another player who was more of a challenge, and thereafter a tennis game was noted in her diary each day, along with antenatal clinics, lectures on perforations, bridge games, going to church, and playing a game called gooseberry. She managed to get to hear Handel's "Messiah" and to go to the theater two or three times, and was invited to the country for the weekend with the intern crowd. She was all dressed to go, "when that abominable conscience of mine told me when I was only here for a few weeks, I'd better not skip off."

She was rewarded by "a perfect day worth ten weekends," which she described to Gwen.

"The 'abnormal' bell rang just as I was going up for breakfast so I dashed up to the labor ward in my blue serge dress. Dr. T. said, 'This is a forceps case. Will you scrub up?' One of the girls gave me a rubber coat so I could take off my dress and no one knew. I did it very well. The only comment was, 'Of course you've done them so often.' I was a heap pleased although I was terribly nervous in front of everybody."

Later a friend called for her, bringing her family and a picnic lunch. "We drove forty miles through exquisite countryside roads to the sea. Had lunch in a sheltered little cove, afterwards all

paddled in the sea. It was a heavenly day, hot sunshine and practically no wind. I slept in the sand in the afternoon in my usual
dormouse fashion. Later, at their place for dinner, they got me
started on Germany and of course I could talk about that for
hours."

Marion was taken off the home-delivery team after her twenty-
first case.

"Some people have to wait two months to get that many and
I got mine in three weeks. That's what it is to be enthusiastic!"
she wrote home. In two weeks she had lost ten pounds, but was
resigned to regaining them the minute she let up. Unreservedly
she wrote, "I surely have enjoyed myself here."

Another triumph in quite a different field had her "up in the
stars all day." She had sent a witty account of her travels through
Europe the previous summer to her friend Lorne Pierce, an editor at the Ryerson Press in Toronto. Now he wrote her that *The
New Outlook,* the United Church magazine, had bought it for
ten dollars.

With a few days to spare, Marion was able to carry out a
plan that had been in the back of her mind ever since she'd
known she was coming to Ireland: to visit the part of the country
where her father's people had come from. She spent four days
with friends in Belfast, visiting the Giant's Causeway—"such a
steep climb it made me seasick"—buying linens, and seeing the
city. Then, on Friday, June eighth, she took an early-morning
train to Enniskillen.

She had always thought that the talk about the greenness of
Ireland was probably exaggerated. Now, on a matchless summer
day, she rode through the countryside and was struck by the vivid-
ness and vitality of what she saw. Later she wrote an essay about
it.

"It was spring time and the hedges dividing the fields were all
in bloom. I can still see the picture of those green, green fields
(there I am, muttering about green fields like everybody else),
surrounded and divided and adorned by hawthorn hedges—a

mass of pink flowers; in this corner and that corner, a clump of lilac bushes all purple and white, and in the midst, the golden rain of the long fragile flowers of the laburnum—and just beyond the rolling hill, the sea. Such beauty hurts, and as its ache remains, so also does the memory, deep down, never to be forgotten."

On the train she had a lively discussion of Irish cities with an old gentleman in her compartment. He thought Belfast a common place—materialistic, middle class, no culture. Marion pointed out that there were practically no slums in Belfast, but certain parts of Dublin shrieked of human misery.

"Ah, yes. Maybe," said the oldster. "But think of Phoenix Park!"

"So like the Irish," commented Marion, feeling that, since she was one of them, she could have her say. "Why worry about the slums when you have the finest park in Europe!"

Enniskillen was "a dear little town looking for all the world like a Canadian village with its Main Street."

She arranged to ride with the mail carrier out to the castle of the Earl of Enniskillen. Hilliard family legend had it that, as a child, Grandfather Thomas Hilliard had been a playmate of the Earl's father, and Marion wanted to see the castle and perhaps the Earl too.

The mail carrier—"an enormous man with bronzed complexion and a motley nose"—made his rounds in an Irish jaunting cart, which took an hour and a half to ride over four and a half miles of rutty clay road through bleak countryside full of peat swamps.

When he learned her destination her driver advised against trying to see the Earl. "He things nought of the ladies," he explained. "He thinks only of the cattle and the fields."

"I decided," commented Marion, telling of the conversation, "that I'd rather trust him than the sort that thought nought of the cattle!"

The castle proved to be a large stone house set on a hill—no turrets, moats, or drawbridges: Marion was disappointed. The

Earl appears to have been as unapproachable as the castle; her conversation with him is scantly referred to in her essay. In one of the small houses clustered at the entrance to the castle's driveway Marion found a hospitable old lady who gave her tea, and she made the return trip to the village with the postman, feeling that, "No matter how dull life may become, for a few hours I lived in a fairy tale."

In Dublin, Marion said farewell to the Rotunda and took a small Irish freighter bound for Plymouth, where the Dearnleys would meet her.

"Seasick. Rose after dinner and saw Land's End and Lizard Point," was the succinct entry in her diary for the following day.

"When we rounded Land's End," she wrote later, "the waves were coming from the south—and unfortunately, also from the west. You can become more or less accustomed to a lateral roll or a forward plunge, but a diagonal spiral will flatten out the best of sailors!"

She was amazed to learn that others among the seven passengers had booked passage in the name of health! She had chosen it because it was cheap; even so, she landed with only one shilling to her name. In their many reunions on both sides of the Atlantic in the years to come, the two favorite jokes Marion and Miss Dearnley shared were this meeting at Plymouth, when Marion arrived literally staggering from her rough voyage, with one shilling left in her purse; and the time, very early in their acquaintance, when Miss Dearnley had invited her to a tennis party at her elegant club. Digging into her trunk, Marion found that in her excitement she had packed two tennis shoes for the left foot instead of a pair.

"It never crossed my mind to make some excuse or try to borrow a pair of shoes," she wrote many years later. "I joyfully bounced out on the court in my two left shoes and played with my usual uninhibited style. The women doctors who watched my strange-gaited footwork have never forgotten me."

For ten days Marion enjoyed the bliss of a holiday by the sea with her congenial English friends. She loved Crantock, the little village named for one of the saints who brought Christianity to the west coast of England, but observed that the Holy Well, which stood in the center of the town, had "lost a lot of its romance by being whitewashed every spring." On the common, which stretched for a couple of miles right down to the sea, roamed horses, sheep, and donkeys. Each evening at sunset she watched the riderless horses gallop up the hill, putting on "a better rodeo than when they are accompanied by the art of man," she wrote home; and the sheep with "those little spindley legs." "I hope never to have to put a splint on one of those," she remarked.

Even for one trained in the rapids off Point Iroquois, the undertow was pretty strong. The vacationers did their swimming in the sheltered little bay, Jolly Porch, that the Dearnleys had discovered. Warned about how quickly the tide could come in, Marion learned to choose a cave high above the sandy shore in which to stow away her clothes. Once she emerged from her cavernous dressing room dressed to go back to their bungalow and found the water so high that she had to get back into her bathing suit to get out of it.

One day was spent exploring through Truro, St. Ives, down the steep and twisty road through Penzance and along the wide boulevard by the sea to Land's End, where Marion saw close up the high, rocky place she had got such a brief glimpse of from the freighter's porthole.

"There is a majesty about this coastline—and a ruthlessness," she wrote feelingly.

Lovingly she recorded in her diary the little things that made this holiday so wonderful—going to bed by candlelight, the luxury of chicken and strawberries in the same meal, playing demon patience, having a nap after lunch. She celebrated her twenty-sixth birthday with a swim before breakfast, and later in the day her hostesses presented her with two paintings and a box of candy.

On her last night at Crantock the sunset seemed more glorious, the night sky clearer, the moon and stars closer than the ones that had gone before.

"I hate to leave this marvelous place," she wrote in her diary. "It seems like the beginning of the end."

Motoring back to London with Miss Dearnley's sister, she went by way of Exeter and Wellington, so she could see "where Alfred the Great burned the cakes," detoured to see Stonehenge, and was treated to a ride through the crush of traffic from the races at Ascot.

For her last two weeks in London she headquartered at the apartment of her Australian friend, Margaret.

Between bouts of packing and shopping for presents to take home, she dashed to Wimbledon to see the tennis matches, and to Windermere for a three-day trip through the lake country. Ruskin's motto, "Today, Today, Today," "impressed me particularly."

Chuck and Mac came from Oxford and took the two girls to the theater. "A gorgeous farewell party," said Marion's diary.

She went one last time to the Royal Free to watch Gertrude operate, and to the Dearnley cottage, where her favorite dessert, ginger pudding, was on the dinner menu. She cried saying good-by to Mrs. Dearnley.

"I'm not the only one to feel sad. I think they are really sorry to see me go," she noted in her diary.

After a final round of farewells—to the two Margarets at Temple Fortune Lane, the interns at Soho, the Queen Charlotte, and The Mothers', Kensington Gardens and her friend Peter Pan, and Margaret, whose hospitality and companionship had meant so much—Marion sailed for home on the *Empress of Scotland* on July seventh, a year and a day after she had left Canada. At the last moment Gertrude's sister appeared on board ship with a huge box of chocolates as a bon-voyage present from the Dearnleys.

"Low in my mind when on board," Marion wrote in her diary. As an antidote she set to work and wrote six letters before dinner.

How wonderful it would be, she began to think, "to have the fun of doing things rather than still learning out of books." She wondered how long it would be before she had a "real, honest-to-goodness patient of my own."

The year of decision was over, and with it the years of preparation.

CHAPTER 9

"To Seek My Fortune"

"Set out to seek my fortune," wrote Marion gaily in her diary. It was August twentieth, the end of a happy, peaceful interlude at Irwanna. Uncle Rob and Aunt Clauda, home on furlough and full of stories of their life in China, and Aunt Luella and her family had helped crowd the cottage to the rafters. There had been weeks of the "ripping good hilarious time" Father had hoped for, with Foster and Leila and the children there, and a visit from Ruth and Wentworth to round out the family reunion. It was wonderful to be home again, in the midst of her loving family and with an exciting future beckoning.

At Toronto's Union Station that August Monday, there was a second great homecoming, when she was met by Maryon and Mike and another of the Vic roommates and her husband. For three days, between dashing trips about town to visit old friends and arrangements by telephone for a reunion with Gwen, she savored long catching-up sessions with Maryon, and got acquainted with her eight-months-old godson. Happily the two girls planned the wonderful winter they would have, and Marion saw the Pearson trio off for Winnipeg, where they were to vacation with Mrs. Moody. Her farewell gift to little Geoffrey was a silver mug from his "Aunt Marion."

The "wonderful winter" was not to be. Only a few days later Mike received his first job offer from the Department of External Affairs, and the little family went directly to Ottawa. From then on, the classmates' devoted friendship had to be nourished by brief visits and hastily scrawled notes, as both the Pearsons' responsibilities of state and Marion's medical career gathered momentum.

The following week she armed herself with certificate 472 from the College of Physicians and Surgeons, showing that she was licensed to practice in Ontario, and a supply of prescription blanks, headed

MARION HILLIARD
B.A., M.B., M.R.C.S. Eng., L.R.C.P. London

Then she set up shop in the office of Dr. Jane Sproule-Manson, on the fourth floor of the Physicians' and Surgeons' Building. It was a well-located, well-equipped office, having even such refinements as a telephone answering service. Dr. Manson, a nose-and-throat specialist, was a prominent member of the Women's College Hospital staff, and was then serving on its Medical Advisory Board, the staff group that determined medical policy. Her advice to this new recruit in the ranks of Canadian women doctors was invaluable, Marion wrote later.

"I admired her more than any other," she said, "and can never thank her enough. I can only help other starters."

Her office "remarkably uncluttered with patients," Marion wrote long letters to every friend and acquaintance she had. Then she tried her hand at mystery stories.

One of her first patients, a Vic student, rang the bell and walked into an empty waiting room. Behind a closed door a great clatter of typing continued for several minutes before Dr. Hilliard appeared. Later, when they knew each other better, Marion confessed that she had reached an exciting point in her story and delayed answering the bell until she had finished the paragraph.

Although she was determined to be an obstetrician, Marion wisely took on everything that came along that first year, promising herself that she would be a specialist when she could afford it. She never forgot her first three night calls, shattering experiences all.

"Bundling myself in my warmest clothes, I climbed on the streetcar at three in the morning with my satchel of instruments and a map of the city. Though I have had a lifelong fear of the dark, I found the house and stood my ground while a police dog leaped and barked around me. I discovered my patient was in an advanced state of delirium tremens. She died a few minutes after I arrived.

"The second one was to another remote and shabby neighborhood, this one happily devoid of watchdogs. The patient was again unconscious, this time suffering from toxemia, and she died a few minutes after my arrival. The third night call was no different. This patient was an old woman with uremia. Like the others, she was unconscious when I reached her and died a few minutes later.

"Optimistic as it was my nature to be, this nevertheless did not seem a very auspicious beginning. Luckily for my confidence, as well as for my patients, my next cases survived."

At Women's College Hospital on Rusholme Road, the erstwhile junior intern was welcomed back as a full-fledged doctor by her old friends Clara Dixon, the superintendent, Dr. Guest, and Dr. Stewart, and was appointed to the obstetrics staff. Her chief, Dr. Marion Kerr, a tall, handsome woman, dark-haired and brown-eyed, welcomed her new colleague, as she had been conducting the obstetrical work alone.

The struggling little hospital was bursting at the seams. A campaign for funds for a new hospital had recently begun, and Marion joined enthusiastically with other staff members, board members, and citizens to help. Because of the depression, it was an enterprise that was to take seven long years before it was fulfilled.

Another challenge that elicited Marion's interest was the effort to lower the incidence of maternal and infant mortality, a major effort of hospitals of North America in this period.

It was a time of large questions and small ones. There were problems of organization: were pregnant women patients of the obstetrical department or the gynecology department? Should the two departments be merged or remain separate? Such knotty problems vied for staff attention with very practical difficulties: only the purchase of more chairs for hospital rooms would end the matter of visitors' sitting on the patients' beds, it was decided. The superintendent complained that married doctors were bringing their children to the hospital and leaving them downstairs to be watched while they made their rounds!

To help pay her share of the office overhead, young Dr. Hilliard took on what she called "odd sidelines." Yet each added a cubit of growth toward the person she was to become. As a speaker on health subjects (five dollars per lecture) she gained the poise and ease that were to make her one of the most sought-after speakers in Canada. As the first doctor employed by the Toronto Children's Aid Society she learned about social problems and social work, which gave her insight into the profound effect a patient's way of life has upon his medical problem, and set her in the direction of seeing a patient as a whole person.

Her duties at the social agency were to hold clinics for both well and sick children being cared for by foster families, to see that hospital care was arranged when necessary, to visit sick children in foster homes and prescribe for and treat them, and to act as general advisor to the agency on health matters. The executive, Nora Lea, one of Canada's most respected social workers, liked the enthusiastic interest the young doctor brought to her job. Even more, she appreciated her sturdiness and stability. As in the clinic years at medical school, Marion was outraged and appalled at the home conditions from which the young wards had been removed and the overwhelming personal and family problems faced by the agency's clientele; but now she could "take it" and concentrate on how her own job could help.

Marion loved "her children" and soon showed a native skill in personal counseling. Adolescent youngsters seemed to be able to spill out to her, and she was willing to listen, just as she had listened earlier to the problems of her schoolmates. The homespun advice she gave was a real help to youngsters whose parents had grossly neglected or even abandoned them. She appeared never to be in a hurry, and, as Miss Lea put it, "She had a spongelike ability to soak up worries and give back a few reassuring ideas."

When boy-girl relationships came up, she went right to the heart of the matter, giving sex education matter-of-factly. She was particularly skillful with unmarried mothers, for she was never judgmental and was able to give them back their self-respect. Then, as later, she believed that when a young person had "made a wrong turning or taken a curve too fast" it was up to the adults around him to help him get back to as nearly normal a pattern of living as possible.

The "odd sidelines" paid office expenses and board at the private home where Marion lived for her first year, but somehow there never seemed to be anything left over for clothes. All Marion's friends came to know well her two "uniforms"—the Burberry suit and a green and black rayon dress. Once toward the end of this first year Miss Lea pointed out to her that the dress was coming apart at the seams. That day the clinic was held up while the social worker, behind her closed office door, mended the dress and Marion sat in her slip, going over the case histories of the day.

Happy to be reunited with her SCM friends, Marion went to the Elgin House conference, helped start SCM groups on the campus when the university opened, and made several speeches about the Schiers conference and her travels in Europe.

One fall afternoon she dropped into the SCM rooms for tea, wearing the Burberry suit and an old felt hat and carrying her doctor's satchel. There she was introduced to a newcomer to Toronto's medical circles. Dr. Eva Mader, a Nova Scotian, graduate of the medical school at Dalhousie University, had won a fellowship for postgraduate work in public health at University of Toronto, and was just beginning a year's assignment.

"You're Madeline's sister!" exclaimed Marion, remembering

back to the night at Elgin House when the young Maritimer had congratulated her on her speech and said shyly, "I have a sister who's just like you."

It was the beginning of a warm, gay friendship. They plied each other with questions, comparing notes on postgraduate work in Toronto, London, Dublin. Their boardinghouses were near each other, and that winter they met often. When Eva fell ill with a bad case of scarlet fever and spent several unhappy weeks in an isolation ward Marion was her faithful correspondent.

Come spring, they decided to give up boardinghouse life and strike out with a home of their own. On the attic floor of an old three-story house in St. Mary's Street, a two-block street digging into the north side of the university campus, they found just the thing—two rooms, kitchen, and bath. The girls were thrilled with their home; it was up so high, it was surrounded by treetops. There was a fireplace. Casement windows looked out over St. Mary's Street and below these a built-in window seat furnished seating space for their many guests—a fortunate provision, since the furnishings, contributed by friends, consisted of two wicker chairs, a card table, a bed for one girl and a convertible sofa for the other. To these they added orange crates for dining chairs, and, after an extensive examination of the budget, a four-dollar four-drawer chest to hold their skimpy belongings. One very ugly wall was triumphantly covered up with one of Marion's souvenirs from England, a decorative map of London. In hot weather life under the eaves, with the sloping roof holding the Toronto heat, was made pleasant by an architectural *pièce de résistance*—a flat roof upon which the kitchen door opened, making a "terrace."

The house budget was a simple one: thirty-five dollars a month for rent and a dollar a day for food. Later on, when their income began to be augmented slightly by a few paying patients, the budget was enlarged to allow for a cleaning woman once a week.

The little apartment became a meeting place for doctors, stu-

dents, and social workers. Up the stairs clattered young women
and men in white coats with stethoscopes in their pockets,
students with books and tennis rackets under their arms, weary
child-welfare workers, university faculty members, and occasionally, although they were rare in these depression days, a beau.
One of the latter, a determined young businessman from the
Maritimes, kept climbing doggedly for two years until he persuaded Eva to become Mrs. Charles Macdonald.

Visitors were always sure of getting a good meal. A favorite
was Marion's recipe for date bran muffins. But the dollar-a-day
budget often left something to be desired. With alacrity the two
girls accepted all invitations to dinner or tea. The arrival of
apples, tomatoes, and fresh vegetables from Morrisburg was a
great event. Marion's favorite invitations for lectures came from
the Health League of Canada. Not only did she make five dollars,
but, "To make sure people attended, they served refreshments,
and I was as grateful for the food as anyone in the audience."

In the living-room corner stood a basket piled with things
that needed sewing and mending, reserved for a domestic evening. The evening never came. Both young doctors were too busy
earning extra money or entertaining guests. Their greatest luxury was reading. They took turns at the newsstand, buying the
women's magazines that then were printing in installments the
current novels of such writers as Edna Ferber and Sinclair Lewis.

The one bone of contention in the otherwise congenial
ménage was that Eva enjoyed an occasional cigarette. Marion
knew that not all young people had been brought up as strictly
as she had, but she had not yet come to accept women's smoking.
Goaded by Marion's silent but obvious disapproval, Eva once
called her a "sticky Methodist," at which Marion left the apartment and clomped down the stairs. Clomping downstairs was
something she always did, whether in good or bad temper.
It appeared to be literally impossible for her to go out quietly.
Since she was often called out at night, there were complaints
from other tenants. Periodically she was approached pleadingly
by the librarian on the second floor, and would humbly apologize

and promise to do better; but when the next night call came, her mind would fly ahead to the patient waiting for her, and the good resolution would be forgotten.

Toward the end of her first year of practice Marion had had an unexpected windfall. Someone gave her a stock-market tip, which in a short time netted her six hundred dollars. Immediately she sold her holdings and bought a Model A runabout with a gear shift and a rumble seat; whereupon, as she told later, "the streetcars lost a good customer."

It was the beginning of life itself for Marion, the "go-go-go girl." The pure pleasure of driving, especially at night, was somewhat like the thrill she had got from ice skating.

"You're getting this letter," she wrote a friend from Iroquois, where she was vacationing briefly at Irwanna, "because I feel peppy, garrulous and not wanting to go to bed. Tonight I was driving over from Morrisburg at 45 miles an hour. The wind nearly blew my hair off but oh! it was fun."

Under Eva's tutelage, she learned to drive, at first making kangaroo-like leaps through downtown traffic, but quickly learning the co-ordination that made her a fast, sure flivver pilot. In her later, more affluent years she drove heavy, high-powered five-passenger cars, but none of them was ever so prized and dear to her as this small secondhand Ford. She drove to out-of-town rugby games, to Morrisburg to show off to the family, to a nearby town to see Margaret Wrong, who had come from England for a visit. In the spring Gwen joined Marion and Eva for a holiday trip to New York, where Marion and Eva visited Marion's sister and brother-in-law, and Gwen, somewhat overawed at the prospect, was expected by her well-to-do relatives on upper Fifth Avenue.

It was too good a chance not to give Gwen, the tease, some of her own medicine. When she arrived in a chauffeur-driven Rolls Royce to pick up the two girls for a dinner and opera party her hostess was giving, the girls appeared, dressed to the nines in new velvet evening gowns (in fact, for this swank affair Marion had plunged into a department store and bought, not only her first not-homemade evening dress, but her first girdle). They talked loudly in affected accents, vied with each other to make pointedly gauche remarks, and gawked out of the windows in an exaggerated takeoff of tourists, while Gwen nervously watched the chauffeur, who, she feared, would look down on all Canadians forevermore. In her eyes they were only partially redeemed by their model behavior at the dinner and opera.

In turn Gwen was invited to the Myers' for dinner one evening, and was presented with an elaborate spoofing menu, headed by "roast leg of lamb (warmed over)."

The cup of mortification spilled over when, in the midst of Gwen's polite leave-taking of her hostess, Marion drove up to the swank address in the shabby car, wearing her English tweed suit, now in its third year and growing somewhat shapeless.

Soon after the advent of the car Marion proposed that she and Eva rent a piano. Eva was doubtful about their ability to scrape together the required six dollars a month, but yielded when Marion offered to teach her how to sing. This was a piece of gross deception; Marion was still a very good pianist, but as she herself confessed once, in describing the Hilliard family singing sessions in Morrisburg, "We all sang, with varying degrees of competence that reached the lowest point in me." However, the small upright that was hoisted up to the third floor paid for itself in the pleasure it gave its temporary owners and their guests, and Eva was able to join, with some degree of comfort, the Christmas-carol singing group Marion organized with her friends on the staff at the Children's Aid Society. For the next thirty years a vintage group of fifty to sixty people, many of whom had long since gone to other jobs, some out of town, returned for this pre-Christmas evening of song and fun. Marion herself never missed one.

Nothing pleased her more than to have someone start a round of singing on a summer evening at the cottage she acquired later. She so loved it that once she brashly applied for membership in the Mendelssohn Choir, accepting her rejection with equanimity, since she knew she was not qualified. All her life she firmly believed that anything was worth a try.

Eva completed her postgraduate work and was appointed to the staff at Women's College Hospital, where she worked hard to convince her colleagues of the powerful potentialities of bacteriology and pathology in preventive medicine. (In time these efforts would lead to her appointment as head of the laboratories.) At the same time she became a public-health lecturer at the university, which brought her into working relationships with "The General" and "Sick Kids." Marion was impressed, and listened carefully to Eva's ideas, especially after their hospital fell upon troubled days.

In a small house the hospital had rented near the site of the new hospital Marion and Eva conducted outpatient clinics on the same days. While Marion saw obstetrical patients on one floor, Eva was holding medical clinic on another, and in still another part of the house Dr. Guest was working with venereal-disease patients.

Clinics were crowded, and Marion often saw as many as sixty patients in an afternoon. When the last patient had left, they took a break for tea and compared notes on their hard-working day. "Do you think we'll ever get any credit for this from anywhere but heaven?" sighed Marion once, as they washed up the tea things and prepared to leave.

The hospital itself was very shorthanded and lacking in equipment. Trying to treat a pneumonia patient in a basement room without an oxygen tent was just one of the everyday problems. One such patient was pulled through only because Eva was able to borrow an oxygen tent from another hospital. There was an outbreak of diphtheria that kept the staff on the jump for weeks. (In another few years such frights would become a thing of the past, for the first of the antibiotics would make its appearance, and shortly afterward Eva, as head of the laboratories of the hospital, would be manufacturing her own penicillin.)

Worst of the crises faced by the hospital was an epidemic of puerperal sepsis (childbed fever) in 1930. It was a heartbreaking, backbreaking experience for the staff and it left Marion with the determination to help raise standards so that her hospital would be in the vanguard of the effort to wipe out maternal and infant mortality. It was a lofty aim for a hospital with such a high percentage of obstetrical patients, but it was achieved.

Back in Morrisburg, Mr. and Mrs. Hilliard and Aunt Sue Hilliard, retired from her millinery shop, rattled around in the big Main Street house. Aunt Laura's son Fletcher, now a teenager, had gone to the States to live with his father, who had remarried, and Irwin, the last of the Hilliard brood, had entered Victoria College in September of 1929. Winner of the college's Blake Medal for science, which included a scholarship, he had begun the biological and medical sciences course, and, to Marion's joy, planned to go on to medical school.

Mrs. Hilliard, now a prominent member of the Dominion Board of the United Church Missionary Society, did some traveling, since she was in great demand as a speaker and discussion leader. Her deeply felt convictions, often expressed with a touch of humor and briskness, made her a memorable and much-quoted leader. In one meeting she chaired there was some difficulty arriving at a concensus on a current issue, and time was growing short.

"I think we should pray about this, Madame Chairman," said one of the ladies.

"Yes, perhaps we should," she replied, "but let's be quick about it."

With three of her chicks there, she turned longing eyes on Toronto, and was always delighted when her travels took her westward.

Then came a turn of fate that not only moved the dwindled family to Toronto but also brought great honor to Mr. Hilliard. For his distinguished service as a leading lawyer in Dundas County and his loyalty to the Conservative party (apparently bygones were to be bygones when it came to his temporary split with the party over the Prohibition issue in 1927), he was appointed Assistant Master at Osgoode Hall, Ontario's Supreme Court. Not without sorrow, they sold the Main Street house, moved their church membership to Toronto's Timothy Eaton Memorial, and promised themselves that summers at Irwanna would keep them close to the roots they so cherished. Into the apartment Marion found for them they moved themselves, Aunt Sue, and young Irwin, rejoicing that neither Helen's dormitory at Vic nor Marion's apartment were far away. It was the first time in thirty years that the Hilliard household had been lacking a child or at least a teen-ager. Then, only a few months later, Foster brought his family home from Japan, his wife hopelessly stricken with cancer. After her tragic death Mimi and Sonny, now seven and nine years old, made their home with the Hilliard grandparents, while their father took postgraduate work in theology.

In his new position Marion's father, too, was brought close to the human tragedy of those depression years. His job was to hear testimony and prepare cases for court hearings on such matters as insurance claims, alimony settlements, and mortgage foreclosures. In the dignified atmosphere of Osgoode Hall, even then a hundred-year-old institution, with its red plush carpet and dark paneled woodwork bearing huge portraits of Ontario's premiers (he must have been pleased at the impressive likeness of his old friend Sir James Whitney), he listened to the lawyers and thought of the people involved. He was, he told his family, "greatly exercised" over their hardships.

Often he would "find for" the underdog, disregarding the technicalities, sometimes winning a mixture of admiration and criticism from his colleagues. Once when he was taxed with having ignored the fine points of property law he replied simply, "I couldn't sleep at night if these people lost their home."

At the end of a year he was appointed Master, in which position he remained until his retirement in 1935.

Eva and Marion went swimming at the "Y," played badminton at the university. Occasionally they extracted money from their tight budget for attendance at rugby games (in years to come Marion would have season tickets, and only one of her babies would keep her from the Saturday-afternoon game), and concerts, for which they were often joined by Helen, who had become a real music-loving Hilliard.

The two young doctors were active in the SCM and went regularly to Old St. Andrews, a United Church, to hear the popular, dynamic Dr. John R. P. Sclater. After church they had a standing date for dinner with the Hilliards.

Together they organized a Bible study group for medical students and young doctors that met weekly on the campus and usually ended up with a heated discussion of eugenics, a much-discussed question of the day. Marion was so impressed with what she was learning about social problems that she invited young colleagues to the apartment to hear informal talks about these. Miss Lea talked to them about adoptions, a subject on which she tried in vain to indoctrinate Marion with a social-work point of view. To the end of her days of practice, complying only with the letter of Ontario's laws, Marion made her own placements of the babies her unmarried-mother patients wished to surrender for adoption. Usually she arranged for them to be taken by her patients who wanted children but were unable to have them. When child-welfare workers involved in adoptive placements asked for confidential information about the child's mother or background, she refused to give it.

"I don't ask you for information from your records," she would point out, sweetly reasonable. "I know my mothers and their babies very well indeed, and when I make a judgment about where these babies will fit happily into a family, you can take my word for it."

She was as appalled as the social workers when, in the 1950s, a "black market" in babies boomed in North America and it was proved that unscrupulous doctors charged fees for the placements they engineered. But in her own practice she continued to match babies whose heritage she knew well but kept secret, with grateful parents who trusted her judgment with no questions asked.

Marion acquired another "sideline": because of the favorable impression her health talks had made, she was appointed the YWCA medical examiner (at fifty cents an examination) for the "gym and swim" departments. At the same time she was appointed chairman of the Physical Education Committee, which automatically put her on the board of directors. Her entry into this women's organization was the beginning of a lifelong enthusiastic interest. Here her talent for organization and creative ideas were welcomed; and her exposure to YWCA philosophy and program helped to widen the framework within which she viewed women and their problems.

It was not long before she began to give volunteer time to planning and taking part in special programs with industrial and office workers among the "Y" membership who suffered from the common maladies of these depression times: unemployment, or infrequent employment, low wages, salary cuts, fear of the future. She helped to organize a first-rate training program in physical education and recreation, whose "graduates" were in demand in churches, settlement houses, and community centers all over the city. Enlisting the interest of her friends who were skilled in personal counseling, or knowledgeable about public affairs, she planned panel discussions and evening education programs. She herself conducted a Bible study group. In board meetings she proposed that use of the swimming pool be extended to Negro girls, that club dues rates for industrial workers be reduced, that the gym be kept open an extra hour a week for members' recreation.

At the end of three years, when she resigned from the job because of pressure of work, she accepted re-election to the board and thereafter maintained almost continuous connection with either the Toronto "Y" or the YWCA of Canada.

Now Marion was a doctor on wheels, often making evening house calls. She liked company on her rounds, and, never one to do just one thing when she could be accomplishing two at a time, she invited friends with whom she was working on such extracurriculars as the YWCA programs to accompany her.

She was distressed at the "so-what?" attitude among some of the young people at the "Y," and persuaded Miss Lea to help her plan a series of discussion evenings that would begin with talks on various aspects of a healthy philosophy of life. Cruising around town on the house calls, she and Miss Lea listed speakers and subjects; then, one by one, each of the speakers became a "passenger" for an evening to plan a particular session. Marion suggested that, in compliment to the audience, the speakers wear formal evening dress and make it a real occasion. The series was a success, and led to similar programs during succeeding years of the depression.

A frequent companion on the evening rides was a friend Marion had first known at the 1923 Silver Bay conference. Now married to a Canadian clergyman and raising a family, with Marion as obstetrician, Sasha Davidson was in demand as a speaker on current events and world affairs. Though their evening talks ranged wide over political trends, social problems of the day, unsolved medical mysteries, and so on, one of their greatest bonds was a mutual struggle against overweight. Both girls were continually torn between love of good food and horror at the consequences of consuming it.

"Even if we do weigh more than we should," Marion would say to her pal of the weighing scales, "we can take more than other people because we've got good covering for our nerves. We'll be whole until we're mechanically dismantled, and when we die, it'll probably be by accident!"

More than once she used the term "practically indestructible" to describe herself, and took it for granted that she would live to a ripe old age in the best of physical health. Her only worry came when she saw that it was probably in her heritage to suffer loss of memory and the waning of her faculties after a certain age.

"You'll just have to tether me," she would say to the younger members of her family.

One hot summer night the two young women fortified themselves for an evening ride with some pastry from a favorite Czech bakery. On the way Marion stopped at the hospital and found that a patient was ready to be delivered. She put Sasha in the students' gallery to watch. Suffering from the heat and a stomach full of delicious but indigestible food, Mrs. Davidson saw her friend deliver the baby with seeming ease and casualness, and carry on her usual reassuring conversation with the mother, holding the baby up and patting it.

"How did you ever do it?" asked Sasha on the way out. "Weren't you just dying?"

"Delivering a baby is a wonderful aid to digestion," replied Marion airily.

It was the end of an era when, in August of 1931, Eva and Charlie Macdonald were married, and the St. Mary's Street apartment lost one of its original settlers. The entire Hilliard family attended the wedding, at Knox College Chapel; for Eva now was like a member of the family.

"Now don't forget, children," admonished Mrs. Hilliard after kissing and congratulating the happy pair, "always put first things first." As her sayings so often did, this became a household phrase to the newlyweds and their close friends—"Handy in a crisis and a good corrective for all hasty decisions," as Eva told Marion.

Two years later, when the Macdonalds' first son was born, Marion, as her friend's obstetrician, had her first really difficult time in the delivery room.

"I was scared pea-green," she would tell the story when the two old friends got together. "Eva was out cold, with the anesthetic. He was a darn big baby and she had been in labor seventy-two hours. It was a terribly hot night and once I stuck my head out of the window and said, 'Lord, help me. Here is one of my best friends in the world and I've got to pull this thing off, and I don't know what to do.' Fortunately, things took a turn for the better; I delivered the baby and they were both all right."

One of the baby's first pictures went to "Aunt Marion" who framed it and kept it in her consulting room.

Ten miles east of Toronto, the Scarborough Bluffs, famed among geologists the world over because of their curious clay-and-sand composition, rise sharply in two tiers from the shore of Lake Ontario. To Marion and her friends the pleasant farmland that lay along the plateau at the top of the first tier, three hundred feet above the lake, was a favorite spot for picnics and weekend walks.

One summer day in 1932 the picnickers strolled along the edge of the bluffs, stopping at one of their landmarks, a spot delineated by a clump of lilacs and a huge old birch tree on a promontory that afforded an admirable view eastward toward Frenchman's Bay.

"I'd love to have a cottage right here on this point of land," Marion told her friends. They had often speculated about the farmhouse that must once have stood here; in Ontario countryside a clump of lilacs was a sure sign of it. Now they looked at their landmark with new interest. Nearby, to the west, a fence smothered with wild cherry and elderberry bushes stood on the edge of a deep ravine filled with white birches that seemed to look up to the great granddaddy of them all, sturdily rooted at bluff's edge. Far to the east a row of Lombardy poplars marked the edge of a property on which stood an old house, the only sign of habitation in sight. A quarter mile to the north, the second tier of bluff rose straight up from the plateau, the gentle curve of a dirt road leading from one level to the other. It would be an ideal spot, they all agreed.

The piece of land Marion had set her heart on extended some five hundred feet along the lower bluff. It proved to be part of farmlands owned by the Muirs, long-time Scarborough residents, and they were willing to sell. The down payment amounted to approximately a year's income, but Marion believed in herself and her future. To anyone who would listen she talked about her marvelous plan. Uncle Rob, home from China on furlough, was entranced with the place and offered to lend her the down payment from his retirement fund, if she would repay it in seven years when he came home next time. Gratefully Marion accepted the offer, and plans for Birch Point moved into high gear.

The simple two-room-and-kitchen cottage was designed around a huge stone fireplace. If she could have afforded it, Marion would have had a stone farmhouse, like the ones along the St. Lawrence that she had loved since childhood. (Her favorite, "the old Loucks place," is now part of Upper Canada Village, an authentic reproduction of an eighteenth-century Canadian town, on the Seaway near Morrisburg.)

The members of the weekend picnic-and-walking club became gardeners and field hands. Even their families were involved in the project. Miss Lea's father dug from his own property a pussy-willow tree and planted it near the cottage. Admiring remarks mingled with groans at the thought of the work ahead when Marion would open the back of her car with a flourish, displaying to her spring weekend guests a hundred pansy plants and other annuals brought back from a foray into the back-country greenhouses. Violets transplanted from Morrisburg gardens grew under the shelter of a covey of spruce and larch trees at the north end of the property where it joined the dusty road.

The telephone company was persuaded to string a wire down from the upper bluff and a shrill outside bell was installed so that Marion would not be out of reach of the hospital. Cedar logs were thrust into the bank in the west ravine to make steps down to the lake shore; it was unthinkable that a Hilliard should be that near the water without a quick and easy way to go swimming. Part way down, a natural broadening of land lent itself to the construction of a small pool that in summertime was stocked with goldfish.

What was to become one of the crowning glories of the place —a blue spruce—was brought down by Mr. Hilliard and planted in front of the cottage midway between the living-room window and the bluff's edge. By the 1950s, when the cottage was rebuilt for year-round living, the venerable tree, nearly forty feet tall, dominated the view of garden, front lawn, and lake. Trimmed with red, white, yellow, and blue lights, it was a Christmas landmark on the bluffs and an admirable background for Birch Point's holiday parties.

Shortly after Marion first determined upon the idea of Birch Point she visited a patient in the hospital one day and exclaimed with delight at a little nosegay of columbine, wild daisies, and delphinium at the young mother's bedside. Her husband was a nurseryman and landscape gardener, Dorothy Hancock explained. He stopped to see her early each morning on his way to his current job, bringing flowers fresh from their own gardens. A few weeks later Marion visited the Hancocks to check on the mother and new baby and to see the gardens for herself. Over a cup of tea she told of the land she hoped to buy and her dream of a garden on the bluffs overlooking the lake.

"When you're ready, just let me know," said Leslie Hancock.

Now, a few years later, Marion and Mr. Hancock paced the cottage grounds and adjoining fields, evolving a ten-year design for planting. From the woods adjoining his nurseries he brought an elm sapling and planted it beside the cottage. No incubator baby ever had more tender care. Marion nursed it through its first years, took pride in its sturdiness and nobility. Twenty years later, when the cottage was to be rebuilt, she told the architect, "Whatever your plan is, I want to be sure we keep the stone fireplace and the big elm tree."

Year by year the little estate unfolded as Marion and Mr. Hancock had envisioned it. Slender white birches and willows whose tender green shoots were the first heralds of spring made a pleasing contrast to the sturdy elm and a few bearers of the Canadian maple leaf. The several flower gardens were planned so that petunias, snapdragons, lobelia, and poppies would be taking the eye from the spots where lately the daffodils, hyacinths, and tulips had sprung up on the heels of snowdrops and crocuses; and these, in turn, would yield to the baby mums, marigold, and purple alyssum.

A barberry bush was placed here, mock orange-blossom bushes there, to line the driveway. A Chinese-elm hedge marked the eastern boundary of the cottage lot, and beside it a two-hundred-foot perennial border showed a preponderance of purple and white phlox, blue lupine, and delphinium, Marion's favorites.

Often Mr. Hancock's visits to Birch Point became a family outing, for they all loved "their doctor" and her country home on the bluffs. A special event for the children each spring was to take goldfish from the deep pool on their own grounds and bring them to Birch Point to stock the shallower pool beside the cedar-log steps.

In Mr. Hancock, Marion recognized a kindred spirit, for his business in life, like her own, depended on ever-growing knowledge of nature's way of work. They shared a deeply felt awe and respect in the face of the mystery and miracle of life. He saw that her trees and flowers were like children to her, and understood it.

"Our jobs are the same," he would say. "Yours is to bring new human life, mine to bring new life out of the earth."

"And the secret of them both is to work with nature's timing, never against it," she would reply. They both enjoyed these philosophic exchanges, and he was frank to say that, of all the gracious estates he had helped to create, Birch Point represented his proudest pinnacle.

Marion loved to plant, but wasn't so keen about weeding, unless someone worked with her and they could talk as they labored. Harvesting vegetables and picking fruit were great events to her. From the first cutting of asparagus in May until the last corn husking in August she loved nothing better than to "harvest" the vegetables for a meal, unless perhaps it was to cook them, which she did extremely well. On summer mornings she liked to go out early and pick raspberries for breakfast, and after gardening in the hot sun her favorite thirst quencher was a melon right off the vine, broken open with the handiest implement and eaten sitting in the grass at the bluff's edge, looking out over the lake.

Birch Point, or just Scarborough, as it was more often known to Marion's family and friends, was Marion's home in adulthood

—her Oak Hall and Irwanna all in one piece, the place where she put down roots, and, as life became more pressing, her sanctuary.

She shared it joyously and openhandedly with family and friends. In twenty-five years it was the scene of hundreds of picnics, large and small parties, wedding receptions, and even a few wedding ceremonies. Countless friends and family members came for weekends, summer holidays; to convalesce from illness; or to "smooth life out a bit," as Marion called it, after suffering trouble or loss.

Yet she managed to keep it the haven of peace, quiet, and relaxation she needed to offset the "go-go-go" life she lived. Much as she exulted in the busy, exciting days, she treasured every moment of the garden tending, swimming, reading, and sometimes just sitting in the sun that she could do at Scarborough.

" 'What is this life, if full of care, we have no time to stand and stare?' " she liked to quote.

She moved to Scarborough as early as possible in the spring, stayed as late as possible in the fall. With luck she could make it to the hospital in twenty minutes, and the nurses allowed for that. At the peak of her career she might be called out three or four times a night. Always she would drive back to Scarborough for a shower and breakfast before returning to her operating schedule at eight o'clock.

"It's worth it," she would say. "It's at its most beautiful in the morning."

In the evenings, when she returned from town, she walked slowly around the garden, looking at each flower bed, each bush, each tree. If there were guests, as there often were, she would take them with her. It was her ritual to observe the progress of each growing thing each day. After that came a quick run down the bluffs and a refreshing swim; then she was ready for dinner and the evening activities.

Even when the spring thaw turned the roads to mud and the gardens to ponds, Birch Point was always a place of beauty to her. Sunsets, especially in winter, thrilled her, and she looked

for the certain moment of winter dusk when the snow-cov-
ered lawns and fields took on what she called "white magic."
A clear summer day when the clouds made patches of green and
dark blue on the ever-changing lake waters sparkling in the
sun was, in her language, "a perfect Scarborough day," often
noted as such in her diary and letters.

It was Marion's sixth year in practice, and her office had begun to move out of the remarkably-uncluttered-with-patients category. On the hospital's operating schedule and the cards over
the newborns' bassinets her name appeared more and more
often. The spring appointment list announced that she had been
named assistant, lifting her one rung up the ladder of the obstetrics department. The staff elected her its representative on
the powerful Medical Advisory Board. Victoria College asked
her to serve as physician for women students at her Alma Mater,
beginning with the fall term.

After five years, "If I have given up my hopes for marriage
and my ideas about being a missionary . . . ," she had written Gwen from the eye of her personal hurricane on that spring
day in 1928, she would settle for a career and get more training. By now most of her men friends had, one by one, married
other girls, and the hurt and disappointment at breaking with
the one she cared about the most had begun to fade. He had
seemed about to propose; then, one romantic evening, she fell
asleep in his car, worn out from four successive nights in the
delivery room, and he had found it unforgivable. Shortly afterward he had married a girl Marion knew well. They asked her
to deliver their first child. To Marion, it was the most hurting
experience she had ever had.

The little girl who intended to be "a married lady with six
children," though she freely admitted that remaining unmarried inevitably brought "a shredding sense of failure," always
felt that the bitterest renunciation of all was to give up motherhood.

The call to the mission field had faded too. Building on the new hospital would begin the following year, and there was no doubt in her mind about wanting to be part of the great days ahead for Women's College Hospital.

Now was the time to do something more substantial than making flying trips to hospitals in the States to observe surgery and obstetrical work; now she wanted to do some work in European hospitals. She wrote to Budapest and Vienna, and to Miss Dearnley in London, getting "come-ahead" signals from them all. Her chief, Dr. Kerr, became interested in the idea, and the two doctors got summer leaves of absence from the hospital in preparation for the big adventure.

In the midst of these spring events Gwen Mulock announced that she was returning to Toronto to practice, and had been appointed to the Women's College Hospital staff. Her father, whose practice she had shared in St. Catharine's, had died. Her fiancé, a university classmate, had died of an obscure disease contracted in a medical-research laboratory. She would like to live among her Toronto friends. Would Marion share an office with her?

The exuberance with which Marion always embarked on a new chapter swept her and her friends into a new whirlwind of plans. When the dust settled she and Gwen, with Eva and Dr. Marjorie McIntyre, another assistant in the hospital's obstetrics department, had rented an office together and invited Winifred DeGruchy to preside over it as nurse and secretary.

Mrs. DeGruchy, formerly a private-duty nurse, had been recruited two years before to help Marion part time. She had had to be persuaded by their mutual friend, Miss Lea, to be interviewed by Marion; she had always worked for men, and was dubious about the job. After one talk, however, they were both sold. For eighteen years, until failing health necessitated her retirement, she was a reliable asset in Marion's office, beloved of all patients for her ready humor and sympathetic ear.

Doctors Kerr and Hilliard sailed from New York on the *Bremen* on June first, 1934, bound for Budapest, where Marion would work at the Polyklinic and Dr. Kerr at a school of mid-wifery.

It was a great send-off. The Myers, Marion's sister and brother-in-law, gave a dinner party before the midnight sailing. Four Toronto friends came to see them off. Cables, notes, and flowers arrived.

As the ship nosed down the Hudson River, Marion looked at everything briefly and went to bed. After four days of almost continuous sleep she awoke one afternoon in time to dress for dinner.

"Suddenly I seemed to come to myself," she wrote her mother cheerfully. "I'm profoundly grateful for the way I can sleep. It certainly has the healing quality. That's one way I'm glad I take after Father."

Budapest was entrancing. From the very first evening Marion loved the old city. The *pension* recommended by a Hungarian-born musician friend in Toronto served delicious white corn. The Danube River traffic was fascinating. It was fun to spend the evenings walking up and down the boulevard, then stop in a cafe for coffee or wine and listen to the gypsy bands ("The lights and the music get right into your bones," Marion wrote home ecstatically), or to walk up to the old castle on the hill in the late afternoon and admire its beautiful marble and woodwork appointments, which were "not overdone in any detail."

The early summer weather was perfect, but psychologically speaking, Marion sweated her way through the first week. The Polyklinic proved to be a large private hospital with a great many public patients, which offered excellent opportunities for post-graduate teaching. Its distinguished chief of obstetrics and gynecology, Dr. Alexander Fekete, who was also surgeon and assistant professor at the University of Budapest, gave the courses, which included observation work in operating and delivery rooms and the opportunity to assist in a certain number of operations in a given period of time.

Then a man in his late fifties, serious, kindly, and a topnotch teacher, he met Marion with undisguised dismay. Because her name was spelled with an "o" instead of an "a," he had thought the application came from a man!

It would be unsuitable for a woman to work in his operating room, he said. He had never been confronted with such a situation before. The hospital was not equipped for women staff members. Why didn't she go someplace and take special work in nutrition? It was a much more fitting specialty. He would gladly refund the five hundred dollars she had paid for the course in advance.

Patiently Marion persuaded him to try her out for a few days. To her mother's advice to "enter every open door," she had by this time added for her own private guidance—"And if it isn't open, give it a shove." Dubiously he agreed and she took her place among the group of men who had come from hospitals all over Europe.

"The work here is first class," she wrote her mother, "but I get nervous when I'm working. There are so many men looking on—usually at least seven or eight. There is so little in private practice that a large number of doctors stick around the clinics. Women aren't very well thought of."

When she was sure she was over the hump, she wrote again, telling of Dr. Fekete's surprise, which "in the beginning wasn't entirely agreeable!!" "Now," she added, "he is very nice to me."

It grew hot and humid, and in the daytime the operating rooms were blistering, but "the work gets better and better," Marion reported in a crescendo of excitement. Dr. Kerr, who was doing considerable work at the Royal Hungarian School of Midwifery, arranged for them to be called when "abnormals" were being delivered. One Sunday morning they hurried to one of the hospitals and observed two Caesarian sections before time for church.

Marion observed her thirty-second birthday with a jaunt to a country town to join costumed villagers at a church service, after which Dr. Kerr took her to dinner at "the best hotel on the banks of the Danube." She was frankly homesick, thinking of the family together at Iroquois Point within sound of the river rapids.

"Won't it be wonderful when we all get together again? . . . When you get away you realize very acutely where your foundations are and of what they are made. Goodnight and may the pine trees give you sweet dreams," she wrote them.

The two colleagues visited an eleventh-century church ("I love to think of the centuries thru which people have gone and knelt in those old places") and spent a happy day with Marion's Hungarian–Canadian friends, who stopped in Budapest en route to the Salzburg Festival. But for the most part they worked.

"Dr. Fekete has insisted on me doing the operating, and altho I'm a wreck afterwards with so many people looking on—I keep going," Marion reported, adding that the experience was worth twice the money and more. As the end of the course neared she had a moment of quiet triumph when the surgeon invited her to stay another month, showing clearly that he was impressed with the caliber of her work. Since it would have meant changing the arrangements the doctors had made to visit Vienna hospitals and Marion's agreement to work with Miss Dearnley in London, she declined, noting in a letter to her mother that "he was very sweet in the things he said."

After a few days in Vienna, where they visited hospitals by day and the opera by night, they went to Munich to start a week's holiday trip to Oberammergau and through Switzerland. It was an uneasy summer in Germany, and, Marion commented, "we breathed a sigh of relief when we got to the border and saw the last German uniform."

In Oberammergau, "Dr. Kerr and I stayed at the home of the man who plays the Christ. He is a marvellous wood carver by trade and an enthusiastic applegrower by inclination. The front garden of his home is really an orchard with large borders of flowers. I was thrilled just to sit quietly under the trees. The Bavarian villages are very quaint. The Passion Play itself is difficult to describe. It is intensely real and those parts which need no staging are tremendous. The scene of the Last Supper and the Garden of Gethsemane left me absolutely shaken up."

Rain spoiled the three-day bus trip through the Swiss Alps, which was too bad for Dr. Kerr, since it was her first trip. Marion thankfully remembered her golden days in the summer of 1928 at Schiers. In Paris, where "I showed Dr. Kerr the Paris I knew, including a whole day in the Louvre," the two colleagues parted and Marion went on to London alone, treating herself to a trip on the fast train, the Golden Arrow.

It was the first of many reunions with her beloved Miss Dearnley, and again she had the fun of seeing London with someone of her own family. Her sister Helen, now a schoolteacher, was on her first trip abroad, with friends. The two Hilliards "tore around" together, stopping for breath long enough to attend services at Westminster Abbey, where Marion reported she "sat right over Thomas Hardy's tomb."

With Miss Dearnley she observed operations at the Royal Free and anywhere else something was going on, and the two friends journeyed to Bournemouth for the annual meeting of the British Medical Association. Miss Dearnley, at that time vice president of the section on obstetrics and gynecology, presented a paper, and, chortled Marion in a letter to Gwen, "A couple of the old boys just jumped on her which showed how jealous they are!" After the meetings Marion spent the weekend with her former employers, "the two Margarets," enjoying the feeling of "going back as a guest," then went to work in earnest, assisting Miss Dearnley in the operating room for two weeks.

Later in August she and Helen sailed for home on the *Empress of Britain,* which was trying to make a record crossing. The girls were in tourist class right over the engines, which shook day and night. Undismayed, they had the fling of their lives, and the last night out, feeling suave and sophisticated and most un-Hilliard-like, ordered crème de menthe in the ship's bar.

CHAPTER 10

Tea and Sublimates

The seventh-floor suite in the Physicians and Surgeons Building was sumptuous, consisting of a waiting room, two consulting rooms, an examining room, and a bathroom that doubled as a laboratory. The original plan was that Dr. Mulock and Dr. Macdonald would have daytime office hours, Dr. Hilliard would have the run of the place from early afternoon, when her operating schedule and hospital rounds were over; and Dr. McIntyre would see her patients in the evening. As it turned out, three or possibly all four would be crowded in together, with patients coming and going and Mrs. DeGruchy acting as middleman.

One of Marion's patients was very deaf. Every detail of their interview behind the closed door of the consulting room could be clearly heard.

"How often do you have periods?" Marion would scream, and at the end of a half hour everyone in the waiting room and the other offices would have had a complete rundown on all the patient's functions and complaints.

Once Gwen sent a note in to Marion: "Pipe down! You're driving everybody crazy." Mrs. DeGruchy brought back a scribbled: "I can't. Might get the wrong answer."

After one long session with the patient Marion came out and, forgetting it was over, yelled loudly, "Is tea ready yet?"

On days when there was a lull, drug salesmen and other such visitors got more of a welcome than they did at busier offices. One such was a beauty-product representative, and Marion was persuaded to let her demonstrate, while the others looked on with interest. At last, her unusually long eyelashes dripping with mascara, her cheeks feverishly rouged, she was a sight to make a chorus girl blanch. Amid shrieks of laughter from her colleagues, she fled for the bathroom, where she took nearly an hour to get peeled down to normal.

In those days she could *take* an hour; in later years she got through a shampoo, with luck, but rarely made it to the hair dryer before being called to the hospital. Her hairdresser, Mr. Charles, became adept at twisting a towel around the heavy taffy-colored hair and covering it with a plastic cap, and away she would go. In an hour or so she would return, cheerful and happy ("Well, we got a fine baby boy"), and slide under the dryer.

In those earlier days, every afternoon when office hours were over, it was the custom to have tea and cakes. The favorite was a tea biscuit topped with jam, called a "sublimate." Marion and Gwen, both still hoping that romance and marriage might be in the cards for them, teased each other about being old maids with their afternoon tea and sublimates.

The banter between the two old friends amused and amazed their office mates. Opposites in personality, they were always worthy of each other's mettle. Along with her growing practice, responsibilities in the hospital's public wards, and work in the hospital campaign Marion energetically rushed pell-mell in dozens of directions. Brilliant, well read, and witty, Gwen was too much of a skeptic to engage herself thus.

"Marion bites off more than the rest of us can chew," she would say in her sardonic drawl.

"Gwen's trouble is she's lazy," Marion would retort. "Things come easy to her, so she never buckles down. If she would, she could do anything in the world. I work hard; Gwen does everything else but."

Gwen was very much interested in her patients and was a great counselor at heart. Beyond this, she couldn't decide where her niche in medicine was. In the space of four or five years she switched from general practice to a specialty in skin diseases, briefly considered going into psychiatry. Then she was asked to

make a series of radio broadcasts on health, and her success
with these led to a teaching post in the School of Social Work
at the university. She was a born teacher, she discovered to her
satisfaction. She continued her teaching and broadcasting for
some time, even when illness put her in a wheel chair.

The hottest arguments between Marion and Gwen were about
religion. Gwen had been brought up in a Baptist family, but had
never so much as been baptized because she was too much of a
doubter, even as a young girl, to take the vows. Unmercifully
she challenged—even ridiculed—Marion and Eva, who were both
still deeply involved in the SCM and the United Church.
Mrs. DeGruchy, a devout Anglican, was often distressed at these
sessions, much as she admired Dr. Mulock, but the SCMers
pitched into them with zest and no hard feelings.

Marion herself had, for some years, been a pillar of Old St.
Andrews Church, and, true daughter of her mother, one of the
minister's right-hand women.

Dr. Sclater, a Scot by birth and Canadian by adoption, had
been pastor of the old church since 1924 and had made his mark
as an eloquent preacher with a gift for friendship.

(At a memorial service following his sudden death in Scotland in 1949 a United Church official said of him, "He loved
people; and many groups who foregather now will be duller for
his absence. A great many people can establish and maintain
friendships with those who think as they do, but only the choice
souls can develop and maintain friendships with those who differ
radically from them. He was one of those choice souls.")

Perhaps because of his Old World upbringing and education, Dr. Sclater did not have, as one of his parishioners put it,
"This cut-and-dried attitude that all women are helpless little
things." He respected Marion Hilliard's intelligence and skill,
was challenged by her dynamic approach to problems, enjoyed
working with her as an equal. He consulted her often about important problems, asked her to take on responsibilities suited to
her skill and maturity, and she accepted him as a valued pastoral
counselor and friend.

A question before the United Church in the mid-1930s was whether or not women should be ordained. Marion, who had expressed herself forcefully on the matter to Dr. Sclater, was asked to appear one morning before a church commission charged with deliberating the matter.

Among other questions, she was asked if she felt that women had the physical stamina for the work of the ministry. Marion arose—"looking fresh as a daisy," one witness reported later— and said demurely, "Gentlemen, since eight o'clock last night I have delivered five babies. I believe that's answer enough."

"But will women accept a woman as minister?" asked a commission member. Without hesitation Marion replied, "You know how devoted I am to Dr. Sclater. But I must say that, of all the ministers I have heard, I remember Maude Royden best of all."

Then and later, in her service to the church she avoided the traditional activities of church women by proposing and conducting such activities as marriage-counseling sessions for young pastors, courses on marriage, love, and sex for young married people of the church, and writing articles for church publications.

"The church is years behind the times," she told an old friend of her university days who had gone into the ministry, "by not recognizing the true importance of women. You keep them busy with missions, bazaars, teas, and suppers but you don't listen to their ideas or give them a voice in making policy. There is practically no place in the church for the professional woman who has a certain degree of intelligence and a tremendous desire to give her best to the work of the church. And the worst of it is," she had to add, "the women accept the role that is thrust upon them."

For years she tried her best to accept all invitations to speak before women's church groups, to spread her personal gospel that a woman should "stop being just a housewife and be a person." Once she got carried away with her message and later wrote a note of apology to the group's chairman.

"My difficulty is that I get disturbed and upset because [women of the church] do not fulfill a great purpose in saving the world. With the power they have they could change this old world in a very short time but they have never realized their potential or been willing to accept the responsibility. It is because of this I mourn."

Eventually, after she had learned "what the inside of every church basement in Toronto look[ed] like," she concluded that she was being invited more to provide entertainment than to offer ideas for thought and study. Thereafter she accepted such speaking engagements only as a favor to her family or old friends.

Marion began an eleven-year stint as the doctor for women students at "Vic" in the fall of 1934. Her duties were twofold: to care for infirmary patients, and to give an annual series of "facts-of-life" talks. Her natural interest in young people, and a close working relationship with the dean of women, Dr. Jessie Macpherson, an SCM friend from her own university days, made it a congenial assignment.

Students enjoyed her brisk, cheerful, matter-of-fact talks and the lively, free discussion she encouraged, and soon found that, though Dr. Hilliard had reached the advanced age of thirty-two, she still remembered how it felt to be a student.

One girl, down with a low-grade virus on the day of the big senior dance, phoned Marion in misery and disappointment. Would she absolutely *have* to miss the dance?

"This is what you should do," came the prompt prescription. "Stay in bed till the last minute, then take some aspirin. Go to the dance for two hours. Then come back to bed."

Like her later lectures and writings on sex, her talks were simple, direct, explicit, with no moral overtones. Her own lack of embarrassment encouraged forthright discussion and frank questions. One perennial was the question of premarital relations. With this one Marion minced no words, explaining what could happen and under what circumstances, drawing on her own experience for case examples of unmarried mothers and women who had abortions, some of whom then married and were unable to conceive.

After the first series she learned to begin by instructing her audience matter-of-factly, "If you feel faint, just put your head between your knees." When a student once protested at her frank discussion of sex relations, she replied mildly, "Isn't it better to hear all this from me?"

One paragraph she always got in sooner or later was to the effect that the summer murmur of "Don't worry, dear, I can take care of you" often led to babies in the spring. She said that this never failed to produce an uneasy ripple of recognition in her audience. Years later, when she wrote "An Open Letter to Husbands" as a chapter in her first book, she whaled into the "zany" methods boys believed would prevent pregnancy, calling these "as imaginative as they are ineffective."

As part of her job Marion emphasized the importance of posture, weight control, and good-health regimes, and dreamed up end-of-the-year programs to make it fun. One such was the year "Miss Annesley Hall" was chosen from among the healthiest physical specimens, and prizes were given for the ten girls who had made the most progress during the year in overcoming health problems.

At Rusholme Road the hospital was within eighteen months of moving to its new quarters and life was made difficult by overcrowding, debates about the structure of services, and the drop in the number of nurses coming in for training. As staff representative to the Medical Advisory Board, Marion launched a campaign for improved nursing services, for it was clear that overwork had brought on a slackening of standards. From the days of her junior internship she had had particular interest and sympathy with the nursing staff, and had continued to sprout ideas for their recreation in leisure time, including periodic winter parties at her apartment and summer picnics at Birch Point. But to her, lowered standards of any kind in the hospital were unthinkable and intolerable.

The matter of structure of the services had been batted about since the mid-1920s. The question centered on the departments of obstetrics and gynecology, which many thought should become one department. Whether it be in the world of business, industry, government, or one of the professions such proposals of merger seem to be a signal for internal struggle, and so it was for the strong-minded women of the second and third "generations" after the pioneers who opened up the field of medicine for women and established this unique hospital in Canada. It was a painful process, but by the fall of 1935, a few months before opening the new hospital, the Board of Governors announced that the union of the two departments was a necessary step and would take place immediately. In their decision they were backed up by Marion's beloved professor Dr. Hendry, who had been appointed consultant to the obstetrics department two years before. Dr. Kerr was appointed chief of the new department, in which Marion was to spend the rest of her professional life.

In the midst of these delicate adjustments the Board of Governors expressed renewed interest in learning whether or not the hospital could be accepted by the medical faculty of the university as a teaching hospital. Three years before, when this question had come up, seven representatives of the medical staff, chaired by Dr. Kerr, had deemed the proposal unwise. Now the board was anxious that the new hospital be accepted for teaching. Once more the elder statesmen of the staff advised that the matter be postponed for the present.

Vital for the hospital's future, the question was fated to be raised and rejected several times in the next twenty years. Just when Marion incorporated the idea into her dreams for the hospital is not known; in time, it would become the goal above all others toward which she worked.

Such growing pains faded into the background and the staff closed ranks with joy and pride to celebrate the crowning event of 1935: the cornerstone laying for the new hospital. In a blaze of satisfying oratory the Prime Minister of Canada, the Honorable R. B. Bennett, paid tribute to Canadian women for "this monument of their courage, vision, and hope," and a copper box was placed in the stone, containing a history of the hospital's "ancestor," the Women's Medical College, written by Dr. Augusta Stowe-Gullen, the first woman physician to graduate in Canada.

At eleven o'clock on the morning of January twenty-second, 1936, the hospital was formally declared opened. The medical profession was received that afternoon, donors of rooms the following day, and, on the twenty-fifth, it was opened to the public. A compact, ten-story structure built of earthen-shade brick, the splendid building stood well back from tree-shaded Grenville Street. From the top floors, where Marion was destined to spend a good deal of hospital time—since the operating rooms, doctors' locker room, and lounge were on the ninth, the delivery rooms on the tenth—one looked south over the downtown area and the lake front some twenty blocks away; north to nearby Queen's Park, the home of the Provincial Parliament; and west to the pleasing spread of the university campus. The dignified marble staircase facing the main entrance and the quietly elegant appointments of the administrative offices seemed a far cry from the worn old Victorian house on Rusholme Road—but best of all were the hundred and forty beds (in less than twenty years it would be necessary to build a new wing to double this capacity), the space, the up-to-date equipment.

One special affair followed another as the hospital was shown proudly to various groups. Marion was the moving spirit behind a tea and tour for a large group of university undergraduates. Enthusiastically she drew out women students who were considering going into medicine to talk about their ideas and hopes, and spoke of the opportunities afforded by "this great new hospital." Always a looker-to-the-future, she saw the proud history of this unique institution as a sturdy foundation on which to build, and knew that all would be won or lost by the caliber of recruits from among the new generation. Already she was aware of how fast the times were moving in Canada's medical world, how quickly the adequate qualifications of yesterday were being outmoded by today's higher standards. From now on she was to pour great energy into cultivating promising young women students and the best of the interns in an effort to enlist their loyalty and enthusiasm for the hospital and its future.

Marion's interest and skill in this direction were recognized. That year, the first in the new hospital, she served as convener of interns and later she was appointed chairman of the intern committee, so that she was in a position to spread her interest beyond the confines of her own department. Taking up the cudgels in behalf of these young women while they went through the lean, hard-working years, living under a strict regime, came naturally to her. She was always not only approachable ("Dr. Hilliard would just as soon stop to chat with a junior intern as with a senior staff member," they told each other), but enjoyed talking shop with the juniors over a cup of tea or on the tenth floor, "waiting for babies." She knew that people often learn as much this way as they do on the job.

She showed her personal interest by gestures that were simple but unforgettable. The chief of one of the departments today still remembers the time she was miserably ill with a strep throat and Marion stopped to see her on the way home from a banquet, bringing some flowers from the table decorations, and stayed to chat for a few minutes about the humorous highlights of the occasion. ("Imagine—and me just a resident intern!")

Though not the fussing "mother-hen" type, Marion worried along with her interns in their moments of crisis, and laughed with them when the crisis had passed. Once when taking care of a young intern down with the flu she asked for a urine sample and disappeared with it to the laboratory. Later she stomped up the steps of the interns' residence, worry writ large upon her face.

"You've got a four-plus sugar," she announced.

There was a thought-filled silence.

"Well," replied the young doctor-in-training feebly, "I did use a maraschino-cherry bottle. Maybe I didn't rinse it out well enough."

Somewhat grimly Marion found another bottle for a second sample, but the next day, when this proved to be normal, she fully shared both the relief and mirth with her intern-patient.

Another time, while working over a patient with a mysterious, as-yet-undiagnosed illness, an intern broke the glass tube while taking a blood sample, and got some of the patient's blood in a cut on her hand. Marion took what measures she safely could and suffered through an uneasy twenty-four hours with the frightened young woman, at the end of which the head nurse on the floor where they were making rounds accosted them.

"Did you hear about Dr. X's mysterious patient? Overnight she broke out with mumps."

Marion and her junior looked at each other and staggered weakly to the nursing station where they could sit down and laugh in comfort.

Some of these young women later became Marion's valued colleagues and close friends, and one of them, Dr. Jean Davey, now the hospital's chief of medicine, became her own physician. Slim, dark-haired, vivacious Jean was a classmate and favorite dancing partner of Irwin, Marion's brother. Marion met her at the party she gave to celebrate her brother's coming of age, and saw her often thereafter. Impressed with Jean's record as a medical student, she tried to interest her in obstetrics, but found that Jean, the daughter of a general practitioner in Hamilton, Ontario, had long since decided to specialize as an internist. When, after internship at another hospital, Jean came to Women's College Hospital for her resident year, before going to England for postgraduate work, Marion worked hard to sell the young woman on returning to the staff. On Dr. Davey's last day as resident Marion came to say good-by and thrust two checks into her hand, one a farewell gift, and the other, for two hundred and fifty dollars, a loan to be repaid without interest after ten years. Marion remembered only too well her own postgraduate days in England a decade before.

When Dr. Davey's tour of study in England had to be canceled because of the onset of World War II, and she opened an office in Toronto instead, many of her first patients were referred by Dr. Hilliard.

Another close friend of these years was Dr. Dorothy Redmond, later Mrs. Gordon Daley. Coming up to her last year in medical school, student Redmond, a petite, gay Maritimer, landed at Women's College Hospital for a junior internship in a summer of intern shortage. Though it was a rotating internship, with a certain amount of time on each service—medicine, surgery, and so on—obstetrics interested her the most. She spent every moment of extra time watching deliveries and left word with the nurses to call her, as Marion had done in London and Dublin, whenever something interesting came up. Because of the shortage, she was called upon to take more responsibility than was customary for junior interns, and reached the end of the summer short on sleep, long on experience, exhausted but happy. Her reward came when Dr. Hilliard, a woman who measured her words under such circumstances, told her, "You'd make a good obstetrician. Why don't you come here next year?"

Dr. Redmond did return for her senior internship, and later became an assistant in Marion's office before beginning her own practice.

Working under Dr. Hilliard's supervision was not all honey and roses, however; she could be as human as anyone else under certain circumstances. Once when she was delayed in getting to the hospital the resident intern and the anesthetist decided that the fetal heartbeat was too weak to wait to deliver the patient. Marion arrived just as the baby was delivered. She examined the patient and the baby to make sure that they were all right. Then, stony-faced, she walked past her colleagues without looking at them and left the hospital.

Another time, when she was on holiday at an isolated spot on a northern lake, the young obstetrician who was caring for her patients went to great trouble to reach her by phone. One of Marion's patients had become very ill and, although the younger woman was doing what Dr. Hilliard would have done if she had been there, she was mindful of the great interest her senior took in her patients and thought she would like to have a report.

"Don't talk to me about patients when I'm on holiday," barked Marion and hung up.

Such irritable moments were few and far between, and today a number of successful women obstetricians gratefully recall Marion's steadfastness.

"When you ran into trouble on a case," said one, recalling her days as resident in obstetrics, "she was like the Rock of Gibraltar —safe, secure, capable. She *always* came if you really needed help and always stuck it out until the patient was safe. And she was all there—never distracted by anything she might have left, like an office full of patients or a medical paper she was working on. Whether it was her patient or yours, the whole world was bound up in that person as long as she was needed."

Marion's unfolding career also brought closer working relationships with other hospital staff members. Of these, none was more mutually rewarding and happy than her teamwork and great friendship with the chief of anesthetics, Dr. Ellen Blatchford.

A graduate of the University of Toronto's medical school, Dr. Blatchford had done special work in anesthesia on both sides of the Canadian–United States border before joining the hospital staff in 1928, and had been chief of her department since 1931.

For twenty years nearly all the mothers of Hilliard babies and most of Marion's surgical patients gained courage and assurance from the serene countenance and quiet voice of this skilled anesthetist, as they sweated out the first few minutes on the delivery table or operating table.

The two doctors were perfect foils for each other: Marion, airy and casual, Ellen, quiet and deliberate; and each appreciated the other's sense of humor and strong personality. Theirs was something more than the teamwork of two competent professionals. They worked as two parts of a single entity, with a kind of unspoken communication. Besides having complete faith in each other's judgment, they shared a warm concern for the patient as a person, which grew out of their similar religious beliefs.

Once when they were having an informal religious discussion with a group of friends someone voiced a doubt that there had ever been such a thing as a miracle. The two doctors who had shared so many life-and-death crises spoke almost as one. "You can't be a doctor and not believe in miracles. We've seen them happen."

Like Marion's Grandfather Hilliard, Ellen's ancestors, the Comiskeys, had hailed from Enniskillen. As one of their friends said, their great compatibility "must have been a case of the Irish just naturally gravitating to each other."

Ellen had married during her internship, and her husband, Douglas Blatchford, a mathematics instructor at a Toronto collegiate institute, and their children, Ann and Bob, became "family" to Marion. They were frequent dinner visitors in each other's homes and were summertime neighbors after the Blatchfords built a weekend cabin on the upper bluffs near Marion's Scarborough cottage. Often Marion joined them at their cottage on a northern lake for part of her summer holiday.

Both doctors preferred being routed out at night to staying in the hospital, "waiting for a baby." They developed a kind of firehouse procedure that went like clockwork. The hospital would call Marion, who would call Ellen, then scramble into her clothes and take the stairs at a run. In a few minutes Ellen, who lived farther from the hospital, would drive up and they would take the twenty blocks to the hospital at a good clip. In twelve to fifteen minutes from the time of the first call they would walk into the hospital, always breathless and usually laughing.

At a nearby restaurant afterward, over cups of coffee, or breakfast, depending on the hour, they would relax, talking over affairs at the hospital, about which they did not always agree, and confiding their personal worries and problems, for they trusted each other personally as well as professionally. They corresponded faithfully when one or the other was away on holiday, or business.

"My dear friend," Marion wrote at the end of a breezy letter to Ellen from the Gatineau Hills, where she was convalescing from an operation for which Dr. Blatchford had given the anesthetic, "you are such a comfort to me. You have no idea how thankful I am for your strength and thoughtfulness and constant kindness. Everything from putting me to sleep to bringing in those pastries at just the critical time!"

The first of a long line of wedding receptions on the pleasant lawn at Birch Point came in early summer of 1938, when Helen Hilliard forsook her teaching career to marry Dr. Burdett McNeel, her brother Irwin's classmate and friend. A specialist in psychiatry, Dr. McNeel had been appointed to the staff of a provincial hospital in London, Ontario, and there the young couple took up residence immediately. The new Mrs. McNeel announced to her assembled family that because she was marrying into a family already replete with Helens, she was falling back on her inherited middle name. From then on she was Barbara, or Barby, to all the family but her mother and father, for whom habit was too strong.

In the Hilliard memory book this was "the summer of weddings," and twice more Mr. and Mrs. Hilliard journeyed from Morrisburg, where they had returned after Mr. Hilliard's retirement from Osgoode Hall three years before, to see a child married and wave a happy couple off to a new life.

Foster, who had won his degree in divinity at the Union Theological Seminary in New York, married an Ottawa girl, and they left for his new charge in British Columbia, taking Mimi and Sonny, now teen-agers, and preferring to be called Mim and Joe.

The last of the weddings involved the youngest of the clan. Dr. Irwin Hilliard, with two years of internship behind him, married Agnes Magee, an Ontario girl, and they left immediately for western China, where Irwin was to study parasitology and tropical diseases in preparation for work in a mission hospital. They were to be gone seven years. Marion, no less than her parents, found the separation hard to bear. Her little brother of childhood had grown into a young man with whom she felt as congenial and close as ever, and she was proud of his excellent record in medical school. (Her pride was some source of comfort to her brother after his parents had expressed astonishment that he hadn't stood first or second in his class, instead of seventh!)

Marion's mixture of joy at her brother's happiness and sadness at the separation had a third personal ingredient: his choice of medical missions brought back her earlier dream of entering that field herself. For several weeks she was preoccupied with doubts. Had she made the right choice? Had she really turned her back on her upbringing in favor of a more comfortable, lucrative career in a place where she could live among her closest friends? It was a conflict that was to return to her periodically for another decade until she finally reached firm ground in her assessment of her choice and the direction in which it had taken her.

Now this period of self-questioning was abruptly terminated by a family crisis. The distraught McNeels phoned to say that Barby was pregnant and so sick that a miscarriage was imminent. This was Marion's bailiwick and she swung into action. After a conversation with her sister's physician in London she sent an ambulance to fetch Barby the hundred miles from western Ontario, with directions to return to her own apartment in Toronto, greeted her at the door, and put her to bed.

Within minutes she appeared at the bedside, a bowl of porridge in her hand.

"Barby, you're going to hang onto this baby," she said firmly, "and the first thing is I'm going to feed you this porridge and *you're going to keep it down.*"

Meekly the sick young woman took the food, spoonful by spoonful. It was the first she had been able to retain for ten days.

"She mesmerized me," she explained to her family later.

It took weeks of close care, including a stay in the hospital, to get the young mother-to-be over the danger period, during which time the young couple's residence was transferred to Toronto because of Dr. McNeel's research assignments. The following May, when Susan Jane McNeel was born, no one was more thankful and jubilant than Aunt Marion.

With Barby and Burdett established in a Toronto apartment, and letters flying back and forth to west China, Marion's world began to right itself. Happily she sent off a Christmas cable to her new sister-in-law and brother, and was rewarded to hear that it had arrived just as they were sitting down to Christmas breakfast. They had observed some of the Hilliard Christmas traditions, Irwin reported, including making patience in their tiny kitchen—and, "The Hilliard luck held."

Suddenly, in the spring of 1939, Marion started to have a rough time of it. For ten years she had been rewarded for her hard work and faithful care of her "mothers" with fine, healthy babies and a fantastically low rate of those whom nature had handicapped at birth. Now, one after another, Marion delivered nine abnormal babies. Sick at heart, she summoned her strength to encourage those saddened parents who could "try again," and to search for ways to comfort those who couldn't. It was a severe test of what she was to call later her "faith in life as a whole."

In the midst of it she was chosen by the medical women graduates of that year to speak at their special service, at Knox College chapel on a Sunday morning in March. She set to work to find a theme. It came naturally to her to try to pass on to a new generation the best of what she had learned and found good. But in such times—with Hitler's armies throwing their menacing shadow over Europe, with whole countries capitulating to his demands, with honest men forced to flee into hiding, with the threat of another terrible war seething beneath the surface of life—what were the truly enduring values?

She tried to imagine what these young women might be called upon to do and to face in the years ahead, and strove to get to some kernel of truth that had served her well and that they might carry with them. She remembered how her mother had fired each of her children to believe that they were born for great things, and how her father had taught them, by word and example, about integrity. The picture of Gertrude Dearnley rose in her mind, a symbol of the high achievement now open to women in medicine. She reviewed the many patients who had come in and out of her consulting room and felt again the ups and downs she had lived through with them. Turning to her well-thumbed Bible, she searched for the words that would help her express her thoughts and feelings. Then swiftly, she wrote the few hundred words of which one member of her audience said later, "I came out of there feeling I was going to be the best doctor that ever was— even better than Marion Hilliard if I could!"

" 'And who knoweth whether thou art come to the kingdom for such a time as this?' " Marion began. Briefly she talked about the present, "when chaos surrounds us and man does not seem to be the heroic figure we believed him to be," and the need for all people to have principles to live by. "Of necessity, they must be few, fundamental and constant, and you must know how to find them and hold fast to them," she added, saying that she wanted to speak of four important ingredients of the doctor's life: time, honesty, steadfastness, and courage.

"Never let time be your master. It is your master if it hurries and worries you. You must always be at ease if you are going to gain that final ounce of confidence from your patient."

A patient's physical symptoms "may be due to hidden fear or panic," and "unless you can wait until she is able to tell you the cause of her fear, she has not received your best attention." A patient must "never leave your presence until you have understood her position and shared her burden." Even if there is no solution to her problem, "if confidence has been awakened, with it comes comfort."

"Time seems to stand still sometimes," because a patient's progress is slow, but "you must learn patience, for the passing of time is your chief assistance, or vice versa—you may be the assistant, and time and nature the powerful partner." On the other hand, "there are times when action must be swift and decisive— when time is pulling against you." In such times, "never forget you can ask for help." It was her experience that help was always graciously given, she said.

She tackled honesty head on. "I don't believe there is another profession in which the scope for dishonesty is greater," she declared, explaining that what she meant was the temptation to avoid telling patients the truth ("We must protect their faith and preserve our own honesty so that we may live peaceably with ourselves"), unwillingness to admit mistakes ("Because it is seldom that anyone else can check up [on you], it becomes more important to be acutely aware of your own thinking processes. Always admit a mistake to yourself. Avoid rationalizing").

"Honesty between women physicians should be easy. We should be able to be simple and direct with each other. But most of us talk too much. We must embroider the tale. We seem to be trying to prove ourselves. We don't need to do that any longer. We must be able to admit our mistakes, give honest criticism, and trust to Divine Guidance to tell us when to keep our mouths shut!"

Steadfastness went to the heart of Marion's philosophy of the practice of medicine. "It means just this: that you will cure your patients if you can, but if that is impossible, you will go with them all the way." Sick patients are anxious, afraid, often unfamiliar with illness and such things as anesthetics, perhaps have never faced the possibility of death. "In this maze of uncertainty, they must feel your presence and hear your voice." More than this, "you have not done your best unless you have . . . taught them to find their feet again, helped them create the ability to achieve their own courageous attitude" toward whatever it is the patient must face.

Whether the patient suffers from serious disease or neurotic imaginings, she said, "the resulting unhappiness is the same, and often the need for steadfastness is more essential in the latter than the former."

Steadfastness in the doctor gives the patient the sense of security that gives rise to true confidence. If it is there, the patient sees it "in the mind's eye." Faith, discipline, and courage are the undergirding of the doctor's ability to be steadfast. By faith she meant, she explained, "Faith in the ultimate truth of the universe. Simply said—faith in God—faith in something more powerful than your own puny efforts. If you lose faith, life becomes a frustration."

As she often did in speeches and writings, she quoted from Masefield's "Good Friday," for she considered the line "But that green blade of wheat, my own soul's courage, that they did not take" one of the most stirring in English literature.

"It does not make any difference how dull the routine of life, how hard the competition, how nerve-wracking your surroundings, no one can take away 'that green blade of wheat—your own soul's courage.' It is the light in a person's life that cannot be hid."

After a sentence or two about the wisdom that would come with experience she paused a moment, then added, "My blessing goes with you, and the blessing of hundreds of women physicians who have found in the practice of medicine a great adventure, an engrossing life work and tremendous joy. Bless you, my children, for who knoweth whether thou art come for such a time as this?"

Shortly after her successful address to the medical women graduates the run of bad luck with babies was terminated when she delivered a fine, healthy baby boy. It was a happy day on the tenth floor, with nurses and colleagues who had watched with pity while Marion stoutly lived through the bad time now joining her in celebration. The sun shone again, and cheerfully Marion planned a trip to the World's Fair in New York with her father and mother.

The usual Hilliard bustle filled the Myers apartment on Riverside Drive while the sizable family group packed a picnic lunch, collected coats and cameras, and prepared for the trip to Flushing Meadows. After an hour's bus and subway ride they emerged in the shadow of the Trylon and Perisphere and stood in the sunshine, planning sightseeing routes through the exhibits and arranging for a meeting place. Suddenly Mr. Hilliard disappeared.

A half hour later, just as suddenly, he rejoined the family.

"Been to see the Magna Carta," he announced. "Very interesting. Well, I'm ready to go home now."

Storms of protest. "But what about our *lunch,* Father?" "Gee, Grandfather, we were going to stay for the *fireworks!*" "Dear, I do think we should at least see the pavilion." Seeing that he was a minority of one, he gave in and grimly plodded through the rest of the day, while the rest of his family chattered, laughed, exclaimed, and discussed their way through the exhibits and pavilions. It was quite a long time before anyone could say "World's Fair" to Mr. Hilliard without getting a snort in reply.

The Long Slugging Hours

"If anyone asked what part of my work had been most rewarding to my patients, I would have to say it was the long, hard slugging office hours I have put in over the years," wrote Marion in the final chapter of her second book.

The scene of most of those long slugging hours was Suite 716 of the Medical Arts Building, to which Marion and the faithful Mrs. DeGruchy moved in 1938. For the next fourteen years until Marion began to taper off her obstetrical work Suite 716 was the stage set for the rising action of a drama, which was more often comic than tragic, and which each year seemed to present a larger cast of characters, most of whom were engaged in producing a new generation of Canadians.

Although many of the forty to fifty babies Marion delivered each month in her peak years were public-ward patients of the hospital, a sizable number were the offspring of her private patients who followed a regular schedule of visits to her office: every three weeks for the first twelve weeks of pregnancy, every four weeks for the next twelve weeks, twice during the seventh month, and once a week during the last two months. Consequently about forty patients a day passed in and out of the office between two o'clock and six, four days a week.

A standard "prop" of this cast of characters was the bottle, usually in a paper bag, containing a urine sample to be analyzed by the nurse to make sure that the mother was not suffering from toxemia, that bugaboo of pregnancy. The nurse's office and the laboratory were always full of labeled bottles. Once Mrs.

DeGruchy mistook a bottle of a testing reagent for a bottle containing a sample. When she heated it in preparation for the analysis, it exploded. For some time the ceiling bore the scars of this misadventure until Marion decided that there was time to have it redone.

Another time a patient with a pixyish turn of mind brought in her sample bottle wrapped in Christmas gift paper. It found its way into the gift cupboard and was not discovered until Christmas Eve.

When Marion began working on sterility cases there were even more bottles to keep track of, as part of the diagnostic job of determining the reason for a couple's inability to have children was to examine the male sperm under a microscope.

One husband, unable to find a more suitable container, left a quart jar. "For Dr. Hilliard—she'll know what it is," he said, making a quick exit. Marion took one look at it. "Wow, what a man!" she exclaimed cheerfully.

There was a homey, community-center atmosphere in the small waiting room. Bulging women of various ages and stages of pregnancy chatted while they waited, and everyone listened avidly to the nurse's end of conversations on the telephone, which seemed to ring every three minutes.

"Oh, isn't that too bad, Mrs. X. You're still sick? Every morning? Did you try soda biscuits?"

Often the waiting was long. The telephone would ring, then suddenly the consulting-room door would open and Dr. Hilliard would bustle through the little room, calling out, "Baby on the way!" as she went through. Although that would mean waiting at least another hour, no one really minded. Each one was thinking, When it's my turn, she'll rush out the same way. When she returned she nearly always reported to the room at large, "Lovely nine-pound boy," or, "Well, we got a nice little girl."

Sometimes a young mother holding a baby or young child would squeeze into the packed room, telling the nurse she "just wanted Dr. Hilliard to see how well the baby was growing," or "thought Dr. Hilliard would like to see her little namesake." (The number of Hilliard babies christened Marion was lost count of midway in Marion's career.) In all the rush and crush, these visitors without appointments were always welcomed.

Occasionally a father-to-be would be a member of the cast of characters for the day.

"I would sit there in absolute misery," recalls one, "surrounded by bulging women, hunched over like a character in a Thurber drawing, thinking just one thing to myself: *My God, why doesn't Dr. Hilliard come?* Then she'd come in and I'd have a minute with her in the office and she would be so cheerful and casual that I'd relax and begin to think this thing was almost fun!"

Getting behind that consulting-room door was worth all the waiting. With phones ringing and a crowded waiting room, Marion centered right down and gave her undivided attention to the patient. She was able to select quickly those who needed her attention the most, and had no compunction about dealing with the others with dispatch, sending them off with a word of cheerful encouragement. Her ability to slough off other preoccupations and concentrate on the thing at hand gave a patient the sure knowledge that, for the time she sat there, she was the only person in the world who mattered, and that her problems —all of them—were important to her doctor. Marion's real concern for her patients never failed to convey itself.

Her concentration was not just to absorb knowledge, as in "the old Maytime grind" of her schooldays. It was to gain as complete an understanding of her patient as possible. Her instinct for "seeing into" people and her ability to sum them up rapidly was part of her artistry. She worked to be able to put her finger on what was basically troubling a patient who couldn't express herself or bring herself to face a problem.

There was a plus to her skill that a doctor has to be born with. Along with her patient's medical treatment she gave good-sized doses of forthrightness, wit, and warmth, a few practical suggestions, and a good deal of wisdom. It bred the confidence that made patients react favorably to treatment. It was no novel experience for her office nurses to see a person come in looking down and out and leave looking cheerful and hopeful. Men who hadn't wanted their wives to be treated by a woman doctor would come in reluctantly for a talk, and go away smiling, satisfied and perfectly happy about the whole thing.

"Each patient comes to your office with new problems and a new difficulty," wrote Marion in *Women and Fatigue*. "Each is asking for your complete attention and all you have to give in skill, competence, and experience. The treatment . . . is not the most important part of the office visit, though of course it is important that it be accurate, definite, and in accordance with the best known therapy of the day. But that is only the beginning. The most important thing is that this person . . . shall have the faith to carry out what is written down on those little pieces of paper. She has to be helped to have that faith."

A woman expecting her first baby is, as Marion once wrote, "in for an experience of special fears, special hazards, special wonder, and a poignancy beyond all other human experience."

It was standard procedure for these patients to appear with lists of questions and to be nervous for fear there wouldn't be time for all the answers.

"But every time the same thing happened over again," recalls one patient. "She seemed to know what my questions were and answer them before I asked. I'd go in full of worry and dragging my feet. Fifteen or twenty minutes later I'd come out feeling I was the luckiest woman on earth, and I'd be full of energy."

One great anxiety is fear of a miscarriage. As Marion wrote in her second book, "Sometimes I wonder if some aren't so scared . . . that they bring it on." Patiently she explained over and over again that there is no need to worry "if you take reasonable care of yourself."

If worse came to worst and the patient did miscarry, she shared the patient's grief, for she understood how discouraging it was, but she let it be known that in her experience miscarriage occurred in thirty per cent of pregnancies, and "Nature knows what she's doing," for in the great majority of these cases the embryos are malformed. Experience had also taught her that one miscarriage didn't necessarily mean the patient would have another.

One patient, early in her first pregnancy, was at a dance when symptoms of miscarriage appeared. She rushed home and phoned Marion.

"Get to bed. Lie still and don't move a muscle," said Marion crisply.

Terrified, the young woman lay absolutely still in one position all night. The next day Marion arrived, having arranged for visiting-nurse and housekeeper service. She made it her business to know the social-agency resources of the city and relied greatly on them for practical assistance to her patients' families.

Fortune smiled on the obedient patient and the determined doctor, and Marion delivered a healthy boy. In time she rejoiced to see him graduate from the university with honors and establish himself in a brilliant career.

Another such patient was not so lucky. After five miscarriages, when she became pregnant a sixth time, Marion put her to bed with instructions not to get up for anything. "And I mean *anything*," she told her patient. When the young woman was well enough to make the regular office visits she had a longer list of anxious questions than the average pregnant patient. On her last visit before confinement the list was headed, "Tell Dr. H. if baby is retarded or Mongoloid, don't let it live."

Six turned out to be her lucky number. With suitable spacing, she had a family of three lusty youngsters. For years the gloomy question list was a family joke with their doctor.

Another patient had a miscarriage following the tragic death of her young son. Well-meaning relatives visited her in the hospital and told her, "Don't try again. Just leave well enough alone."

She and her husband had cherished the hope of having a large family. The advice sent her already lowered spirits down several more notches.

Shortly afterward Marion came in to see her. After examining the patient she sat down beside the bed and took the patient's hand. "You be a good girl and get back on your feet. Then you can try again," she said. Actually it was some time before she felt that the patient's recovery was complete and another pregnancy was safe, but eventually the woman and her husband had a family of six.

"The important thing was that Dr. Hilliard said exactly the right thing at the right time to help me throw off depression and look to the future," the patient told a friend.

Apprehension does not fly out the window the minute the new baby safely arrives. New mothers can always find things to worry about, and Marion knew when to laugh them off.

Once she came in to find a patient sitting up in her hospital bed, anxiously studying the face of her two-day-old daughter.

"She hasn't any eyebrows," wailed the new mother. "Will she ever have?"

"My dear friend," replied Marion, "my babies *always* have eyebrows!"

Sometimes Marion felt that it was part of her job to answer a question in a way that would set the patient thinking about an underlying problem. To a woman who had several children and yearned for a new baby, half consciously believing that it would be a solution to family problems, she said, "I don't believe the happiness of your home depends on the number of children you have. It's the type of home you make that matters."

To another young woman, who was putting off having a family, she said, "Why not really try to get pregnant, or at least give up the idea of trying not to? It will be a miracle if you do, but let's have a miracle."

In other instances she took a practical approach.

A highly intelligent eighteen-year-old once came to her the day before her wedding for premarital examination and counsel. In spite of her high intellectual capacity and performance, she was almost completely ignorant of the facts of life. Marion went to the heart of the matter, "managing to convey the information as if I already knew it, which of course I didn't," the patient later confided to a friend.

At the end of the interview Marion handed the young woman the necessary equipment and said, "Now before you do another thing, go home or someplace where you can lock yourself in and practice."

The most famous example of her practical advice concerned a patient she told about in her first book. The patient and her husband, a minister, "enjoyed each other once a week on Sunday night," but the woman found she was always too tired to do the washing on Monday. Could Dr. Hilliard suggest something?

"Certainly," replied Marion. "Wash on Tuesday."

A thoughtful patient of Marion's once observed that such practical solutions could really be called "psychiatry at its best," as they helped a patient get insight into herself.

"When you are covering up the *real* reason for a problem by a *good* reason and an understanding person like Dr. Hilliard removes the obstacle posed by the 'good' reason, you're that much closer to solving your problem," she said.

CHAPTER 12

The Turbulent Years

For Canadians, World War II began September tenth, 1939. For Marion, as for most other people who kept things going at home, it was six years packed with overwork and worry.

Although both her brothers were now in the mission field, Reverend Foster Hilliard having gone to Trinidad under the auspices of the United Church of Canada, one of them, young Dr. Irwin, was located in a theater of war in the Orient even before the onset of the European war. In midsummer of 1939 he wrote from Fowliang Szechwan, where he had been appointed physician in chief of the Canadian mission hospital, that bombings had begun but that their small settlement had a "perfectly good air-raid shelter." And indeed, "the Hilliard luck held," throughout repeated Japanese air raids.

As time went on, Marion's nephew Joe went into the RCAF; her New York brother-in-law, Wentworth Myers, was sent to China with the American Air Force; Dr. McNeel enlisted in the army Medical Corps and went to England, after training in the Maritimes; three of her colleagues at the hospital enlisted in the Canadian women's services; and Jean Hall, the friend with whom she had shared an apartment for some years, was recruited from her social-work job in Toronto for war service in Ottawa.

All Canada watched with despair and horror while, in the spring of 1940, Hitler's armies invaded Norway, swept over Belgium, Holland, and France, and pushed the British armies onto the shores of Dunkirk. And then they wept with pride at the courage with which nine hundred vessels of what surely must have been the most fantastic flotilla of English history rescued over a third of a million troops and skippered them to the temporarily safe side of the English Channel. Then, as the London bombings began, they counted the hours from one BBC broadcast to the next and asked each other if it could be true, as it was whispered, that Hitler's invasion barges were ready to go.

Marion thought of Miss Dearnley, her "two Margarets," and the other friends of her happy year in England, and of Maryon and Mike Pearson, who had gone to London in 1938 when Mike had been appointed first secretary to Canada's high commissioner there. Busy as she was, she lent time and energy to organizations in which she could, as the World War I phrase had it, "do her bit." One such was the Committee for British Overseas Children, which, in Toronto, was chaired by Mrs. Peter Sandiford, a member of the hospital's Board of Governors and one of Marion's good friends.

July, 1940. The blacked-out *Monarch of Bermuda* plowed through the North Atlantic, bound from the besieged British Isles for Halifax—and safety, safety for its precious cargo of women, babies, and children.

Among the masses of crying children, and the mothers and "nannies" clamoring for food for their young charges in the *Monarch's* stripped-down, trestle-tabled dining room, was Pauline Shapiro. The young wife of a University of Birmingham faculty member, and herself a professor and writer, Mrs. Shapiro was traveling with her small son and was within days of having her second child.

Though fortunate that her child was safe and that she had been invited to bring him to Toronto by the university's Committee for British Overseas Children, she was about as desolate as a human being could be. She had left home fearing that she would never see her husband and parents again. She knew no one in the city of her destination. In her possession was a gloomy letter from a Birmingham gynecologist reporting her long and difficult confinement with her first baby and offering a cheerless prognosis for the one to come. Moreover, she could barely tie the straps of her life jacket around her bulky waistline, and her typewriter was lost in the hold!

For five days, as the ship zigzagged its way across the ocean, the young mother staggered from jam-packed dining room to crowded sun deck to her berth on D deck, five flights below the lifeboats, seasick, homesick, trying not to think of torpedoes and mines, and doing her best to keep up with a bright, alert little boy who was having the time of his life. She took heart a bit when her typewriter turned up in the purser's office and a kind nurse on board told her that she would make it to Canada before having her baby.

A thirty-two-hour train journey brought the Toronto-bound contingent of evacuees into Union Station at seven o'clock on a hot, steamy Sunday morning, where they were met by members of the committee and whisked off to the quarters arranged for them. Mrs. Sandiford had one question for Mrs. Shapiro: Would she mind having a woman obstetrician?

Study of the feminist movement in Britain and great appreciation for its significance was part and parcel of this young woman's background. "I'd prefer it," she replied.

Out at Birch Point, Marion was enjoying one of her rare lazy mornings when the telephone rang.

"How would you like to deliver an English baby as a contribution to the war effort?" asked her friend Mrs. Sandiford.

"I'd love it," was her unhesitating answer. Before lunch she was at Mrs. Shapiro's bedside. Sensing that her young patient was "keeping a stiff upper lip," she concealed her dismay at finding a very large baby and a mother in a toxic condition, and embarked on a typical Hilliard procedure.

"Her manner was superb," recalled Mrs. Shapiro later. "She cast aside the doctor's letter so quickly that I thought she had hardly read it. She was completely reassuring and told me just as much of what was true as was good for me then. She sensed my desperate fatigue and weariness of spirit and had the wisdom to leave me to rest for a week before induction, in spite of the size of the baby."

A week later the patient checked into Women's College Hospital, rested, relaxed, assured about the committee's arrangements for care of her little boy. Medication was begun in the evening and by five o'clock the next morning she was in labor. Being a stoic type, the patient "held tight to the bed and thought of air raids," so that her nurses did not realize how near to delivery she was, but at seven-thirty she was trundled into the elevator, bound for the famous tenth floor.

The next half hour she described a few days later in a letter to her husband.

"Still in the middle of a terrible pain I was wheeled out onto the tenth floor. Shouts of 'No, not the labor room, straight to the delivery room.' As I emerged from the pain, I got a glimpse of a scene straight from an American film—chromium gadgets, shining surfaces, an army of masked nurses and the commander-in-chief, Dr. Hilliard, with barely anything on except her white topcoat, saying rather severely to my attendants, 'You should have brought her here before this.' Then, so kindly, to me: 'Tell me as soon as the next pain is beginning and I'll give you something.' They barely had time to transfer me to the delivery table before the next pain and I signalled. It was terrific, but by this time the anesthetic apparatus was going and I knew no more until eight o'clock when I was lying over on my side being sick into a kidney tray, and then I saw a very fat, very pink baby, squealing and kicking on the scales. 'A fine baby boy, eight pounds, eleven ounces,' someone said, and that was that."

When the lusty young man was a week old his mother wrote home again, to say that she would like to name the baby partly for her doctor.

"I couldn't have had more kindness and attention anywhere," she assured her husband, "and I was sustained by complete confidence in Dr. Hilliard. A marvellous woman—the ideal type that the woman's movement has set free. I should think she's about forty, so brisk and untiring even in this weather, fine features and the most beautiful blue eyes I've ever seen. She's as kind and understanding as she is quick and efficient, discussed everything with me very honestly, yet showed discrimination.

"People are pleased about my enthusiasm for Dr. H. and the hospital. Sometime I'll write more about the delightful equalitarian atmosphere that prevails. There's none of that beastly hospital hierarchy with the doctor as semi-divine. Dr. H. prefers to go her rounds unaccompanied and rings for a nurse if she wants one. Also I noticed she apologized to a nurse for leaving the bell light on, on one occasion!"

Young Jonathan Hilliard Shapiro, with his mother and brother, spent the first three years of his life in Canada. Pauline Shapiro's typewriter turned out articles for Canadian magazines and programs for the Canadian Broadcasting Company, and she and her children made fast friends of their Canadian hosts. For one summer the little family boarded with cottager-neighbors of Marion on the bluffs, and the doctor-patient relationship grew into a family friendship, joyfully renewed each time Marion returned to England with a visit to Birmingham on her schedule.

It was not the first time, nor would it be by a long shot the last time, that Marion's intuitiveness for the hidden feeling, the unspoken word, would turn a woman's despair and fear into hope and confidence. And it was by such experiences that her own unquenchable joy of living was constantly reinforced.

Marion's steadily growing practice shot up rapidly as the war baby boom gathered momentum and she took over work for her colleagues who went into the women's services. Obstetrical patients gradually overcrowded the hospital so that post-delivery care had to be reduced from ten to seven days. Beset by staff shortages, the hospital board decided to make no permanent appointments of women of military age, and the Medical Advisory Board, of which Marion was again a member, voted to allow staff members to work on two services where necessary to keep the work covered.

Once for a period of nearly two weeks Marion never went to

bed at all, visiting her apartment only to change her clothes, catching catnaps in her office or the doctors' lounge at the hospital. As she edged past her fortieth birthday, even the strong and energetic Dr. Hilliard began to show the strain.

"I saw you grow old and then grow young again," one of her long-time patients told her when the postwar years had revived her.

In spite of the pressures, she retained a farsighted attitude that the future of the hospital depended on highly qualified people in all departments. A member of the surgery department whom she had known well from the time of the latter's intern days asked her advice about an offer for a year's special internship with a top-flight surgeon at another hospital. It was a year when the hospital was very shorthanded, but Marion unhesitatingly told the young woman, "Don't pass up this opportunity."

If the ill wind of war took away some of the hospital staff temporarily, it also blew some good new recruits to the doorstep. On the eve of war the first of these, Dr. Elizabeth Wiley, had emigrated to Canada with her husband, an Austrian businessman. In her own country Dr. Wiley had had a successful practice as an orthopedic surgeon. Seeking an internship as a first step toward certification in Canada, she was referred to Marion, then chairman of the intern committee. She arrived for an office appointment just as Marion was rushing to the hospital for a delivery. Together they sped through the six or seven blocks, Marion rapidly firing questions about the young woman's experience and training. When they pulled up at the hospital Marion asked, "How soon can you start?"

"But you don't know enough about me!" protested the young doctor.

"Yes I do," replied Marion, dashing for the door, then calling over her shoulder, "It will be all right! You'll see."

Two years later, after completing a resident internship in obstetrics, Dr. Wiley joined the staff, opened her own office, and later won certification in two specialties. She and her husband and son became Marion's devoted friends.

One wartime winter a severe blizzard brought Toronto transportation to a standstill. The snow began late one afternoon and by three o'clock the next morning, when Marion was called to the hospital, it was waist deep. There was nothing to do but walk. For the last few of some twenty blocks she was fortunate enough to be able to follow in the wake of a snow plow. Her patient safely delivered, she and the night nurses set up coffee and sandwiches for the doctors who struggled in for the next three hours, arrayed in a variety of odd costumes. Dr. Wiley, schooled on the slopes of the Alps, won top honors for the day, and a headline in a Toronto newspaper, by arriving on skis.

Marion's Bible study group at the YWCA reflected women's interests and problems in wartime now, just as during the depression it had delved into the causes of unemployment. One series dealt with the meaning of Christian marriage. One question was preoccupying the young women: If their husbands who were overseas had affairs with other women, what were they expected to do about it?

Marion was forthright about the answer. "You jolly well better take them back and say nothing about it," she said earnestly. "You have no idea what they are going through while you are safe at home. Your biggest job is to start thinking about what we can all do to rid this world of war so these family separations won't have to take place at all."

She was among the representatives chosen by the Canadian YWCA to attend a conference called by the World's YWCA in Washington to discuss the effect of war on the life of women. Although she was interested in the subject, and later wrote a series of articles about it for a church publication, she was, as a friend expressed it, "like a cricket on a hot griddle" in the face of gatherings that were long on speeches and discussions and short on action. One night after a long session she gathered up a group of friends to drive out to see the Lincoln Memorial in the moonlight. Another day, en route in a taxi to a meeting, she passed down Embassy Row, asked to stop at the Canadian Embassy, where Mike Pearson had been installed as ambassador to the

U.S., and kept the taxi waiting while she ran in for a chat with her old friend.

After returning to Toronto she and her friend Sasha David-son organized a small study group to consider the findings of the Washington conference and recommend to the YWCA what action it could take as a follow-up.

"No one has ever adequately described the beauty of travel by air. To be suspended under a vault of intense blue which shimmers in the brilliance of sunlight and a temperature of forty degrees below zero is really beyond description. Sometimes there were banks of clouds beneath us, sometimes lonely stretches of forest, but always it was beautiful. If one cannot describe the beauty neither can one appreciate the incredible annihilation of time and space. At ten o'clock in the morning I was finishing my rounds at the hospital and at five-thirty in the afternoon I was happily drinking tea in the home of a faculty member at Manitoba. Canada no longer should have the excuse that she is too large and unwieldy to be a nation."

Thus Marion wrote of what was probably her first plane trip, in January, 1941, on Trans-Canada Airlines, which had begun spanning the continent with regular flights two years before. Thereafter she rarely traveled any other way.

On this occasion she had been persuaded by two old friends from the SCM days to take part in a mission to the University of Manitoba in Winnipeg, the purpose of which was to give students an opportunity to "think through the challenge of the Christian faith." The committee planning the mission had written her that students, as well as their elders, were troubled at the kind of place the world of the 1940s was turning out to be, with mankind in constant terror of air raids, tides of refugees wandering from country to country, unemployed men and women thronging towns and cities.

"We are helpless and confused; we have no plan or perspective. We bargain for our lives from day to day; conflicting loyalties and prejudices or sheer indifference determine our actions.

Even if we strive for high ideals, we are confronted by the fact that what we believe or intend seems to alter but little the kind of world in which we live. Does it make any difference what we believe or what we live for?"

At first Marion refused the invitation, feeling that she was not qualified to speak with young people about these things. Further persuaded by her friends, she took stock of what she had to bring to the experience: her own faith; the knowledge gained under the tutelage of Professor Hooke and Dr. Sharman; the weekly sermons by Dr. Sclater, whom she thought of as "one of the world's great preachers"; and finally, her knowledge of the Bible, "gained by the fact that my mother supervised our reading as children, night after night, until we had completed it three times including even the 'begats.'"

As usual, she decided that what one lacked in armament, one must make up in courage. But the idea of getting up and preaching a Sunday-morning sermon to a congregation full of university students seemed more formidable than a major operation. It was reassuring to find that the minister knew and admired her parents, and she was grateful for the note he slipped into her hand as they sat in the chancel: "This is the kindliest congregation in Canada, so feel right at home, as much as if you were talking to a group of probationers in a clinic."

Nevertheless, her knees were shaking as she rose and announced her text: "For I know whom I have believed, and am persuaded that he is able to keep that which I have committed unto him against that day" (II Timothy, 1:12). Her sermon was a testimonial to her faith.

"My belief in God," she said, "comes out of my deepest thought and experience. It is the tower of my strength. It is a rock in a weary land. I believe in God the creator, or you may say I believe in an ordered universe, ordered by a mind which takes pleasure in creating—and that is the only answer we have as to the reason. God is an ever present, all-sustaining power, and I recognize that power for the world is dynamic and full of change. Where there is evil it is because God's love has made us

free and where there is freedom there is sin. God is continually
at work turning evil into good."

She spoke of the beauty of God's world as seen through the
child's eyes; the sense of God's power that one feels in a storm or
in the pull of gravity; of how one sees goodness and love in people: "My mother's face, the smiles of old friends, the sudden
awakening to a kindred soul."

Elaborating her idea of God's gift of freedom to His people,
she said, "God plays the game by the rule He laid down and is
willing to suffer for it. He feels that love shall be free and that
He does not want His children to be puppets, so He sees them
sin and He suffers."

In the confusion and disillusionment of the post-World War I
days Marion and her SCM friends had thought of themselves as
"seeking the utmost realities and sincerities of religion and feeling after the pure heart of Christianity" in an effort to bring the
kingdom of God on earth. Now, as World War II raged across
Europe, she declared stoutly, "We are fighting to save our religious freedom and Christian principles. We are willing to sacrifice everything in order to have a second chance to help build the
kingdom of God."

But wasn't the sacrifice ridiculous, she asked the students, "If
the younger generation coming along have no idea what they
believe?"

She spoke of her medical experience, the trust patients have
in their doctors, and confessed that eventually one looks back at
the medical-student period and wonders at the arrogance in feeling that just training and knowledge can sustain a doctor's
power.

"I have seen in people that something that is part of God that
makes them strive for perfection. Nothing can prevent the human soul from preferring creativeness to happiness and that is
because it is part of God. Christianity's greatest strength will
come when we realize the futility of man in his own endeavor:
he learns something, only to destroy himself; but with God, all
things are possible."

Back home in Toronto after the three days of student discussions Marion laid it on the line to the church and student movement groups in whose behalf she had gone in Winnipeg.

"It is difficult to change in a flash from a doctor to a missioner. I kept feeling you must diagnose the situation before you apply the treatment. Bitten into my mind forever is the obligation to diagnose accurately. Even if the patient is dead, the diagnosis must be confirmed if humanity is to gain knowledge. When will the church wake up to the fact that this is a universal principle, and as essential to saving the soul as it is to physical healing? The attitude of always emphasizing the bright spots is about as sensible as looking for diphtheria when your patient has measles."

Then she offered her "diagnosis."

"Students have acquired an amazing defense against emotional impact. If they hadn't, they would be a mass of shattered nerves. I still remember my two days in bed after seeing my first movie, 'The Birth of a Nation.' How these students have survived the funnies, radio and movies we have these days, I can't imagine.

"The problem put plainly is this—they are not anti-religious, they are just not interested. Religious experience seems irrelevant to their lives. No amount of pounding at that defense in the old-fashioned way will break it down. Only an understanding of its weakness will give us a chance, and this brings me to the second conclusion: they are ignorant. They have no knowledge of the Bible and the personality of Jesus has no shining transcendental quality of leadership to them. He is a dull person who said stupid, misleading things like 'The meek shall inherit the earth,' and is reported to have done miracles of healing which they don't believe. They see no glorious adventure in the early church and have no faith in God, either as a power or a personal revelation. The word 'Christian' has become synonymous with an easy, comfortable, protected good way of life which they take for granted as they do holidays and their education.

"If they accept you as a thinking individual, or rather if you have acquitted yourself in a way they respect, they listen with all their mind and all their heart. They have no pre-existing theological walls to break down. The way can be lit up for them with a radiance we couldn't achieve in our day because so much of our thinking was a made-over thing and never won without a certain sense of loss. Imprinted on my mind forever will be that theater filled with the best-looking group of students I have ever seen and not a shuffle out of them, not even a pin dropped while I told them that science is really not enough.

"Our generation is still running on the faith of our fathers and mothers whether we know it and admit it or not. What have we done to strengthen it and pass it on? The generations coming after us are losing out because of it. I come back to my church saying, 'Take us laymen and laywomen, teach us, demand our best, and see to it that we achieve it in order that all together we may build a new and better world where ignorance and lack of faith gradually disappear. And please hurry!'"

After Dr. McNeel's departure for overseas duty, Marion kept closely in touch with Barby, who, with her two little girls, lived near Marion in the city and spent many of the wartime summer weeks at Birch Point. Marion delighted in being close to her small nieces during their baby days, and hugely enjoyed the lessons she learned about being an aunt.

One summer day at Birch Point she suggested to four-year-old Sue that she pick some flowers to take home.

"As many as I want?" asked the youngster.

"Yes, of course," said Aunt Marion.

Fifteen minutes later the sisters glanced out of the window and discovered that the child had gone methodically down the perennial border, picking every blossom, carefully arranging them in five or six piles on the grass.

"Wait," said Marion to her sister, who was about to hurry out and stop the proceedings. "It's my fault. She asked and I said, 'As many as you want.'" She strolled out and admired the tasteful bouquets, learning that they were designated "for Mummy," "for the neighbors," "for my best friend," and so on, then asked if Sue would be willing to leave the rest for Aunt Marion.

At the other end of the age scale was her grown-up niece Mim, who came to Birch Point for a short holiday before entering nurse's training at Toronto Western Hospital. Aunt Marion undertook to bring from town the supply of new nurses' uniforms ordered from a department store. The large package (along with a crock of gherkins and a jug of vinegar for the fall pickling at Birch Point) was stolen from her car in front of the hospital. Crestfallen, she returned to Scarborough, then brightened up and briskly called friends on the nursing staff to borrow enough uniforms to get the young student nurse started on her career. As her sister Ruth was fond of saying, "It's hard for a Hilliard to look helpless!"

The family gathered at Birch Point in June, 1943, to celebrate Mr. and Mrs. Hilliard's golden wedding anniversary, and Marion began a two-year campaign to persuade her mother and father to move to Toronto. Although he was seventy-two at the time of his retirement from Osgoode Hall, Mr. Hilliard had bought back his law practice in Morrisburg. Now his memory began to fail, and Marion worried about his driving, which had been erratic even in his prime years, as well as his trying to practice.

In the spring of 1945 she purchased a house on Lonsdale Road in Toronto, where "all the old folks can be together." (Mr. and Mrs. Hilliard were eventually joined by her brother, Uncle Rob, and his wife, now retired from their years in the mission field, and her sister, Aunt Luella, following the death of Reverend Warner.) Every day or two Marion stopped in to see them, and periodically had them to her apartment for dinner and the evening. It was the custom for these devout and gentle folk to end family evenings with "a word of prayer," although Uncle Rob still showed the fire of his earlier years of preaching and "a word" became many words. Marion usually entered into the custom wholeheartedly, for she loved her old folks.

One evening, however, Uncle Rob proposed that they now

pray for the recovery of Mrs. X, an elderly friend from his mission days, who had lived a full life and was now in the terminal stages of illness. For some reason—perhaps it had been one of those days when Marion had had the sad task of telling a husband that his young wife had cancer and could not recover—she balked at Uncle Rob's suggestion. Mrs. X was a very old lady, she said, and it was clear that she could not get well: praying for her to recover, or even to live any longer, was not humane, and she, for one, would not join in any such thing. The evening ended abruptly. Marion drove the stunned older people home, returned, stomped up the stairs, angry with herself, burst into tears, then had to laugh at the whole performance. The next day she called and apologized to Uncle Rob, who forgave her though he did not understand her.

The war years brought Marion the only illnesses she had in adulthood until the one that ended her life.

One day in the 1940s Jean Davey received a summons from Toronto General Hospital, where a patient, a Miss Wales, wished to consult her. Who in the world was Miss Wales, Dr. Davey asked herself; she'd never heard of her. Still, it was quite a plum to be called to "The General," after having been in practice only a year. In her best professional bib and tucker, carrying her doctor's bag, she presented herself at the hospital and was ushered to Miss Wales' room.

Sitting up in the hospital bed, convulsed with laughter at the sight of her young friend's solemn demeanor quickly followed by openmouthed surprise, was Marion Hilliard. When she could catch her breath Marion explained that she was having an operation the next day and she hoped that Dr. Davey would give a lecture a few days later in her place. A leak in the nipple of one breast had led her to discover a small lump and she had made arrangements quietly and quickly to have it removed by Toronto General's famous surgeon, Dr. Roscoe Graham. She did not think it was serious (it proved to be a benign tumor) but she had not told anyone but Ellen Blatchford, who was going to give the anesthetic. Sworn to secrecy and agreeing to give the lecture, Dr. Davey prepared to leave. "But why 'Miss Wales'?" she asked, turning at the door.

With the greatest enjoyment of her own wit, Marion replied, "Because the national symbol of Wales is the leek."

Twice more in the next three years Dr. Graham had his mysterious patient admitted to the hospital under names that Marion made up herself and enjoyed hugely, and Dr. Blatchford hurried over to preside as anesthetist for her friend. Once, part of her thyroid had to be removed because of a small growth; the second time she had a fibroid tumor and a hysterectomy was recommended. On these hospital trips, when doctor turned patient, Marion enjoyed her anonymity, joked about her assumed personality, and remarked cheerfully, "Some people get viruses. I grow lumps."

"Dr. Gwen," who always kept close to affairs on the university campus, was very popular among the students and keenly interested in their ideas. The women medical graduates of 1940 persuaded her to follow Marion as the speaker at their traditional spring Sunday service, choosing for the topic: The Philosophy of Living for a Woman Doctor.

Gwen took her assignment seriously, working concentratedly on it for several weeks. Her colleagues, who had noted her quiet, abstracted demeanor while the speech was in preparation, were right on hand to hear her speak. Thunderstruck, they heard her say that a doctor must have the courage to reach for a power outside the self and must cultivate faith in that power.

Later, when she saw her old friends among those crowding around to congratulate her for her stirring sermon, she said with a Gwenlike twinkle in her eyes, "The preacher converted no one but herself!"

And so she had. She began instruction at the Church of the Holy Trinity, an Anglican parish, and was confirmed the following Easter. The rector, Canon John Frank, and his wife, Patricia, became her fast friends. In no time she was a pillar of the church, and was spending much of her spare time in Trinity Square, a tiny, quiet enclave just off Toronto's main thoroughfare.

Before their very eyes Marion and Eva saw the former doubter and scoffer become an ardent churchwoman, and then an out-and-out proselytizer. She was the same old Gwen—ready witted, fun loving, teasing, sharp minded—but a new dimension had been added to her personality.

Only a year later, Gwen fell ill with amyotrophic lateral sclerosis, the progressive neuromuscular disorder that was to cause her untimely death.

"I suppose," she said to Marion with a sigh, "people are going to say I got converted because I got sick." Then she added, with typical irreverence, "And I must admit I did it in the nick of time!"

For the next half dozen years, as her incurable disease slowly progressed, Gwen continued her teaching and broadcasting, even after she had to be in a wheel chair. With the help of her three office mates, Canon and Mrs. Frank, and her many other friends, she managed to maintain herself in her own apartment. As her body grew weaker, her spirit grew stronger. Her wisdom and sharp wit made her the lively center of colleagues, students, church associates who looked upon her as a valuable confidante and a source of strength and inspiration.

To stave off hospitalization as long as possible, the Franks arranged for Gwen and her elderly mother to live at the rectory for six months. There her room was the center of family gatherings and impromptu parties when her friends came to visit. She continued active interest in Holy Trinity's Social Action Committee and put to work the skills that had produced so many good Daffydil shows at the university, helping Mrs. Frank with the final touches and staging of "The Easter Story," one of the two annual dramatic presentations of the church.

Finally, in 1947, she entered Women's College Hospital, where she died three years later.

During these long years of illness Marion supported her

friend's lively interests by arranging frequent outings, even taking her to the movies. Marion was so impressed by *Scott of the Antarctic* that she saw it twice, then brought Gwen in an ambulance to see it. Nothing daunted, she persuaded the management to allow the stretcher to be placed at the head of an aisle, which was then roped off. After Gwen could no longer ride out to Scarborough in a passenger car, Marion had her brought out by ambulance for an evening or a weekend. She rarely missed her daily visit to Gwen's hospital room and often spent evenings reading to her. After the twentieth reunion dinner of "Meds, '27" Marion and their old friend and classmate Bill Keith, by then a celebrated brain surgeon, gathered up samples of the food and flowers from the table decorations and had a second celebration in Gwen's room at the hospital.

It was during these crowded war years that Marion fell in love for the first and only time as a mature woman. A long-time friendship with a man not of her own profession and who lived some distance away suddenly ripened, perhaps as she described in her own writings, "while a man and woman share a companionable chuckle or happen to touch hands."

Circumstances made it impossible for anything to come of it. She accepted her situation with realism and dignity, had no confidants, and after a time she and her friend saw little of each other.

Long afterward, when she wrote her famous chapter "What Women Don't Know about Being Female" for her first book, a chapter packed with hard-hitting, realistic wisdom, she spoke of the time in life when a woman realizes that she will probably never marry.

". . . the path her life is taking . . . never looked more unpalatable. Her friends have small children and she is tortured by the knowledge that she will never hold her baby. She is calling herself a bachelor girl, but she knows the synonym is old maid. At this point in her life passion is going to sear her to the bone.

She is bound to fall in love and her love is almost sure to be married, that's how fate always seems to set it up."

She went on to enumerate the factors in such a situation that add up to "paying a bleak price."

"Yet," she added, "if a woman understands the sacrifice that will be demanded of her and is deeply in love, I cannot in any sincerity condemn the relationship. If tarnish can be avoided, and disillusionment and doubt, she will have a brief love to cherish and remember all her life. Such a love must be held gently and relinquished, when the times comes, without tears."

Midway in the war, through mutual social-work friends, Marion met Opal Boynton, a New Yorker and program director for the far-flung USO operations conducted by the YWCA of the United States. "Poppy," as she was known to nearly everyone, was a native of Washington State and descendant of adventurous New Englanders who migrated to the West Coast in the 1850s. She had inherited intact the gusty humor, *joie de vivre,* and itching foot of her forebears. She and Marion took to each other on first meeting.

A raconteur of sorts, Poppy told stories that delighted Marion —stories of life on the Boynton ranch, of her starting to medical school halfway across the country on a three-hundred-dollar scholarship and hastily switching courses when her money ran out, of her vintage years in Greenwich Village and her job in an East Side settlement house, of her hair-raising experiences on a trip through the tinderbox of Germany and Austria in the summer of 1938.

In turn Poppy, perhaps because medicine had been her own first choice as a career, took a keen interest in Marion's stories from hospital, consulting room, and medical convention; and her own experience in administration made her intelligently appreciative of the problems of a rapidly growing hospital.

A sports enthusiast, she initiated her Canadian friends into the mysteries of baseball and, in turn, learned the fine points of ice hockey. When she found that they had never been trout fishing she arranged for Marion and her housemate Miss Hall to meet her for a holiday at her favorite fishing camp in Laurentide Park, a hundred miles north of Quebec City. Marion promptly adopted the camp as one of her own favorites, and for the next ten years returned again and again to this secluded, beautiful spot. She loved the sleepy hours spent trolling quietly from a boat on a lake surrounded by such dense, silent woodlands that the forest animals often appeared on the shore; and gloried in the days when, equipped with waders, the party fished the turbulent trout streams. It was a poor day that did not see them return to camp with a catch of thirty to fifty good-sized beauties, the best of which would come to their dinner table, perfectly grilled.

On her visits to New York, Marion began to divide her time between her sister's family and Poppy and her circle of friends. To nearly everyone she issued invitations to "come to Scarborough next summer"—and many of them did.

One spring holiday in 1945, as Marion and Poppy sat over a pre-dinner cocktail in a small place in mid-Manhattan, the news of President Roosevelt's death came over the radio. Like a great many Canadians, Marion admired and loved FDR, and now she was one with the handful of Americans in the restaurant who, in shock and grief, drew together as a group, talking from one table to another. The next afternoon, arriving at Carnegie Hall for a concert, she and Poppy were privileged to hear the New York Philharmonic Symphony orchestra give the now-famous memorial concert to the great president, beginning with the second movement from Beethoven's Symphony in A Major and ending with the Brahms Symphony in D Major. To Marion it was a never-to-be-forgotten experience. After her death the concert program was found, folded over and over, tucked away in a pocket of her wallet.

That summer, trudging back to the Quebec fishing camp after a final morning on a lake, Marion asked Poppy, "What are you going to do after the war?"

The war-weary Poppy, whose job had kept her on the move

for four years from one military post and industrial location to another, found herself giving voice to a dream of long standing. "What I'd really like to do is retire to the country somewhere and raise bees."

It sounded like the typical New Yorker's escape dream, but Marion suggested that the fields along the Scarborough Bluffs would make a likely site for a bee farm and invited her to stay at Birch Point and try it out.

On that August day of 1945, they came into camp to find the place in great excitement. The one person on the staff who spoke English as well as the patois of the area was absent, so it was the next day, en route to Scarborough, that they finally found a newspaper with the account of the bombing of Hiroshima. In a matter of days, along with all of Toronto, they celebrated V-J Day.

Like most days, this one brought an emergency call from the hospital for Marion. But for Marion it was a very special call, for she found that she would deliver, a bit early, the newest of her growing group of "adopted" nephews and nieces. As the bells rang and whistles blew she delivered Dr. Dorothy Redmond Daley's second child.

"Hurray for us, Dotty!" she exclaimed to her friend as the premature baby was borne away to an incubator. "The war's over and you have a grand little boy. And this one," she added, with that instinct for giving her patients something interesting to think about, "is all Redmond!"

For the Hilliard family the war was indeed over. Before the month was out Dr. McNeel returned from his last Army assignment, treating men suffering from battle fatigue in France; and the Irwin Hilliards finally arrived, having been en route from China since the previous New Year's Eve. Young Joe Hilliard settled into the Lonsdale Road ménage and began his university studies, which would eventually lead to a medical degree and his becoming the third Dr. Hilliard in the family. At Irwanna, where the family gathered for a brief reunion, the old cottage echoed with laughter, tears, prayers of thanksgiving, and a steady hum of conversation as three generations began to bridge the gap of the war years. Ann and Bob, the "little Hilliards" who had been born in China, began to get acquainted with the aunts, uncles, and grandparents they were now meeting for the first time. Burdett McNeel began a particularly delicate getting-acquainted job with his three-year-old daughter, Carolyn, who had been a baby when he went overseas and now took a somewhat dim view of the strange man who had joined the family circle!

Marion and the other "stay-at-homes" listened incredulously to the account of the long journey home from China, complicated by the dislocations of war and the low travel priority of a medical missionary. At one port city Irwin had signed on as ship's doctor on a vessel bound for England, neglecting to tell the captain that he was traveling with his wife and two small children until he brought them aboard an hour before sailing time (and too late to find another doctor).

By fall Marion in her apartment on Clifton Road and the older generation on Lonsdale Road were settling down to enjoy having so much of the family close together again. The McNeels returned to the home they had left six years ago, where Dr. McNeel resumed his career with the Ontario mental-health service. Irwin took the Fellowship examination to test himself out after seven years and, to his astonishment and his sister's pride, passed them. Shortly afterward Aunt Marion delivered the third "little Hilliard," who was named John. Dr. Hilliard opened a practice in Toronto and the family settled into a house a few minutes' drive from Marion's apartment.

Now all but one of the ten nieces and nephews on whom Marion lavished so much love and attention had come into the world. The Myers' son, named for his father and called "Young Went" by the family, was a teen-ager. A son, Franklin, had been born to Foster and his second wife in Trinidad. When Marion delivered the fourth "little Hilliard," another Barbara, in 1952, she had five nephews and five nieces covering an age span of twenty-nine years.

Marion Hilliard's career spanned a transition period in Canadian medicine. The generations before hers had usually done a year's internship after medical school before beginning practice. In the 1920s more and more graduates sought postgraduate training in France, England, and the United States. Many attached considerable value to fellowships and memberships in the British medical colleges, such as Marion had won by examination.

By the time Marion retired from the hospital staff, a medical graduate planning to specialize could take it for granted that he would do five to seven years' internship, after which he must win certification by examinations of the Royal College of Physicians and Surgeons of Canada. If he sought the highest qualification—a Fellowship in the college—he must sit for examinations so demanding in character that an average of only fifty per cent of the candidates succeeded in passing them on the first try.

Growth in influence of the college, established in 1929 on the initiative of the Canadian Medical Association, was largely responsible for the rapid upgrading of standards and greatly increased requirements for preparation to practice. From the beginning the college standards were exacting; its history records that in the two-part examination given in the early 1930s for the first time, eight of twelve candidates failed the first part, and all three candidates for the second part were unsuccessful.

In the early 1940s the college moved to giving certification examinations, and in 1947 assumed the function of approval of hospitals for graduate training.

By the mid-1930s, Canadian hospitals began offering postgraduate training. One of the first to do so was "The General" in Toronto, where the late Dr. William Edward Gallie, then its chief of surgery and professor of surgery on the university's medical faculty, gave the "Gallie course," graduates of which now hold senior surgery posts in Canada and elsewhere. In a few years it was no longer necessary for Canadian medical graduates to go abroad for postgraduate work.

Rising standards of practice are, of course, a source of pride in any profession. Inevitably, however, in such a transition period, some practitioners will find their technical qualifications out-moded, perhaps midway in their careers. Many Canadian doctors of Marion's vintage found themselves in what could have been a dilemma; to Marion, it was nothing of the kind.

She welcomed these exciting developments, cherishing the best for her profession in her own country. She looked forward to the day when Canadian women in medicine would have their place in the sun, like Miss Dearnley and her colleagues in the London hospitals. Now she bent her energies toward encouraging new generations of women doctors to win the highest quali-fications and toward helping her hospital achieve high standing. It was with the greatest satisfaction that she saw, one by one, the important posts at the hospital filled by highly qualified young women: in 1941, as associate chief of surgery, Dr. Jessie Gray, a graduate of the "Gallie course," veteran of seven years' intern-ship at "The General," and the first woman in Canada to pass the Fellowship examination for surgery; shortly afterward, Dr. Marjorie Davis, an assistant in surgery, became a Fellowship holder; in 1945, Dr. Davey returned to civilian life from the Canadian Air Force, won her Fellowship, and came back to the staff as associate chief of medicine.

Marion threw herself energetically into the work of the medi-cal groups to which she belonged, particularly the Canadian Fed-eration of Medical Women, and reached out in all directions to learn from and exchange ideas with those working on the medi-cal problems she found among her own patients and those of her hospital department. With Miss Dearnley, now at the peak of her career at the "Royal Free" in London, she exchanged medical papers and descriptions of new gynecological surgery.

Nearly every year she slipped away for a week or ten days to work with Dr. Joe Vincent Meigs, Boston's famous gynecologist. Dr. Meigs, professor (now emeritus) of gynecology at Harvard Medical School, who was then chief of Vincent Memorial Hos-pital, the gynecologic service of Massachusetts General Hospital, did notable pioneering in surgery for cancer of the cervix, one of the most common types of cancer among women of middle age.

With Boston colleagues, he was the first in the United States to
publish supporting data on successful use of the "smear test" devised by Dr. George Papanicolaou for early detection of cancer
of the cervix and uterus, and to recommend its use in routine
physical examination.

Similar in its simplicity to the tuberculin test, used to detect
tuberculosis in children and young people, the "Pap" test—or variations of it—is in common use today. The years have shown that,
given early detection, cancer of the cervix is curable in a very
large proportion of cases.

In the late 1940s, Marion was to devise, in collaboration with
Women's College Hospital colleagues, a simplified adaptation of
this method of early cancer detection.

The Boston visits were stimulating and heartwarming to Marion. At Vincent Memorial she observed Dr. Meigs at work in
the operating theater, accompanied him on rounds, spent long
hours in the laboratories, watching and working with cytology
specialists. Often there were other visitors, and she met and became friendly with medical people from other parts of the world.
A particular highlight to her was meeting Dr. Bernhard Zondek
of the famous team that developed the first pregnancy test, an
indispensable tool of Marion's trade.

Part of Marion's enjoyment was in the dignified old city of
Boston itself. In free time she joined friends for sightseeing, walks
in Boston Common, and the seafood dinners that she relished.

A warm friendship sprang up between Marion and Dr. Meigs
and his staff. "We were proud to know her," he once wrote a
friend. In lulls between operations his surgical nurse, Mary Ross,
would bring Marion a cup of coffee, and Marion drew her out to
talk about nursing education and what gynecological information should be added to the curriculum. Years later Miss Ross was
astonished and pleased to find some of her suggestions in Marion's writings.

As Marion's hospital responsibilities grew more pressing she
made the trip to Boston less often, but regularly arranged for her
interns to visit Vincent Memorial and observe Dr. Meigs' work.

14. Mrs. Hilliard's eightieth birthday party, October 22, 1953: with her are (left to right) Dr. Irwin Hilliard, Mrs. Burdett McNeel (Barby), Marion, Mrs. Wentworth (Ruth) Myers, Rev. Foster Hilliard.

15. Women's College Hospital, Grenville Street, Toronto, after the
new wing was added in 1956. *(Photo by Les Baxter, Toronto)*

16. Marion at her retirement party (1957) given by the Hospital's Board of Governors. (*Toronto Telegram photo*)

17. Dr. Hilliard talks with a patient in her consulting room, at the time her first book, *A Woman Doctor Looks at Love and Life,* is published. *(Photo by Everett Roseborough, Ltd., Toronto)*

18. Birch Point, Marion's home on Scarborough Bluffs, overlooking Lake Ontario, after the original cottage had been made into a year-round house. (*Panda, Toronto, photo*)

19. End of a happy day at Marion's favorite fishing camp in northern Quebec (1945).

20. Marion displays her catch on a fishing holiday (1957).

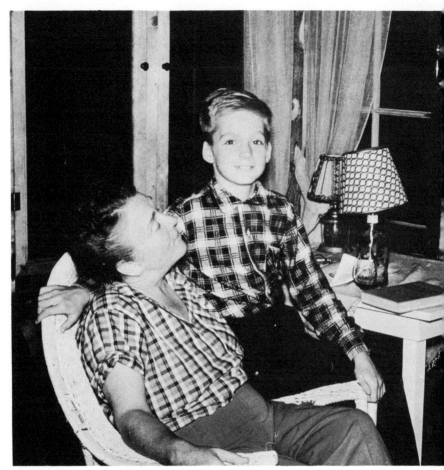

21. Aunt Marion relaxes with nephew John Hilliard (Irwin's younger son) at a family reunion.

"As I have told you so often," she wrote him in 1950, when asking permission to send two of her staff to visit, "you will never know how much I owe you for the improvement in my own work. I am still striving to do my best. . . ."

In the mid-1940s the Royal College instituted a Fellowship examination in obstetrics and gynecology. The first year, all nine candidates failed it. Even the old pros in the field admitted that it was a very tough examination, chiefly because only half the questions were in the field of the specialty, the others being drawn from the fields of surgery and medicine.

With her friends who were also practicing obstetrics Marion talked over the pros and cons of sitting for the examination. All would have had to do additional postgraduate work even to qualify as candidates. Some had families, which made it impossible. Marion considered it briefly and decided that a woman in her forties was too old. It was rumored that Women's College Hospital would soon set a retirement age of under sixty for its staff; to backtrack into further training and study for the examination would take too many of the valuable years she had left.

In these years the college was accepting for certification without examination those specialists who had graduated from medical school five years or more before, held diplomas or high degrees, and had established a local reputation in the specialty. After this period passed, all certification would be by examination. Marion applied for and received, in April 1946, certification as a specialist in obstetrics and gynecology. If she couldn't be a "Fellow," at least she could be the next best thing, a certified specialist.

By this time she was deeply involved in the only true crisis of her career at the hospital, the struggle to become chief of her department that would give her a free hand to achieve the goals for the hospital she felt were absolutely necessary to assure its future.

While they had been learner and teacher, junior and senior, Marion and her chief, Dr. Kerr, had had a good partnership. After the reorganization that had combined obstetrics and gynecology they had, between them, set up a first-rate department, and after five years Marion had been upped from assistant to associate. There came a day when, as far as competence was concerned, they were on a par, and both had large and successful private practices. Dr. Kerr, who was eight years older than Marion, had indicated that she expected to retire in the mid-40s and would recommend Marion as chief.

The two women were opposites in temperament. Marion was quick and breezy; for her, to think was to act. Dr. Kerr, a quiet, motherly person, was slower to come to a new idea. In earlier days the chief had been a good brake on her impetuous assistant's pell-mell tendencies, and Marion, recognizing that she was getting excellent experience, turned to outside interests to exercise her capacities for leadership. Marion was an initiator, an experimenter; Dr. Kerr was conservative and cautious. Marion was friendly and informal with people in the lower echelons of the hospital; Dr. Kerr was dignified, kindly, and a little remote with her juniors.

There were the usual minor disagreements between the two doctors, and one major issue of divergence. Marion was passionately devoted to the idea of having the hospital accepted for teaching by the university's Faculty of Medicine, a step that many staff members saw as a threat to their careers. Since 1932 the question had been broached at intervals by the Board of Governors, and each time the staff had insisted that it was "not wise," or the hospital was "not ready for it." Knowing that their own qualifications would probably not be acceptable in light of the ever-tightening requirements, they formed a kind of mutual protection association to stave off the day as long as possible.

In the mid-1940s, the election for chairman of the Medical Advisory Board became a hotly contested issue. The position was one of considerable power, since the incumbent would represent the medical staff at meetings of the Board of Governors. The board was pressing to take the first step toward Women's College Hospital's becoming a teaching hospital. When Marion, whose views on the matter were well known, was nominated, a doctor representing the opposite view was persuaded to run against her.

On the day of the election the meeting was astonishingly well attended. It was said that some members who did not usually come to the meetings had been recruited to vote for Dr. Hilliard's opponent. Marion lost the election and retreated in dignity, but wept behind closed doors because so many of her colleagues had joined together to defeat her, solely because she held a conviction that she honestly believed to be for the good of the hospital.

Gradually, over a period of years, Marion felt her way through her dilemma. She talked with a few trusted friends and pursued a course of disciplined silence when it came to matters on which she and her chief did not agree. It was a distressing time for those who respected both doctors and loved the hospital. Many tacitly, some openly, thought it was time for the older woman to leave the field to Marion Hilliard. It was becoming very clear that the rapidly rising standards of Canadian medicine were challenging their hospital. Since it was the only hospital in Canada staffed entirely by women doctors, there was even more at stake. The hospital had become a symbol of opportunity, a rallying point for women doctors. If they allowed it to become an ingrown institution, to fall behind the pace setters, the cause of women in medicine would suffer.

Yet the careers of many would be threatened by the very process of lifting the hospital up to a new level where it could compete on equal terms with the best in the country. Marion stood to lose as much as anyone else; the technical qualifications that were adequate in 1928, even with her successful experience and her special work in cancer added, would no longer be so. She was quite aware that she and many others would probably not be eligible for the indoor attending staff of a teaching hospital. But she felt that if she could be accepted even temporarily as chief of a teaching department, she would be willing to step aside in favor of a better-qualified doctor.

In the spring of 1947, Marion faced a turning point in her career. In June she would have her forty-fifth birthday, and it was now in the cards that the new retirement age for department chiefs would be set at fifty-five. She had calculated that, at the very least, ten years were needed if she were to accomplish what she deeply felt needed to be done for the department and for the hospital. If her appointment did not come this year, the direction of her life would have to change. She saw three possibilities: to seek appointment at another hospital and make a new place for herself; to make an open fight for appointment as chief; or to remain humbly in her present status and turn her energies to her private practice, research, and outside interests.

Even as she debated these alternatives, two developments took place.

The Medical Advisory Board recommended to the Board of Governors that department chiefs be appointed for fifteen years or until the age of fifty-five, whichever occurred earlier, and that retiring chiefs have the privilege of applying for appointment to the active staff. The recommendation was accepted.

Shortly afterward Dr. Kerr resigned and, on Marion's motion, was appointed chief consultant to the obstetrics and gynecology department.

Marion's appointment as chief came two months before her birthday. The long wait was over. She had the precious ten years and a clear field before her. It was full steam ahead.

CHAPTER 13

The Hub of the Hospital

Marion moved into the chiefship of her department quietly, and became thoroughly acquainted with all aspects of her domain before making more than minor changes.

She felt keenly her responsibility, not only for her own work, but also for the work of younger, less experienced doctors, and arranged regular staff meetings, inviting medical researchers, men and women with special experience in practice, and medical faculty members to discuss their work; and held rounds of the public-ward cases weekly. She cheerfully accepted the fact that the chief was on twenty-four-hour duty, in the sense that she must be ready to meet an emergency at any time. Her talent for going to sleep instantly and coming wide awake instantly became one of her greatest assets. As time went on, she deployed her staff in such a way that a gifted and skilled doctor was easily available to the delivery rooms and operating rooms for consultation. Slowly, over a long period of time, rules were tightened up, and it became apparent that the new chief was not going to be satisfied with anything short of perfection.

One hazard to the department's work was that some of the rooms in which obstetrical patients went through early stages of labor were on a lower floor, and when the mother was ready for the delivery room she had to be brought to the tenth floor on an elevator that had been known to stop unaccountably between floors. Several babies had been delivered in the elevator while the maintenance crew worked frantically on the recalcitrant mechanism. Marion had the tenth floor rearranged to accommodate all patients in labor.

Though this first change was greeted with relief by the staff, her first real innovation aroused considerable controversy among both doctors and nurses. It had long been a pet idea of hers to have a fathers' room where husbands could be nearby during the hours of the mothers' labor, and would be right on hand to hear the news within a few minutes of their offsprings' arrival. In Marion's practice there was no such thing as "the forgotten father," and she always made a beeline from the delivery room to the telephone or the downstairs lobby to carol the glad news to a waiting husband. Once she called the new baby's grandfather by mistake.

"You have a lovely baby boy," she told him gaily.

"I know," he replied. "I've had him for forty years now."

The idea of having fathers around, urging the nurses to call the doctor when it was still too early, or asking them to give sedatives that might not be good for the mothers, raised doubts in the minds of the nursing staff. Even Marion's great friend Evelyn Galbraith, who was appointed night supervisor on the tenth floor shortly after Marion became chief, argued that the nurses were too busy to cope with nervous husbands. Other critics pointed out the danger of infection in having a fathers' room on the same floor as the delivery rooms (this fear proved to be unfounded), and still others said that the average woman would just as soon not have her husband around until it was all over and she had had some sleep, got washed and combed, and put on her lipstick. Marion knew that this was true for some women. She also knew that others would feel better to know that their husbands could come in and chat with them during the wait in the labor room, and wanted to share with them that euphoric time after the delivery when, as one patient put it, "you feel you're the most complete person you ever have been or could be, and you want your husband with you because you've done this together."

The fathers' room was finally approved on a trial basis. Marion, always on the lookout for people who could be interested in contributing money to the hospital for special purposes, dug into one of her many "little funds" for the money to fit it out with comfortable furniture, extra-large ash trays, and a television set; and a pay telephone was installed in one corner. In a short time the room became such an accepted part of the scheme of things on the tenth floor that its temporary nature was forgotten.

One place Marion drew the line was on the question of husbands coming into the delivery room. Earlier in her career a husband had insisted that he wanted to go through the entire experience with his wife. Marion had tried to dissuade him, then reluctantly given permission for him to be present. Hardly had proceedings begun when he fainted and a nurse had to be summoned to care for him, while the others stepped over or around him.

She was willing to make such a mistake—once—rather than run the risk of underestimating the importance of a prospective father and his feelings. Her approach did not meet with lack of appreciation.

"Frankly, I could never have got through the experience of our first baby without Dr. Hilliard," one father said. "I was panicked. But eventually she had me sitting up nights, reading *The Canadian Mother and Child* as though it were the latest novel, and manfully wringing out hot towels for my wife when she had leg and backaches."

Another put the emphasis on Marion as a person.

"Dr. Hilliard was not only a family doctor to us when she was bringing our babies. She was a kindred spirit, and just the opposite of the slightly pompous doctors and cramped specialists I had known. We could talk about music, art, and travel right along with the items about the care of my wife and the babies."

Sometimes Marion was amused at the antics of a father-to-be, but carefully reserved her amusement until he could join in the fun. Once a young couple having their first baby arrived at the hospital hours before any real action could be expected. Marion had the patient admitted, then suggested to the young man that he take his wife out to lunch. Delighted, the girl asked to go to a posh restaurant a few blocks from the hospital, and they set off. They returned in twenty minutes. The scared husband had refused to go any farther than the first lunch counter a block away. Marion kept a straight face and a soothing manner. Hours later, after the baby had safely arrived, the new father happily took a ribbing from his wife and their doctor.

Her reassurance was as valued by husbands as by her patients. Once a man whose wife had got pregnant for a second time against Marion's advice wrote in panic. What should they do?

"Don't be discouraged or apprehensive," replied Marion. "I felt the last time it was wiser not to have any more children but since this is an act of God, I am always quite happy to feel that it will be the best act of God that ever happened."

Husbands of high-strung women sometimes wondered if Dr. Hilliard was some kind of magician.

"She would look her in the eye," said one husband wonderingly, "and count off on her fingers, 'Now, you've got to do this—and this—and this,' enumerating exactly what she was to do and when. And, you know, she would. It might be something the whole family had been telling her, but somehow Dr. Hilliard could get through to her."

"My wife has no confidence in anyone in your profession but you," wrote a husband from a foreign country where he was on a long assignment. "She needs whatever it was you gave her for hot flushes. Can you send a prescription?"

Marion and Miss Galbraith became congenial teammates. Marion never quibbled over the supervisor's recommendations for changes; if they meant improvement, she saw the reason for it immediately and never hesitated to go to the Board of Governors for whatever was needed. Even in the dead of night, she answered the telephone cheerfully and came directly, knowing that Miss Galbraith had timed her call accurately. In the summertime she could come from Scarborough in half an hour, and it was predictable that she would arrive clad in slacks and sneakers, whistling or singing to herself.

"It might be the middle of the night to some people, but when you go to work it's always the middle of the day to you," Miss Galbraith told her.

They enjoyed teasing each other. Marion knew Miss Galbraith liked being literal and precise on the job.

"Tell the truth," she would say when a patient's contractions were good and strong, "isn't that a beautiful thing?"

"They are good contractions," Miss Galbraith would reply, "but I don't see anything particularly beautiful about them."

In turn Miss Galbraith teased Marion about "the Hilliard stitch," which was not, as some stories about Dr. Hilliard had it, a special kind of suture, but just a way she had of using the same tools and sewing the same way each time to make sure the sutures were tidy, held well, and were easy on the patient.

When Marion's white hospital shoes began to look disreputable Miss Galbraith would remind her to get a new pair. Obediently she would turn up in the next day or two with the new shoes, muttering a bit about dispensing with the old ones that "were just getting comfortable."

The hospital was going into its fifth decade now, and Marion was part of a new generation of its leaders. The year before her appointment as chief, Jessie Gray had been made chief of surgery, with Marjorie Davis as associate; and a few years later Jean Davey became chief of medicine. Marion saw in these, the hospital's first Fellowship holders, the spearhead of a move to bring the hospital to an assured future.

It was a time of high *esprit de corps*. It was not at all unusual to find the chiefs of three or more departments all at the hospital in the middle of the night, concentrating on a critically ill public-ward patient. Mutual trust and friendship and their shared dedication to their profession and their hospital rose above departmental delineations. A department chief knew that ultimately she alone was responsible for the sick patient, but she knew too that she never had to live through an anxious night alone, that if she needed help all she had to do was to ask for it.

The hospital as a whole claimed even more of Marion's interest after she assumed responsibility for her department. No possible improvement or opportunity for development failed to evoke a chain reaction of enthusiasm, ideas, and action from her. When she saw something that needed to be done she talked her way past indifference and resistance until she got others to take an interest along with her. Lack of money was no argument with her; with a letter or a few telephone calls she could raise it, and the bookkeeping department had yet another "special fund" to keep track of. Sometimes she got a promise of a contribution first, then came into meetings of the Medical Advisory Board asking for a list of needed equipment or new projects.

As one of her colleagues said of her, "She thought of all the going ideas current at any one time around the hospital. It drove people nuts because she was always generating new ones before they had recovered from the last one. But she was the hub of the hospital because of all her qualities, with her sense of fun and the light touch."

Toronto doctors returning from war service soon learned that Marion Hilliard had one of the largest obstetrical practices in town. There was some grumbling in medical circles when it became known that the topnotch women specialists were getting her referrals, and she was helping a half dozen younger women obstetricians to build up their practices. Marion herself rarely discussed the matter, but one of her colleagues, when complained to, gave a succinct answer. "Why shouldn't she? It was women doctors, not men, who referred patients to help her get started."

In her first ten years of practice Marion had decided that, as she expressed it, "to get anywhere in this profession, a woman has to be about twenty-five per cent better than her men competitors."

She had countless experiences with patients such as the one for whom she had cared in a first pregnancy during the depression, charging a rock-bottom fee. The patient returned to say that her husband had got a good job and was back on his feet financially and she was pregnant again.

"This time we're going to have a real obstetrician [i.e., a man], but I wanted to thank you for all you've done for me," she said happily.

Marion would wish them luck, see them out smilingly, then make a good story out of the incident for the enjoyment of her doctor friends.

Sometimes the husbands of her patients balked at the idea of a woman surgeon. Many times when Marion's diagnosis showed the need for a gynecological operation, the patient would visit or phone uncomfortably to say that "my husband insists on getting a man surgeon." To their undying gratitude, such patients learned that Dr. Hilliard had but one concern: their comfort and well-being. If they had their operations in her hospital she dropped in to see them briefly almost every day, even though her status was that of a visitor.

"I wonder if you can imagine how I felt," one patient reminisces. "It was a rainy spring day. I was twenty-two. I lay in my hospital bed after a hysterectomy, and tried to realize I could never have any children now. My surgeon was good, but too busy to do more than pay a check-up visit each day. My husband was sympathetic but would have been amazed to know I felt life had come to an end.

"One day Dr. Hilliard suddenly breezed in. She knew me well —I had been her patient for several years—and sensed how I felt. After a few minutes of ordinary chitchat, she said, 'What are you going to do this summer?' I dreaded to face the future, and tried to avoid talking about it. In a half-bullying, half-sympathetic way, she made me talk, and after a while I just found myself making plans for things I would really like to do.

"Her job was to help women have babies, but she helped me feel this wasn't women's only business in life. She made me feel like a person, and that that was the first, most important thing."

Another patient whose story was the same (long-time patient of Dr. Hilliard's—Dr. Hilliard makes diagnosis calling for operation—husband insists on man surgeon) was sitting up in bed on the third day after her operation, staring at her untouched breakfast tray, when Marion came in to say hello. She took in the whole scene in a glance.

"What's the matter?" she asked gently, calling the patient by name.

Feebly the patient replied that she didn't seem to have any appetite. Marion sat down beside her, took up a spoon, and fed her the breakfast, diverting her with cheerful, encouraging talk.

"Somehow that was a turning point for me," recalled the patient. "I snapped out of my depression and got well in record time. She wasn't my doctor at that time; she was a friend who understood me. My surgeon didn't know me at all. He came once a day and that was it. Her friendly attention helped me immensely in a way that's hard to describe."

Marion's schooling in sports from the earliest days on the tennis court-hockey rink at Oak Hall had taught her to play hard and play to win, but to be prepared to lose gracefully. Her goal was simply to be a good doctor—not a good woman doctor, but a good doctor. Sometimes she was hurt by incidents of discrimination, or, later, professional resentment of her success, but eventually she came back to the creed that never failed her: Do your best, stick to your own standards, keep your conscience clear, and above all keep your sense of humor!

When she won applause on merit she enjoyed it to the utmost. Once she presented one of her own case histories as an illustration of the subject under discussion at a medical meeting attended by both men and women doctors. A visiting bigwig, a noted diagnostician from another country, expressed surprise at the ingenious diagnosis made on the case.

"Marion said nothing," reported one witness to the incident, "but just sat back looking like the cat that swallowed the canary."

In later years when she was called in as a consultant specialist on a case being handled by a man less skilled than she, she was the soul of tact, and really worked at timing her suggestions so that the host physician would ask her to take over before the crucial moment of a delivery or operation had been reached.

When her professional reputation was secure she was serene about taking her rightful place in a medical group.

"She was good and she knew it, and she spoke right up. It never occurred to her to mince matters or soft-pedal things the way some women do," said a male colleague. "She could be aggressive, but it was not in a masculine way. She was a very feminine person."

When she heard that a professional society for which she and several other women doctors would be eligible was being organized she dropped in to see some of the men who were spearheading the move and asked matter-of-factly why no women were being invited as charter members. They "just hadn't thought about it," they told her. Shortly afterward she and the other women received invitations to join.

It was a sly little item, tucked away in a corner of a small Toronto gossip sheet. "What doctor from what famous temperance family was recently instrumental in getting money from a beer company for her hospital?"

When Marion Hilliard saw it she threw back her head and laughed delightedly. She took it as a tribute; she was one of that rare species, a born fundraiser, and she knew it. She had only one prerequisite before launching into a campaign: she herself must be completely sold on the cause.

Women's College Hospital, a private community institution, was financially dependent on receipts for service, and on the efforts of its various auxiliary groups. Any new or experimental programs had to be underwritten by special contributions. The blueprints for the Cancer Detection Clinic were waiting to be brought to life by some fairy godmother, when, one day in 1947, it was announced in the newspapers that a large Canadian brewing company had offered a sizable contribution to the United Church of Canada and had been turned down.

Within minutes of reading the item Marion was on the phone to Mrs. Sandiford, who was president of the Board of Governors. "Why don't we ask for that money?" she demanded.

The Board of Governors was hastily polled. All but one member, who later resigned on moral grounds, were for it. Marion hurried downtown to see a board member of the company. There were meetings back and forth. Very shortly it was announced that the company would make a substantial annual contribution to the hospital for the next five years, enough not only to start the new clinic but to put into action some other hospital projects awaiting financing.

"Who needed the money more than we did, or could put it to better use?" Marion declaimed to an interviewer some years later.

At this time Marion was engaged in another cancer-detection project. The Papanicolaou smear test, about which her friend Dr. Meigs had written, was being more and more widely used by gynecologists as a tool for early detection of cancer of the cervix and uterus. The test involved a laboratory procedure of some twenty processes and called not only for a special setup but also for technicians trained in cytology to read the results. The lack of both facilities and technicians posed a real problem to many Canadian hospitals. Marion and her old friend Dr. Eva Macdonald, now director of the Women's College Hospital laboratories, decided to try to devise a similar test that would be foolproof yet manageable within the laboratory and staff limitations.

With the collaboration of the hospital's consulting pathologist, Dr. W. L. Robinson of the Banting Institute, a simplified procedure that could be handled by any well-trained pathologist was developed in the fall of 1947, and in January, 1948, the test was put into use with outpatients of the hospital and private patients of members of the gynecological staff. A progress report of the first six months' work was given at the 1948 meeting of the Canadian Medical Association, and in March, 1950, the CMA's *Journal* published Marion's paper, "Cervical Scrapings Test," describing the laboratory technique and reporting the results of the first two thousand, ninety-six tests. Nearly ninety per cent had been negative; the eight women who had been found to have cancer in its very early stages could be treated immediately; and those whose tests were "suspicious" could be followed up carefully at regular intervals.

"We present," the paper concluded, "a simple accurate method for the detection of carcinoma of the cervix. It can be done by the gynaecologist or the general practitioner. The diagnosis can be made by a well-trained pathologist . . . [it] may be more conclusive and give a better picture of malignancy than the biopsy [and] is of great value in the early diagnosis of cervical cancer. It is painless, harmless and the procedure may be carried out with impunity."

Shortly after publication Marion was receiving inquiries from doctors of countries on three continents.

A third of these two thousand-odd tests were done in the new Cancer Detection Clinic, first operated on a small scale as an outpatient clinic and opened to the public April seventh, 1948. ("A Big Day," said Marion's diary.) Marion's friend the late Dr. Elise L'Esperance, who established the Strang Memorial Cancer Prevention Clinic at Memorial Hospital in New York City, was guest of honor at the ceremonies. To Marion, who was to be in charge of her new brain child, fell the proud task of cutting the ribbon across the entrance to the new clinic's quarters. News photographers recorded the little ceremony, the entrance of the first patients escorted by a group of nurses, and showed the four-member staff headed by the chief of medicine, Dr. Florence McConney. Reporters interviewed Dr. L'Esperance, who gave a lecture that evening at a dinner for the hospital "family."

The "Big Day" had not come about easily. When Marion had, with Mrs. Sandiford's enthusiastic support, first proposed the idea it sounded simple and sensible to the lay person: a clinic to examine well women for the purpose of discovering cancer symptoms in the early stages of the disease, and to refer the patient for whom it was found to be necessary to the doctor of her choice. However, some staff members at the hospital and others in Toronto's medical circles opposed it as a waste of time for a busy hospital or because "it is not possible to detect cancer anyway." Others were afraid it would give patients "a false sense of security." Explicit and implicit in some of these medical arguments was the fear that such a service might take patients away from their private doctors. In time, experience and public opinion were to allay these fears and overcome the opposition.

The new clinic's complete physical examination took two days and cost five dollars. So many women came on their own initiative or by referral from doctors all over Canada—the clinic was the first of its kind in the country—that in five months blueprints were drawn up for alterations to a nearby building owned by the hospital to provide expanded quarters. There was a brief period of worry because the proposed quarters would allow for five times the number of examinations, and how would the hospital man the operation? Shortly afterward the Ontario Cancer Treatment and Research Foundation, satisfied that the Hilliard-Macdonald-Robinson cervical scrapings test had passed its experimental period, recognized it officially and began contributing to the cost of each test.

Six years after opening, the clinic reported that it had completed fourteen thousand examinations involving ten thousand women (many returned for an annual check-up). One per cent of the women had been found to have definite symptoms of cancer and been quickly referred to a physician they chose.

To the few remaining critics who muttered about spending all that money and professional time to discover so few cancer cases, Marion always stoutly replied, "It would be worth while if it were only *half* of one per cent."

CHAPTER 14

A New Chapter

Birch Point had also entered upon a new chapter. Marion's fishing companion, Poppy Boynton, had purchased a large piece of land along the bluffs adjoining Marion's property and, after demobilization from her war job, had begun her bee business. Soon the acres to the east of Birch Point were dotted with the first of a hundred and twenty bee colonies. Marion was fascinated with the project. She studied Poppy's beekeeper's library, helped wrap the hives for the winter, and took a turn at the hand-operated extractor that strained the crop from the honeycomb.

As Toronto began the spectacular growth that was to triple its population in the first fifteen postwar years, the city crept eastward into Scarborough Township and new settlers moved onto the broad plateau on the lower bluffs. Marion's first neighbors—a young widow and her two small boys, a builder and his family, a young department-store executive and his wife—often joined with her visitors from the city for swimming parties and corn roasts. The youngsters helped care for the bees. One neighbor who liked working in the garden evenings and weekends took on some of the heavy work, for the gardens now extended onto Poppy's land. There were sizable plantings of corn, melon, and squash patches, and a small orchard.

One day the neighbor brought a friend, Maurice Brown, with whom he had worked on a war job. A Yorkshireman by birth, Mr. Brown had emigrated to Canada in the 1920s, where he had worked as chauffeur, butler, mechanic, and painter. The Scarborough farm lands seemed like home to him, and soon he was coming out from the city each weekend to work in the garden, mow the lawns, and do whatever else he could for "the Doctor," to whom he was devoted.

A Birch Point diary was begun, to keep notes on weather, crops, plantings, and harvesting. After a mid-March snowstorm an entry read: "Snow drifted over road, bees, and half way up cherry tree. Rabbits had eaten shrubs. Some cave-in of bluffs to southwest. Crocus up in west garden." A month later: "First weekend at Scarborough. Heaters and stove going. Back to town to see Barbara Ann Scott skate and get ready for nurses' party." In May: "Crew of five working to set up hive boxes. Robin's nest in blue spruce. Wonderful steak dinner." Summer entries recorded progress of flowers, vegetables, arrival and departure of visitors, and, in August, the extracting of the honey crop. Wrapping the bee colonies for the winter began in late October and finished in mid-November.

As Poppy was harvesting her first crop of honey the late Harry Cassidy, director of the University of Toronto's School of Social Work, came to call with an offer of a lecturer's job in his pocket. He had calculated carefully so that the job would begin after the honey harvest and finish in the spring, when the beekeeper's busy season begins. He left with Poppy's promise to try the teaching assignment for a year. In time she joined the faculty as an assistant professor and became, as she jokingly put it, "the woman who came to dinner."

For a time, following Miss Hall's departure to seek graduate study and pursue her career in the States, Marion had lived alone, cared for by a succession of housekeepers and her "staunch Scots friend," Helen Paterson, who had come weekly since 1941 to do the cleaning. Marion loved home coming on Thursdays; after "Mrs. Paterson's day" in her apartment she once wrote, "The gentle radiance in my living room uplifts my heart and dispels my fatigue." Over the years they had become great friends.

Now, with the congenial Poppy to make a home with her, and the extraordinarily hard-working war years behind her, Marion entered zestfully into the party-giving and partygoing of the postwar years, and began to attend more plays, symphony concerts, and ballet performances. She followed the football and hockey seasons from the first games to the Grey Cup tussle between the football teams of eastern and western Canada in November and the Stanley Cup hockey play-offs in the spring, and, with an American in the house, never missed the World Series broadcasts.

As her social life expanded, her interest in clothes grew. She found congenial saleswomen in department stores and specialty shops who would save her shopping time by telephoning when her kind of suits, dresses, and hats came in. She bought the rich tweeds she had always loved, slenderizing sheath dresses, often in a lively shade of blue, and crisp cottons with straight lines. She had let her hair grow, and now experimented with hairdos until she finally settled for an upsweep with a French knot, which gave her height, dignity, and smartness. She discovered with glee that she was a "hat person," and could wear even the most outlandish creations and carry them off with an air.

Her list of annual parties for interns and nurses, as well as her famous Christmas party for her colleagues' children, was augmented by parties for Poppy's graduate students and fellow faculty members. Nearly three-quarters of the hospital staff were married women, and now, in place of the small informal get-togethers of wartime, there were large dress-up parties with husbands invited. Marion loved the gaiety and good conversation, the party atmosphere.

"I like it when things are merry," she would say, half to herself, looking around at a happy, chattering group of friends or family, almost as though she were soaking up enjoyment to sustain her in the times when life would be difficult.

There were holiday parties, bon-voyage parties, welcome-home parties, parties for out-of-town visitors, new staff members, retiring staff members, and, of course, a parade of bridal and baby showers. One day in the doctors' room Marion said that she had been to at least five hundred showers, but had never had one herself. "Do you have to get married or have a baby to rate one?" she demanded.

Shortly afterward a dozen of her friends gave her a surprise shower. In the corner of the hostess's living room stood the portrait of the "bridegroom," a caricature drawing of a man with a handlebar mustache, with the fanciful name "Herbert De Wolfe" lettered in at the bottom. A mountain of packages was presented as "trousseau" gifts, such as cumbersome suits of long underwear and green silk panties trimmed with several inches of lace. Marion was presented with a bonnet trimmed with what might be referred to as the tools of an obstetrician's trade.

As the hilarious evening was drawing to a close Marion held a spur-of-the-moment auction of the gifts for the benefit of the hospital, and the donors, caught up in the spirit of her rapid-fire persuasiveness, bought back their outrageous ten-cent-store gifts for enormous prices.

It became the custom in her social circle to serve cocktails before dinner, and "little Prohibition Anna," after a time, adopted it. Long since, she had decided that when in Rome, she would do as the Romans did, and had learned to enjoy a drink before dinner. Being of an experimental turn of mind, she had tried several concoctions before deciding that Scotch and soda was her favorite. Once during the war, when she and a colleague were attending a medical meeting in New York, they had tried a "pink lady" and found it very tasty. Suddenly, on the way back to the hotel, a bell rang and Marion saw her amazed friend being lifted up from the sidewalk by the automatic doors leading into a store basement. Marion doubled up with laughter and teased her friend about how one pink lady sent her up in the air.

The older generation on Lonsdale Road, still ardent temperance supporters, were not apprised of this development in Marion's social life. She was careful not to offend them, for she had always held their convictions in great respect. Her office nurse, now her valued friend, took her to task about what she felt was Marion's deception of her parents.

"What's the use of upsetting them?" protested Marion. "They

are too old to change, and it's not that important. I can respect their way of life and still have my own way of life in my own home."

Her friends knew that when they were invited to her apartment for a Hilliard family party the Scotch bottle would be relegated to the corn-flakes box, the ash trays to the kitchen-table drawer, and everyone would be served tomato juice before dinner. Marion herself was too interested in food to have more than one or two drinks before eating. When she was invited to a party where she knew the cocktail hour would be extended, she went late. At her own parties no one ever drank too much, probably because they knew that they would not be invited again.

She loved the feeling of leisure and relaxation in the hiatus between the end of the day's work and dinnertime, when she could exchange with Poppy and the friends who dropped in, stories of the small happenings of the day—which were as enjoyable to her as the large events—and read her mail.

"Your letters are an event in this household," she wrote a friend. "We read them aloud over our cocktails before dinner and you are really here with us."

For the six weeks before Christmas Eve she thought, talked, breathed, and lived Christmas plans. In a kind of grown-up version of the old pre-Christmas stories of their childhood Marion and Barby got together in mid-November to match ideas about surprises for family members, old and young, and the location, dinner menu, and schedule of events for the family party. Then she dreamed up a dozen plans and, like a happy juggler, kept them all whirling at once: reunion lunches with old friends; suppers or evenings "just to talk" with people as busy as she was; a trip to take the nieces and nephews downtown to see the department-store windows; the carol-singing evening with the Children's Aid Society group; parties for nurses and interns; special holiday concerts or theater parties. Her apartment abounded in scrawled lists of guests, decorations, menus, big gifts, small remembrances, reminders about Christmas letters, cables, and telegrams she wanted particularly to send.

Her favorite party was a tradition she started during the war years for her nieces and the youngsters of her colleagues and closest friends, and which now included the "little Hilliards." Since she chose for many of her small guests the noisemaking toys so dear to childish hearts, and entered wholeheartedly with them into the program of games, carol singing, and consumption of satisfying refreshments, it was an uproarious and memorable event for both guests and hostess. Once on the way home from the party a small boy clutching his first football reverently told his mother that he believed "Aunt Marion is even better than God."

On Christmas Eve she made the rounds of her friends' homes to deliver her gifts and went on to midnight church service, and on Christmas Night, after the family party was over, she and Poppy took the train for New York and a holiday week of theater and concertgoing and visiting with their American and transplanted Canadian friends.

She and Poppy began to plan extensive holiday trips, beginning with a tour of the West Coast, where, in company with Poppy's family at a mountain fishing spot in Oregon, Marion celebrated the twentieth anniversary of the day she "set out to seek my fortune." Looking ahead, they sketched out visits to England, Italy, Greece, Turkey; and Marion began to watch for opportunities to combine such holidays with meetings of the International Medical Women's Association, of which she was a member, and of other international medical groups.

No summer was complete without at least a week at the Quebec fishing camp. When medical meetings were held in eastern Canada she promoted a fishing weekend before or after the event among her colleagues. Sometimes the fishing parties started from Toronto and stopped for lunch in Morrisburg. If Von were not at home, the picnic lunches would be carried out to the point of land where the old Fairview Cemetery stood and Marion would look over the row of blue spruce trees her father had planted there, while the picnic lunch was spread out on the grassy bank where the Hilliard youngsters had sat on Sunday afternoons, back in those "glorious years."

When Von was home there was a great reunion. The two old friends kept in touch with each other somewhat irregularly, secure in the feeling that if the other really needed her, a sixth sense would tell her so.

"Nothing crucial or important ever happened to me," Von told a mutual friend, "but what I'd hear from Marion in twenty-four hours. Sometimes she would hardly let me enjoy being sick a few hours before she would be on the line. 'I dreamed about you last night, Vonnie,' she would say. 'Are you all right?'"

A few times such calls revealed that things were definitely not all right and once Marion got right in her car and drove to Morrisburg, examined Von, called an ambulance, and brought her back to Women's College Hospital for an operation.

A gay time was in store for them when they met for the Morrisburg lunch stopovers or in Toronto, where Von spent a week or two each year. Von's salty, sophisticated descriptions of people, places, and incidents encountered on her annual winter junkets and her accounts of home-town happenings, and Marion's witty stories drawn from life at Birch Point, the office, and the hospital flew back and forth in gusts of hearty laughter.

Often Von would trail the party a few miles east to join in a pilgrimage Marion always made; standing on the grassy bank above the canal at a special vantage point near a huge old gnarled apple tree, she would gaze her fill upon the Longue Sault Rapids that extended a mile from the canal's edge to the islands in mid-river, and watch the ships from the four corners of the earth lock through. The sight and sound of her beloved swift-flowing river were the sweetest in the world to her.

Driving downtown to do her Christmas shopping, Marion noticed an elderly man walking along the street.

Isn't it awful how old folks go around looking so shabby? she thought to herself. Don't they have anyone to take care of them?

Then she did a double-take. The man was her own father! Horrified, she hurriedly parked the car and ran down the street after him. Father Hilliard, now in his eighties, lighted up at the sight of his daughter, as always, and they exchanged a few words about how things were going that day at Lonsdale Road. Then she told him they were going straight to a store to buy him some new clothes as a kind of extra Christmas present. It wasn't really necessary, he protested; these clothes were perfectly all right. But she insisted, and he fell in with the shopping expedition, actually enjoying it after they got started.

In the midst of the trying on and getting fitted she asked him where he had been going.

"Why," he replied briskly, "your mother and I thought we'd give a special Christmas contribution to the church this year [he named a sizable sum] and I was on my way to the savings bank to draw out the money."

Ruefully Marion told the story as a great joke on herself. Actually she loved her father and mother as much for their consistency as they grew older as for any other reason. In spite of failing faculties and partial dependence on his children, her father felt the obligation to share his savings with the church just as strongly as he had when he was at the height of his professional career.

A year later, one November day, Mr. Hilliard wandered off when he and Mrs. Hilliard were downtown shopping, and could not be found. For a day Marion and her brother, Eva Macdonald, and Poppy took their several cars and drove in every possible direction he could have taken, watching carefully for him. Then, frantic with worry, they appealed to the police and the search was on.

Detectives, Mounties, and the local police went through the city with a fine-tooth comb. Marion gave an interview to the newspapers,

"People have been magnificent. Both city and provincial police have followed up every clue. You would recognize him by his shaggy eyebrows and short, quick steps. People talking with him would find his conversation was short and to the point. He is not a man to stand spinning long, reminiscent stories as some old gentlemen are. Not that he is gruff or dour, but even in politics he was not good at kissing babies or carrying on long personal conversations with voters."

She told about his wandering away once before, but finding his way back home eventually, and offered as another clue the possibility that he might have said he was going back to Morrisburg—"Or perhaps, because of failing memory, to Osnabruck, where he was born."

The Toronto police flew back and forth in helicopters across the many ravines that stab into the heart of the city from the north and east, and one hundred and fifteen volunteers from Boy Scout troops over the city combed the deep gullies on foot.

Twenty-nine anxious, heartbreaking days later, when the weather had turned cold and the first snows had fallen, the police found his body in one of the western ravines. He had apparently found a secluded spot in which to lie down and rest, and had died of exposure in his sleep.

The news came three days before Christmas. A service was held the following day in the Hilliards' own church at Morrisburg and he was buried in Fairview Cemetery, beside the row of blue spruce trees he had planted there himself.

A favorite patient whom Marion had taken care of for fifteen years through seven pregnancies said that one of the two times she had seen her doctor weep was "when her father was lost and I asked for news of him and she broke down completely."

A few years later Marion and her brothers and sisters had a stained-glass window put into the east side of the Morrisburg church they had all loved so dearly, "In honour of Mr. and Mrs. Irwin Hilliard" (Marion's mother was to survive her famous daughter by two years).

The subject, executed in rich blues and reds, is Christ's charge to Peter, with the text "Feed my lambs," which was the theme of the dedication by the Reverend Maxwell Allen, then pastor of the church. Before a small group of family and close friends

Reverend Allen spoke feelingly of the great influence of these two remarkable people, not only on their own children, but on so many other children of the community.

Her father's death under such tragic circumstances cast a shadow over Marion's life, and she set about prescribing for herself. Early in the new year she and Poppy began planning a visit to England, Marion's first return in fifteen years. For six weeks, beginning late in May, she would combine visits to hospitals in London and on the Continent, reunions with Miss Dearnley and her other old friends, and a refreshing holiday. It was a bumpy plane trip, and Marion, for the only time in her life, was sick— "over Ireland, of all places," she said. She recovered speedily, arriving in London for lunch and finding crepes suzette on the menu!

A three-week, two-thousand-mile jaunt through England and Scotland constituted the holiday part of the visit. It began by retracing Marion's 1928 trip (even including the traffic jam at Ascot) to Cornwall, where Marion delightedly roamed through Newquay and Crantock and tried in vain to find Jolly Porch, the cove where she and the Dearnleys had had their tea and swimming parties. At a country inn near Winchester she celebrated her forty-seventh birthday with a bottle of champagne, and after a performance of *Othello* at Stratford there was a reunion visit with Pauline Shapiro and her family. The travel diary noted "honeysuckle in the hedgerows" and "peaceful hillsides of foxglove, buttercups, and daisies" as they passed through the lake country and on to Inverness and Dundee.

Back in London, Marion attended meetings of the International Medical Women's Association, called on the surgeons with whom she had studied twenty years before, and took long walks with Gertrude Dearnley to revisit her favorite London spots. After an elegant farewell luncheon—"hare in wine—magnificent," wrote Marion—they flew into Toronto to be met by Scarborough neighbors who had prepared a welcome-home dinner.

CHAPTER 15

The Rewarding Hours

"If anyone asked me what part of my practice of medicine over the last thirty years had been the most rewarding to *me*, I would have to say they were those hours I spent in the delivery room," wrote Marion in *Women and Fatigue*.

She liked coming into the brightly lighted room, liked the feeling of working concentratedly with a well-trained team, and cherished especially, as she wrote once, "the heightened sense of friendliness and tenderness rarely found elsewhere."

"You'd think we were having a party," a patient reminisced. "She'd be laughing and talking and cheering me on. Just at the last, I'd have some anesthetic and I always 'went down' listening to that lovely laugh."

Another patient on the delivery table was diverted by Marion's story to Ellen Blatchford about the event of the day at Scarborough: the birth of a puppy to Marion's dog. A nurse came in and called Marion aside, interrupting the story.

"Oh, no, not another one!" said Marion in loud surprise. "Why, I diagnosed that as a single birth."

"Twins!" gasped the patient, leaning up on her elbow.

"No, no, not you!" cried Marion. "The dog."

Stories about Scarborough often eased delivery-room moments for Marion's patients. A young woman having her first baby was brought from the labor room at night and left alone on the delivery table for a few minutes with a strong light glaring down at her from the ceiling. Feeling like the heroine in a horror movie, she was about to cry out, more in terror than pain, when she heard the bustling footsteps all Marion's patients knew so well.

"She started right in telling me about Scarborough and the bees, and I relaxed," the patient recalls. "It may sound exaggerated, but it is true it was a complete surprise to me when she said, 'It's a girl!'"

Marion's patients, especially those she had known over a long period of time, were her friends and she never felt that it detracted from her professional position to let them know it. Once a patient whose several children Marion had delivered was brought into the delivery room too soon. After examining her Marion confessed she hadn't had lunch that day and thought she'd run down and get some supper. She left, but was back in a few minutes.

"I got on the elevator, then got off and took the next one back," she said. "You and I have been through a lot together. I couldn't leave you now."

When she knew that sympathy would be no help she was ready with a verbal astringent. One morning she rushed upstairs from the operating room where she had done two operations to the labor room, where three of her patients were in different stages of labor. One, who was having her second baby, had lost all control and was moaning over and over, "I can't go through with it."

After trying in vain to soothe her and make her more comfortable Marion finally said sternly, "Look, you've been through this before. You know that when you get to a certain stage you *have* to go through with it."

One of the other patients in the room that morning was impressed—not just that Marion's words helped the patient get hold of herself, but that "it showed Dr. Hilliard's respect for people, trying to answer a person even when what she said didn't make sense."

Because of well-placed confidence in her own instinct for nature's timing Marion did not hesitate, under certain circumstances, to induce labor, a practice once in disrepute but now used more widely. Sometimes this was for medical reasons, such as to terminate an overlong pregnancy; sometimes to save another long ride for a patient who had come from some distance, and a few times for the parents' sentimental reasons.

For some, the blessed event is twice blessed if it occurs on the father's birthday, mother's birthday, or St. Valentine's Day. The few instances where Marion was able to turn this romantic trick, certain that it was safe, gave rise to stories about town to the effect that "you can go to Dr. Hilliard and she will see to it that you have your baby on your own birthday."

For most of her patients in the delivery room Marion preferred a spinal anesthetic, because the mothers could relax and still remain conscious; she felt that there was value in staying in communication with the mother during delivery. To avoid difficult and painful repair of torn tissues, she often chose to do a midline episeotomy, a straight cutting of the tissues, which then requires from ten to twenty stitches immediately after the delivery.

One of her patients just back from the delivery room, a bit groggy from anesthetic and uncomfortably aware of the sutures, overheard the cleaning woman chatting with the new mother in the next cubicle.

"How many stitches do you have?" she heard the woman ask.

"Exactly one hundred and twenty-eight," replied the young mother.

Unsteadily Marion's patient raised up to gaze with awe upon her neighbor. When her eyes focused, she saw that the woman was sitting up in bed, knitting a baby's coverlet!

Marion enjoyed her hospital rounds of mothers and new babies, when she and the mothers could glow with their respective feelings of accomplishment, and exchange admiring comments on the babies' appearances and personalities.

Once, however, she paused at the door and left on the verge of tears, unseen by the mother. The girl had come to her, desperate because of her illegitimate pregnancy. Marion had arranged with her employer for a leave of absence, got her a place to live during the last weeks before confinement, and, with her permission, had set in motion the wheels for adoption of the baby. She had told her that she need not nurse the baby, as it might make it that much harder to give up the child, but the girl had said it might be better for the baby and she would rather do it.

"When I saw her sitting up in bed nursing the baby, in that wistful Madonna-like attitude," Marion told her office nurse, "I had to leave. I'll just have to go back later."

On the whole, however, Marion never felt terribly sorry for unmarried mothers. She maintained that having a baby was the most glorious thing that could happen to a woman, the most basically creative experience in life. She never sat in judgment on these mothers, but put the emphasis on facing up to a firm decision on whether or not to keep the baby, making plans for the future, and, at all costs, keeping a feeling of self-respect.

Over and over again she picked up people stuck on the shoals of tragedy and set them afloat again in the main stream of life—always with brisk common sense, good judgment, great humor, gentle understanding—and no nonsense!

"I am glad you wrote me," she concluded a letter of information and practical help to a girl in another city who had appealed to her. "It is always tragic when a boy friend changes his mind about getting married, but it is far better for you than to be tied to an unhappy marriage."

To another girl, who was in an agony of indecision about placing her illegitimate baby for adoption, she wrote, "I realize how desperate you must be feeling, but you must remember you are young, that you have a profession and a future. You must not let your own personal need blur your picture of the need of your child. I know this is not the comfort you were wanting but I must give you my experienced decision."

The day before a patient was to be discharged she had a special visit from Dr. Hilliard. Whether she had had a baby or an operation, she was left with no doubt as to what she could and could not do during her convalescence.

"I can see her now," reminisces one patient, "standing at the foot of the bed, saying, 'Get a paper and pencil or else commit this to memory: on the first day home, you may be up and dressed for one meal only; on the second day, you may take a drive if you come home directly and rest for two hours,' and so on."

"You were so busy following directions," says another, "that the next thing you knew you were feeling fine—just as she said you would!"

Another laughs to remember the time she checked out of the hospital before Dr. Hilliard got there to make her "do-this-and-do-that" speech. "She was very cross with me," she recalls.

Usually D (for "discharge") days were happy events for Marion and her patients. Once, however, it brought tragedy. Marion was just about to go under the dryer at the hairdresser when the hospital called to say that a patient she had visited a few hours earlier had died of a sudden heart attack as she was dressing to go home.

To see the gay, brisk, confident Dr. Hilliard look so distressed, fight for control, then burst into tears, was a shaking experience for Mr. Charles and his staff. Someone ran for a cup of tea, and Mr. Charles found himself in the unique position of talking soothingly and sympathetically to the woman who had been a tower of strength and reassurance to thousands of people. She never forgot her friend's kindness, which is probably why she once found herself addressing a national convention of hairdressers, charming them with her wit and common sense just as she had so many other audiences.

CHAPTER 16

Office Team

It was the end of an era for Marion and her patients when the cheery, sympathetic Mrs. DeGruchy became ill and left her job as office nurse in the summer of 1949. Her successor, Miriam Darlington, was a graduate of that year at Women's College Hospital and had been on private duty, caring for Marion's friend Gwen Mulock.

Like other student nurses at the hospital, Miss Darlington regarded Dr. Hilliard with a combination of affection and awed respect. Probationers soon learned, by experience or hearsay, a kind of Who's Who item for nurses that went something like this:

"Dr. Hilliard's patients have to be looked after a certain way, or you hear about it, not in any roundabout way, but firsthand and straight from the shoulder. But she never reprimands a nurse before a patient or another doctor, and if you take the trouble to do things exactly right, she always shows her appreciation. She never calls nurses by their first names, not even the office nurse she's had for eighteen years, or her own niece when she's on private duty for Dr. Hilliard. It takes nerve to work with her in the operating room—she operates so fast, you have to be on your toes every minute. But she's very methodical; she arranges her instruments the same way every time, for instance, which makes it a lot less nerve-racking.

"She gives marvelous parties, at least two a year—one at Christmas and another at graduation, and even though the president of the board and the superintendent are there, the lid's off for the evening. She always has good food and lots of it, then all kinds of games, singing, and skits with take-offs of bigwigs around the hospital.

"But, mind you, the next day on duty, there's not a crack in discipline. She may mention the party in a friendly way, but you know you're back on the job."

The new office nurse's first encounter with her employer had been during her training when she and another nurse had been on night duty. At three A.M. all was quiet on the floor, and the two sat in abandoned relaxation with their feet on the desk at the nursing station. Suddenly there was a slight clearing of a throat. There, in her slacks and sneakers, stood Dr. Hilliard, who had come in from Scarborough for a delivery and stopped to see a very sick patient.

"All she said was, 'I'd like to see my patient, Mrs. X,' in a very quiet tone, but you never saw feet hit the floor so fast!" Miss Darlington told the story much later.

Along with the new nurse, Marion employed a bookkeeper-secretary, Olive Maltby. After a crisp rundown of instructions as to their duties she told them, "After two months I expect no mistakes."

In a short time the three had been welded into a team, Marion giving both girls considerable responsibility, and, while holding them to top performance, encouraging them to learn and to use initiative when it was appropriate. Before patients she addressed them formally, but as time went on and they became friends she used their first names in private.

Between ten and twelve each morning except Friday, having finished operations and rounds at the hospital, Marion got off the elevator a dozen steps from the office door. Both staff and waiting patients sat up and got ready for things to hum; everyone knew her step. Once Gwen asked her why in the world she didn't wear rubber-soled shoes like everyone else.

"I like my patients to know I'm coming," replied Marion.

Until six or seven o'clock the office team worked steadily. The nurse got a patient undressed and seated on the table in one of the two examining rooms. After the examination the doctor returned to her consulting room, the patient's card in hand. By the time the patient had finished dressing the chart would be filled in and Marion would take ten or fifteen minutes to answer the questions that nearly always were predictable. When she said good-by to the patient, another would have been got ready for her to see in the second examining room.

It was a new and different regime. Some of the community-center atmosphere disappeared from the waiting room, to the patients' sorrow. Young Miss Darlington was very conscious of Dr. Hilliard's strenuous life and many responsibilities, and she concentrated on protecting her from all but the really important interruptions. She and her boss were two of a kind, liking to work at a fast, steady pace and to stay on routine.

The tea-and-sublimates half hour of Marion's earlier days was now replaced by a ten-minute coffee break in mid-afternoon. Sometimes the girls took their coffee into the consulting room and the team relaxed together. Other days they left Dr. Hilliard's coffee on her desk, closed the door, and kept the office quiet, sensing her need to be alone. Those who worked closely with her knew well how much of herself she gave to each person and how drained she sometimes felt, even as they marveled at her resilience.

Monday was the big day of the week; somehow its list of appointments always seemed longer. When the last patient had gone Marion would say, "There's another Monday gone. The week's half finished."

The comradely feeling spurred the young recruits. Miss Darlington took pride in learning to know Dr. Hilliard's procedures so well that she was often able to anticipate her requests. Gradually she increased the per cent of telephoned questions she could discuss with the doctor, and then relay the answer herself. This left the doctor more time to spend on the call backs that warranted her full personal attention. Marion encouraged her to ask questions and make observations. Once when they had finished going over some patient charts the nurse asked why it was that

such a high percentage of fibroid tumors occur in unmarried patients. Pleased at her making this independent observation,
Marion launched into some interesting theories she had read,
and added some of her own ideas.

"Of course nobody really knows how these things start," she
mused, "but sometimes I think it's nature's way of filling a
vacuum."

Marion came to depend on her team to pass on her choice
of clothes, order flowers, make beauty-parlor appointments, and
see that she got off on time and properly dressed for dinner parties and evening engagements.

They egged her on to keep the becoming red hat whose price
tag she had misread as being half what it was, and to buy the
mink cape she coveted. (Expensive as it was, it cost less than
half of what she spent on the education of only one of the many
young people she befriended.) They made a special effort to be
on hand to help her dress and wave her off when she was making
a speech; they knew she always had nervous pangs.

"I'm having the most awful pyloric spasms," she would say
cheerfully. "I'm sure it's going to be a good speech."

The high point of the year for the team was "that wonderful
six weeks" before Christmas. In mid-November they sat down to
make three gift lists: one for remembrances for interns, nurses,
and orderlies at the hospital; a second for the young guests who
would come to the children's party; and a third for their friends
around the Medical Arts Building, such as the switchboard
operators and the boys at the service station next door who saw
to it that Dr. Hilliard's car was always strategically parked for a
quick getaway.

Marion never gave money, always personal gifts. Miss Darlington happily spent her lunch hours doing the shopping, and
each day, between office chores, the girls wrapped gifts and
stacked them in a cupboard set aside for the purpose.

All year long Friday was a great day; there were no office hours,
and all three could use the time to catch up with correspondence,
get records in order, and relax from the pressures of the previous

four days. The Friday before Christmas was the best of them all. In the late morning the office was closed, and the team delivered the great pile of packages, then went off for a long, leisurely luncheon, to laugh together about all the ups and downs they had been through together during the year and to plan excitedly for the new year coming up.

CHAPTER 17

A Place in the Kingdom

The gay, unquenchable spirit of Dr. Gwen Mulock finally flick-
ered out, after nine long years of illness. Marion and Poppy, who
were at her bedside when death came in early June of 1950, had
fulfilled her dearest wish two months before, when they were
confirmed at Holy Trinity Church, Marion wearing Gwen's
prayer shawl and Poppy carrying Gwen's own prayerbook.

A vigorous, unashamed proselytizer since her own conversion, Gwen had focused her main efforts on Marion, who, by
the late 1940s, admitted herself to be searching for a more satisfactory means of expressing her faith.

Over the years Marion had come to feel very much at home
in Trinity Square, often attending services with Gwen and visiting her almost daily during her residence at the rectory. Their
mutual concern for Gwen's care and comfort had drawn Marion
close to Canon and Mrs. Frank, and she now counted them
among her dearest friends.

Marion's old friend had been right. As Marion wrote to an
acquaintance, at Holy Trinity she "found [her] spiritual home."
The twin Gothic towers of the old church, the mellowness of its
brick exterior, and the dark wood of its interior vaulting and
galleries, hewn from Canadian forest timber, were pleasing to
her. High above the transept the faded blue legend in Gothic
lettering, "This is none other than the house of the Lord. This is
none other than the Gate of Heaven," and the Beatitudes lettered above the stained-glass windows circling the church, invited her quiet reflection. From her favorite pew she could

glance up to read, "Blessed are the meek, for they shall inherit the earth." Perhaps this was the source of inspiration she told about on a radio broadcast she and Canon Frank did in the early 1950s.

"My private prayers," she told the radio audience, "are really not for publication, I'm afraid. I have my own language. One prayer of great significance to me came to me once as I sat in my own church. It was this: 'O, Lord, I think I talk too much and write too much and if I am not careful I will be a windbag. O, Lord, help me to be an instrument and not a windbag.'"

Although well-to-do worshipers were among its communicants, Holy Trinity traditionally also had been a church of the poor. A bedraggled down-and-outer wandering off the street into a service, far from being ushered out by discreet sidesmen, was likely to find the rector leaving the chancel to offer him a hymnbook opened to the right place. Much of Canon Frank's time during the depression went into the recreational center for pensioners and older unemployable men and the shelter for transient boys in the parish hall. One of the church's most active groups was the Social Action Committee, which had sparked Canada's Malvern Conference of 1943, an inquiry into religious thinking on social problems.

The esteem in which John Frank was held went far beyond the boundaries of the parish. A graduate of the London School of Economics, he had great concern for people in their everyday lives mingled with a firm belief in realistic Christian social action. He had served as city alderman for one term, and was a familiar figure on the picket lines in labor disputes and at rallies for peace and against the use of nuclear weapons.

He had a special affinity for children. Once when he was swinging down the corridor of a children's hospital, his cassock over his arm, a small boy walking toward him looked up in awe. "Hello, God," he said.

Canon Frank beamed down at him. "Hi!" he replied genially.

Of all Holy Trinity's traditions, the best loved by Marion was "The Christmas Story." Mrs. Frank, daughter of the vicar of St.

Martin's-in-the-Field in London, had brought the script for this pageant of the Nativity from her father's church when she came to Canada as the bride of Ontario-born John Frank. She herself produced the "Story," which attracted full audiences for ten days each early December. Bearing no marks of the amateur, the story was told simply and directly in a series of tableaux linked together by scriptural narrative done by Canon Frank, accompanied by carols and hymns from the unseen gallery choir. The beauty of music and costume and the quality of performance so enchanted Marion that it became a high point in that best part of the year for her. It gave her especial pleasure that her favorite carol, "In the bleak mid-winter," not only was included among the children's carols in the *Book of Common Praise*, the hymn-book of the Church of England in Canada, but also had its own place in "The Christmas Story."

The best way to begin a Sunday, to Marion's mind, was to attend the eight-o'clock communion service in Holy Trinity's chapel, her favorite place of worship—an ell-shaped upper room accommodating no more than fifty people, its white-painted walls made whiter by the slashes of cerulean blue, faded pink, and jewel red made by three stained-glass windows. Candles towered from pedestals on either side of the altar, as well as from the silver candlestick on the altar itself. The wide floorboards creaked and the wood of the pews and appointments glowed from years of loving care.

The lovely familiar words and phrases of the service, Canon Frank's strong, sure, cultivated voice, the stillness and peace of the little chapel were refreshing and moving to Marion; often she came away from the communion with tears in her eyes.

Before the drive back to Scarborough it was her custom to have coffee with the Franks in the big, old-fashioned rectory kitchen. It was characteristic of these devoted friends that she and Poppy and the Frank family could give themselves completely to the service, and a few minutes later crowd around the kitchen table together, plunged into uproarious conversation about church affairs, local politics, and stories of the past week's experiences.

It was some time after her private confirmation that word began to filter beyond Marion's immediate circle of friends that she
had joined the Church of England. For many the name Hilliard
was closely identified with the United Church; they wondered
if Marion's move had not distressed her mother, perhaps even
"broken the old lady's heart." Such speculations would have
astonished both Marion and her mother. The staunch, far-seeing
woman who, thirty years before, had declared publicly that "The
kingdom of God is not contained within the bounds of any 'ism'"
received her daughter's news imperturbably, glad only that she
had found a happy affiliation within the "kingdom."

No one appears to have remarked—and it is possible that Marion did not even know—that the church she had now chosen was
the church of her paternal grandparents, Thomas Hilliard and
Charlotte Gillespie.

Now Marion renewed her interest in Bible study. A few years
after their confirmation she and Poppy began meeting weekly
during Lent with eight or ten friends for dinner and an evening of free-wheeling discussion held together by a knowledgeable religious educator. Known to its members simply as "The
Group," the institution flourished for five years.

Each year some part of the Bible—the Acts, Paul's Epistles,
the Psalms—was chosen as the focus of study. The members, who
were of varying church affiliations, personal philosophies, and
levels of knowledge of the Bible and religious history, learned
from the leader and from each other.

Although explicit herself about her simple, deeply felt faith,
Marion was accepting of those friends who took a more intellectual approach and had honest doubts.

"Marion is not an intellectual," one of the Group's leaders
once said of her. "Rather, she has what I call intelligence of life.
She is not afraid to face the big questions of life and death."

Reveling in an atmosphere of uninhibited—sometimes hilarious—discussion, which was reminiscent of her SCM days, Marion

and her friends cherished the experience for its free exchange of
ideas, questions, doubts, and convictions.

Marion's motivation for much of her writing, speaking, and
teaching was to help people be more at ease with what she felt
to be the two most emotion-fraught subjects of our times: sex
and religion. To such groups as the School for Brides and
Grooms, which she conducted annually for some time for the
United Church, she brought candor and what she called "light-
heartedness," and she consciously employed fun and humor to
dispel tensions so that her audience could be free to listen more
closely and think more clearly.

She felt strongly that the same frank, explicit, unsanctimoni-
ous approach was needed to bring religious beliefs out of a seg-
ment of life barricaded by conventional forms, and integrate them
into everyday life. When, in 1953, she was elected to the national board of the YWCA of Canada and appointed chairman
of its Committee of Christian Emphasis (a group charged with
finding ways for members who are of all confessions to bring the
organization's religious purpose closer to its program in explicit,
practical ways), she entered joyously upon the task. The job
was just what she had been working at all her life.

A brand-new experience awaited her. Her idea of good discussion was a vigorous give and take; she responded frankly to
others' ideas and expected them to do the same with hers. Her
instinct was to get to the heart of the matter, and her training
had taught her to make rapid assessments and adopt and follow
a course of action, assuming responsibility for the consequences.

In the YWCA, whose way of work is the inevitably slow
process of reconciling differences of opinion and arriving at a
concensus with full democratic participation of group members,
the impact of Chairman Hilliard and her committee members
upon each other was an unforgettable experience.

During her four-year term, she alternated between excitement
at "the potential vitality of this committee work if we can ever
get at it," and frustration at the slow progress.

"Thank goodness," she fumed after one meeting, "after nine months of pregnancy you have a baby. In a committee nothing happens that soon."

Always a valued committee member because of her enthusiasm and original ideas, she was not the ideal chairman. Sometimes she got carried away with her own large ideas, and her friends had to remind her that the chairman's job was to invite the ideas of others. The bubbling humor and fun she had used so successfully as a speaker or teacher in a stiff, overdignified situation often sounded flippant coming from a chairman, and the kernel of wisdom beneath the surface of her remarks went unrecognized. On the other hand she was taken aback when ideas she intended as trial balloons to provoke discussion were accepted as though an oracle had spoken.

At the end of the first year the committee sponsored a seminar in which outstanding Protestant and Roman Catholic clergymen interested in the ecumenical movement joined with organization members to open up new avenues of thought. In her report to the national board, Marion waxed enthusiastic about the "atmosphere of freedom and warmth" of the seminar, and said it was "evident we all needed to become more articulate about expressing our faith and more at ease in feeling it."

Once during her four years on the committee, Marion was visiting a friend, a staff member of the World YWCA in Switzerland, to whom she complained that this work was so complicated "when it should be so simple."

"The discipline will do you good," said her friend briskly.

There was a silence. Marion was accustomed to think of herself as an extremely well-disciplined person. Finally: "I guess you're right," she replied humbly.

Eventually her hard work, force of character, and joyous vision gave the committee an impetus that still carries on. In 1959, the year following her death, YWCAs across Canada held a series of study groups on Christian emphasis in the organization, which, in her honor, were called the Marion Hilliard Seminars.

CHAPTER 18

"Life Begins at Fifty"

"There were even fireworks at the lively party that celebrated Dr. Marion Hilliard's fiftieth birthday the other evening at Dr. Ellen Blatchford's summer home in Scarborough," reported one of the Toronto newspapers a few days after Tuesday, June seventeenth, 1952.

It was Marion's theory, with which she comforted many a woman struggling through her menopausal forties, that life begins at fifty. The end of cyclic life relieves a woman's emotions of a great burden, she believed, and brings her to a plateau where she can depend on her moods and her stores of energy. Married women, no longer fearing unwanted pregnancies, enjoy sexual relations with their husbands. The unmarried woman finally accepts her status, the married but childless woman realizes that it is too late for children, and though "these are unhappy truths to accept, there is great peace in the knowledge that the struggle is over." She had found that many women have a sense of rebirth, new exhilaration. A feeling of well-being and stability cancels out some of the urgency about "keeping up with the Joneses" and the small pretenses that formerly seemed important.

"It was a great moment for me," she wrote several years later, "when I reached the age of fifty and could say fearlessly, 'I don't like ballet.'"

It is an understatement to say that she anticipated this particular birthday; she talked of little else for several months beforehand. It could hardly have been other than a major celebration, and Dr. Blatchford rose to the occasion. A special guest was

Gertrude Dearnley, who arrived from England in May to attend medical meetings with Marion in Banff, spend a theatergoing holiday in New York, and make a long visit at Birch Point.

At the Blatchfords' cabin on the upper bluffs, preparations were made for a large picnic supper party, with doctors, interns, nurses, husbands, and some close friends outside the hospital family on the guest list. An orderly who was a special friend of Marion's was pressed into service as bartender. Dr. Davey, who could not come to the party, sent a large collection of fireworks, and Mr. Blatchford spent the afternoon setting up skyrockets, spaced along the edge of the bluff, in preparation for the display that would conclude the evening. Just as supper was being served, a high-spirited young man among the guests went merrily down the line, setting a taper to each one, and Marion was treated to the sight of two dozen skyrockets simultaneously blazing away in celebration of her big birthday.

In comparison with a nine-week trip abroad the previous year, this summer was a leisurely stay-at-home affair, with two brief fishing holidays interspersing visits by holidaying family and friends. For Marion the only cloud over the summer was the departure of her brother Irwin and his wife and the four "little Hilliards" for Saskatoon, where Dr. Hilliard had accepted an appointment as professor of medicine at the University of Saskatchewan's School of Medicine. Once more she accustomed herself to nurturing this precious family tie by letter writing, thankful that they were close enough for weekly telephone conversations and occasional flying visits. In a few years her feeling of "having the family scattered to the four winds" would be greatly changed, when Dr. McNeel would be appointed deputy of Ontario's department of mental health, and she would welcome her sister and her family back to Toronto.

The second of the long trips Marion and Poppy had planned began on Poppy's fiftieth birthday, in early May of 1951. After a bon-voyage luncheon party given by old friends of Poppy's in New York the two were waved off from what was then Idlewild International Airport on the first flight of BOAC's *Monarch of Britain.* Their travel diary noted that they finished a celebratory seven-course dinner at ten P.M. and were awakened for breakfast at two-thirty A.M.—"a little too early even for me," wrote Marion. After a few days with Miss Dearnley in Surrey they took off for Turkey.

"Breakfast in Rome, lunch in Athens, dinner in Istanbul, and all airports are alike," Marion summed up the day.

For ten days they reveled in the pleasure of awakening to the sound of Istanbul street cries and morning tea with English and American friends who had made their home in Turkey for many years. Marion noted particularly the "overwhelming blueness of the Blue Mosque," the excitement of meeting Turkey's first woman lawyer, Byzantine art, delicious artichokes, moonlight on the minarets, a swimming party on the shores of the Sea of Marmara and the drive home "where I saw a house of coral and white making a wonderful picture against the blue sky and water." They wandered through the bazaars, had supper with the president of Robert College, and drove up the Bosporus.

"Though it is really not a river," Marion told an interviewer from a Toronto newspaper when she returned, "it kept reminding me of our lovely St. Lawrence." She had found Turkey "a fascinating land of contrasts of the old world and the modern," she said, and observed that it seemed to be a man's world, "since men ride the donkeys while women walk."

The next port of call was Athens, where Marion's old friend Helen Nichol was headmistress of Pierce College. The travelers were first taken to see "the old olive tree where Plato taught," and to the Acropolis by moonlight, where Miss Nichol's sister gave them a memorable talk on ancient Athens. Dining with their hostess's Greek friends, Marion learned to hoist a glass of ouzo and offer the toast, *"Stin y yassas,"* before plunging into delicious meals of fetta, salad, souvlakia, and fruit. Stories of the occupation and the civil war impressed upon the two North Americans forever the great courage and sturdiness of the Greek spirit; several of the people became Marion's friends, with whom she was in touch each year at Christmastime.

Before she left, Marion held a clinic, at Miss Nichol's request, in which she examined and prescribed for eighteen women suffering gynecological difficulties as a result of the long years of tension and starvation rations. Later she used the experience in her writing, as an illustration of her belief that fatigue is often the cause, not the result, of menstrual disorders.

Two weeks in Italy gave them just time to hit the highspots from Amalfi and Sorrento to Rome, Assisi, Florence, then north to Milan and the lakes. As they drove past carnation farms and geranium trees en route to Nice, where they were to meet Miss Dearnley, they agreed that the next trip must include a return to Italy.

With Miss Dearnley they visited Monte Carlo. Marion won seven dollars, then lost it, and decided it was "more fun to watch."

"Take it from me, gals," she wrote gaily to friends on a Monte Carlo postcard, "it's better to stick to the horses. At least you can see them run."

With friends in Geneva the party celebrated Marion's beginning her fiftieth year, then she and Miss Dearnley went on to Paris to medical meetings, where, as she told her newspaper interviewer later, she enjoyed meeting and comparing notes with gynecologists from all over the world.

A year later, the skyrocketing birthday celebration behind her, Marion began to plan for retirement. There were still five years to go, but, as she wrote, "a busy and intriguing program should be planned well in advance" to prevent "the sweeping sense of being suddenly cut adrift."

Birch Point must be made ready for year-round living; it was unthinkable that Marion's home base should be anywhere else. Second on the list was to find a way to combine the two things she most wanted to do: see more of the world and offer her services in a place where they were really needed.

When she told her mother that she would be retiring from the hospital in a few more years the gentle old lady replied, "That's nice, dear. Then you can do the Lord's work."

This exchange tickled Marion and she repeated it delightedly to friends. In her own way of thinking she had been "doing the Lord's work" ever since she had begun practicing medicine, yet she had never relinquished the girlhood dream that came closer to her mother's ideas. When she had finished doing her best for the hospital she would see to it that this dream too would come true.

CHAPTER 19

Breezy Campaigner

The hospital was beginning to outgrow the building that had seemed so ample and splendid in 1935. Twice in the late 1940s staff groups met with board members to discuss the possibility of expansion, but there were more urgent problems to be solved. Postwar rise in costs had greatly increased the bills for food, wages, and salaries. Reluctantly the hard-pressed superintendent proposed a raise in rates for rooms and services. In a heated staff discussion Marion and Ellen moved for a raise in rates for private rooms, rather than an across-the-boards increase.

Meanwhile beds lined the corridors on some floors, and doctors kept a sharp eye out to see that their very ill patients were left in these overflow facilities as short a time as possible.

By the end of 1951 the hospital was operating at 105 per cent of capacity, caring for six thousand patients a year, three-quarters of whom were obstetrical and gynecological cases. In sixteen years there had been a hundred and five thousand patients and thirty-three thousand babies had been born. For all the volume of patients, the mortality rate was so low, as one reporter put it, "it compared favorably with the most advanced Scandinavian countries." In more than six thousand deliveries only one mother had died, and she had suffered from an incurable medical disease. Infant mortality had steadily declined too. Of the twenty-three hundred babies born in 1950, one had died; of twenty-five hundred in 1951, there were no deaths.

Because of increased obstetrical bookings the hospital went back to the wartime practice of allowing new mothers to stay just seven days after delivery; even so, a dozen or more obstetrical cases had to be referred to other hospitals each year, because of overbooking.

A row of seven old houses nearby the hospital, which served as living quarters for the nurses, had long since ceased to be adequate. A recovery room was urgently needed on the ninth floor. Laboratory equipment had become outmoded. Clinic attendance had risen rapidly each year, and the outpatient department desperately needed additional space.

The opening gun of a campaign for four million dollars to meet these drastic needs was fired in June, 1952, by the late Mr. C. L. Burton, chairman of the board of a Canadian department store.

"This hospital has built up a Dominion reputation as the outstanding institution of its kind in Canada," he told Toronto newspaper reporters, announcing that he would chair the campaign. For the next ten months, until the campaign went over the top, members of the hospital's staff, board, auxiliary organizations, and community leaders and other friends of the hospital fanned out through the city, soliciting contributions from corporations, businesses, industry, community agencies, and individual citizens.

Every few days newspaper readers learned something more about this unique hospital and often, in addition, gained some new knowledge for themselves. The prenatal clinic had been one of the first to test for the Rh factor in the blood of expectant mothers. The new infertility clinic, directed by Marion's friend Dr. Daley, now a well-known endocrinologist, was described under the headline, "Worries Keep Couples Childless." A story about the Cancer Detection Clinic told of the test devised by members of the hospital staff, and Marion, Eva, and Dr. Robinson had obligingly posed for a photograph. The test was now a routine part of the clinic's examination, and a review of thirty thousand cases in which it had been used had shown it to be accurate.

One feature writer was struck with the atmosphere of the

hospital, which she attributed to high professional standards and the fact that "doctors and nurses pride themselves on their willingness to subordinate personal ambition to the good record of the hospital." She quoted a staff member as saying this was no place for a woman doctor simply because she was a woman.

"She's got to be a good *doctor,* ethical, hard-working, co-operative, and available when we need her in a hurry," the staff spokesman added.

Marion sailed into the campaign with throttles wide open. In addition to the highly visible problems of overcrowding and lack of special facilities that, as head of a department, she had to cope with every day, she had another impetus: she had learned that one of the requirements for a teaching program in the hospital would be at least one hundred public-ward beds.

She was asked to chair the committee soliciting contributions among the staff doctors and given a quota of fifty thousand dollars. Five months later, Campaign Chairman Burton announced to the newspapers that the forty-nine doctors had oversubscribed the quota by more than twenty per cent.

Freely using her reputation as an entertaining speaker to get into places where she could tell the hospital story, Marion made countless addresses to countless groups all over town. With other staff members she put on panel discussions for women's audiences.

One memorable evening she and three other staff members took part in a panel discussion before a packed audience in one of the schools. It was a hot evening and the stage where the panelists sat was boxed in by curtains. Marion arrived late, swept into her part of the presentation with vigor, suddenly stopped, wiped off her forehead, and said to the audience, "Maybe it's not really hot in here. Maybe I'm just having a hot flush."

The room rocked with laughter, and she was off. That night she coined a phrase that later turned up in her writing. Describing the "medium" and "all-out perspiration" flushes, she confided that she used to bet with herself ("for moderate stakes") when she felt one coming on, whether it would be a straight flush or a royal flush. It brought down the house; for many in the audience it was the first time they had been helped to laugh at an experience they either looked back on or forward to with dread.

It was one of Marion's first broadsides against the hush-hush atmosphere traditionally surrounding discussion of menopause.

About once a week Marion turned up with a new idea for publicizing the hospital in an unusual way. Her fellow staff members felt as though they barely had time to recover from one before she would spring the next. One that will long have a place in the annals of the hospital was the radio broadcast of the birth of a baby, which she persuaded the Canadian Broadcasting Company to arrange.

Taped in a delivery room on the tenth floor with herself as the obstetrician, the program was first run on November thirtieth, 1952, on CJBC's program "Let's Find Out," and repeated on "Trans-Canada Matinee" the following January thirtieth. Marion was very pleased with the tape, because all performers, including nurses, doctors, the mother herself at the actual time of delivery, and even the baby could be heard clearly.

The hospital's switchboard was jammed with calls even before the broadcast was over, expressing either high praise or scandalized disapproval. The following day during a session of Parliament a Member criticized both the hospital and the C.B.C. for having sponsored such a broadcast. Letters to the C.B.C. showed great extremes of audience response.

"Thank you for the most impressive broadcast our family has heard together. It explained to my children how a mother feels in the depths of pain and despair and then at the moment of birth, such elation and happiness. I truly believe our children felt that together with their parents they were just about the most important people on earth," said one letter.

"How disgusting can you get? This is a flagrant violation of moral and professional ethics," said another.

Later Marion wrote to the technician who had taped the program saying that she was "completely unprepared for the adverse criticism," and telling him how much she personally appreciated the way in which it was done.

"I have worked for twenty-five years in the practice of obstetrics in and out of the delivery room day and night," she told him, "and I have always wanted to have a permanent record of the tenderness and lovingkindness which is present when a baby is born. I think that you have caught that in a remarkable way and I wanted to thank you for doing this wonderful thing for us. I wish that all people could hear and understand your recording."

One of Marion's friends, the headmistress of a girls' school, heard the record and asked her if she would present it to the girls as a special evening program. Later she wrote to a friend: "The girls were age twelve to seventeen, about fifty of them. They listened intently to Marion's introduction; her wholesome approach to sex was like a fresh, clean breeze and they responded raptly to her personality.

"They were spellbound at the record itself and though one might expect it in this age group, there was no giggling and laughing—they were so caught up in an atmosphere of awe and wonder. When they heard the first cry of the baby, one little girl said delightedly, 'It sounds like a little lamb!'

"Later they expressed wonder at this being a natural and wonderful flowering experience for the mother. It was evident that what they had heard about birth had left an impression of its being primarily a painful experience. One of their reactions was that more people should hear it as it was such a rare and wonderful thing. When Marion told them it had been broadcast over the C.B.C. and many people were extremely critical of it, saying it was in poor taste and young people should not hear such things, the girls were horrified."

It was the hospital campaign that began Marion's career as an author. In the early 1950s the husband of a patient, who was then editor of the Canadian women's magazine *Chatelaine*, had asked her if she wouldn't write down some of that advice that always seemed to make his wife feel so much better.

"Impossible," Marion told him. "I haven't the time."

At intervals for two years he tried to persuade her to find the time. The campaign to raise funds for the hospital was in full swing when he suggested that, to save time, she dictate an article to June Callwood, a Canadian writer whom Marion knew well.

"It appeared to my aroused sense of the mercenary," wrote Marion in the introduction to her book, several years later, "that writing a magazine article would be an excellent way of earning money for the hospital and possibly of attracting further donations." Coupled with the prospect of a congenial and time-saving collaboration, the idea of putting her experience and talents to work for the hospital appealed to her.

"Woman's Greatest Enemy—Fatigue," by Dr. Marion Hilliard, was featured on the cover of *Chatelaine's* issue for January, 1954, along with a prize-winning recipe for a seven-layer casserole. The article was "a groan that came out of my bone marrow," wrote Marion; at that time her day began at eight o'clock in the operating room and ended—if she did not have to return to the hospital in the evening—when she arrived home long after dark, too tired to eat her dinner until she had rested. On both the editor's page and the first page of the article it was made clear that the author was donating her fee for the article to her hospital's building fund.

The magazine was sold off the stands in a few days. In time the article was reprinted in seven countries.

More than a year later, in April, 1955, the magazine printed "Woman's Greatest Blessing," a heartening, humorous article on menopause. (This time Dr. Hilliard shared honors on the cover with feature stories on "Spring Beauty Makeovers" and "The Women of Ottawa.")

"Away back last January when your letters began arriving to tell us how helpful you found [the first article]," wrote the editors, "we started in pursuit of Dr. Hilliard for another article. . . . Last summer she attended a meeting of the International Federation of Medical Women [where] she found doctors from many lands so concerned about women's unnecessary apprehensions about the menopause that she came home determined that her next article for Canadian women would be written on this subject. We believe you will find the result . . . the most informative and surprising treatment you've ever read on the subject."

Through the editors Marion conveyed regrets to readers that she had not been able to answer all the letters she had received after the article on fatigue was published. The stack of a hundred or so letters to which she referred was dwarfed by the mail that now poured in to the magazine and to Dr. Hilliard at office and hospital.

"My memory deserted me, my powers of concentration almost reached the vanishing point. However, you know all the symptoms. I didn't. Along came your article and I was very comforted to find that other women did just as silly things or even sillier," wrote one reader. "If other people eventually become normal again, possibly I would too!"

"This is the first fan letter I ever wrote in my life," another letter began. "I realize if everyone sat back and just thought how wonderful your articles are, it wouldn't be much encouragement to you. It is such a help to know that other women are muddling along through this trying period, so God bless you, Dr. Hilliard."

"Bless you, Hilliard," came from the pen of a Vic schoolmate, "I feel as though I'm normal because you say so. My sincere thanks for your enlightening treatment of our real and imaginary ills in such a humorous vein."

"If I had read this article five years ago," wrote another reader, "I'd have got a very large chip off my shoulder and been in a better mood all this time."

A great many letters contained questions "too embarrassing to discuss with my family physician." These Marion did her best to answer. The most frequently expressed dilemma was that of the woman in menopause who loved her husband but had lost interest in sex. Over and over Marion patiently replied, "You may be sure this is temporary and will soon pass, just as I have indicated."

Others were worried that menopause might just seem to be over, and that they might still become pregnant again.

"You may be sure at your age and this long after cessation of your periods that you may put your mind at rest on this count," Marion assured one of these readers.

Knowing that these popular articles, despite their educational messages and the fact that they were not written for personal gain, were probably being frowned on by certain of her medical colleagues, Marion was particularly grateful for approving letters from doctors. Many wrote to arrange for reprints of the article on fatigue for distribution to patients, congratulating Marion, as one said, "on the topic, the understanding and clear way in which it is presented, and your generosity in doing it for the hospital."

A doctor in another Canadian province whose wife had brought the menopause article to his attention said frankly that "it answers many of the questions which are baffling to the inexperienced male. We who must meet these patients almost daily in our general practice can fully appreciate the value of your article. It is a real morale builder to the women of this age group."

Marion replied she was happy if the article had helped to "answer unasked questions," adding chattily that she was "amazed at the response to this common-sense and lighthearted approach to menopause."

One day the mail brought a poem signed "Grateful Patient," and dedicated "To Dr. Hilliard, with all due respect."

> "Sisters, don non-blue attire
> And flock to give me your applause,
> For I've achieved my heart's desire,
> My merry, merry menopause,"

it began, and through succeeding verses told about the "royal flushes" which "make me glow to be alive" and how "adolescence, though such heaven, never was a patch on this," ending by imploring her "sisters" to share her jubilation at "my greatest blessing, grandest thrill, comic peak of my creation." Marion took it home and kept it on display for the enjoyment of visitors, and finally tucked it away to keep.

When the articles were reprinted in a British woman's magazine a spate of mail came from former patients. Several were mothers of babies, now of university age, whom Marion had delivered in the 1930s. One former patient sent a contribution to Women's College Hospital, with a note saying, "But for Dr. Hilliard's care, I shouldn't be the lusty 79-year-old person I happily am."

At intervals for the next two years gustily written pieces flowed from Marion's tape recorder: "Woman's Greatest Hazard—Sex," "Dr. Hilliard Talks to Single Women," "Don't Be Afraid of Growing Old," "The Four Main Fears of Women." The series grew, swelling the hospital building fund and piling up the fan mail far beyond Marion's resources of time and energy for answering. From several publishers came proposals to print the series in book form, and in the fall of 1956 Marion signed a contract and spent a week at home to write some additional chapters that she and the editors had agreed were needed.

"When I was elected to this position last year," said Marion in her report as chairman of the medical staff for 1954, "I undertook it with a great sense of earnestness and a weariness of spirit at the idea of all that lay ahead—change, noise, tearing down, building up. This worry was needless. There was change and noise, there were problems of parking and lack of beds but the total harmony has never been stronger. The enthusiasm of the staff as they have watched day by day the new wing's growing higher and sturdier, has been unbounded."

It was nearly three years from the day of the cornerstone laying to October thirteenth, 1956, the cool, bright autumn day when the new hospital wing and the nurses' residence were formally opened. The nine-story wing ran north and south along the west end of the hospital, making an L-shaped building. A few steps away, on the next street, the splendid new residence, named Burton Hall in honor of the campaign chairman, would accommodate two hundred nurses and house the nurses' training school.

All the needed additions and improvements were there. Well over one hundred and fifty beds had been added, more than doubling the hospital's bed capacity. One hundred new bassinets graced the gleaming, modernized nurseries, where one old-fashioned note had been preserved—the rocking chairs where nurses sat to feed the bottle babies.

The tired, proud staff trouped through the corridors, checking off all the long-awaited additions and improvements: the six-bed recovery area, the modern laboratories, the new outpatient department, the new social-service department, a small psychiatric unit, new laundry and kitchen space. At every turn it was obvious that this had been a community affair; gifts and equipment had been donated by a dozen service clubs, civic and fraternal groups, corporations and foundations, as well as the hospital's own auxiliaries. The staff's own gift had been a new medical library, given in memory of Dr. Kerr, who had died suddenly while on holiday in 1950.

As the day of the grand opening approached, a speakers' stand and a bandstand were built along the two inner sides of the L. Early that morning the crowded parking lot was cleared of cars and filled with chairs for the audience. Gay bunting and flags went up to decorate the entrance. Flowers from the Parks Department nurseries filled the lobbies. Long before the colorfully uniformed members of the Governor-General's Horse Guards band struck up "God Save the Queen" to open the ceremonies, patients with their nurses moved to the windows, and staff and technicians crowded onto the balcony above the speakers' stand to gain a good point of vantage.

The president of the Ontario Hospital Association, Mrs. Charles McLean, presided. Right Honorable Louis St. Laurent, then Canada's prime minister, cut the ribbon over the doorway at the moment of formal opening.

On the speakers' stand, along with Ontario's premier, Toronto's mayor, the president of the university, the campaign chairman, the hospital board president, and chairman of the staff sat a beaming little figure, stylishly clad in a peacock-blue wool suit and mink stole, perky hat cocked over one eye. Dr. Marion Hilliard was enjoying to the hilt the culmination of an endeavor for which she had worked hard for more than four years.

CHAPTER 20

Eventful Year

One of the best parties on Toronto's winter social calendar is "January Nite," when the Women's College Hospital Auxiliary takes over a downtown hotel and puts on a benefit evening designed to bring gaiety to young and old alike. A formal, white-tie affair, it offers two dance bands—one for teen-agers, another for those who like their dance music sweet and slow, a large room set aside for bridge players, a midway where youngsters and their elders mingle to buy chances on donated luxuries, and sometimes a program of entertainment. Guests are greeted by a formal receiving line of hospital bigwigs, and the atmosphere is a happy family one, since the nucleus of the party is the staff, their husbands and wives and youngsters.

The twenty-third annual January Nite, held at the Royal York Hotel on January twenty-eighth, 1956, featured a gay floor show. Between acts a group of people filed onto the stage and a most unusual event took place: the presentation of a check representing gifts from over a thousand patients and friends to establish the Marion Hilliard Trust Fund.

The idea had been thought up by three suburban matrons, each of whom had had several "Hilliard babies" and counted themselves among those who felt their Dr. Hilliard was the best obstetrician in the world. Since the previous spring they had written hundreds of letters to patients and former patients asking them to contribute to a fund "to be used for the benefit of medicine in whatever field Dr. Hilliard herself chooses." "Our hope is," they said, "that this would serve as a constant reminder to her, while she is still very active in medicine, of the great admiration her patients have for her both as a woman and a doctor."

Since no medical files or records could be made available to them, they adopted the chain-letter device, asking each person they reached to suggest other names. The response was immediate and generous. With legal help they had a declaration of trust drawn up and arranged for contributions to be received by a trust company.

For months contributions kept streaming into the trust-fund coffers, the great majority from patients and their husbands in Canada, the United States, England, Switzerland, Greece, and the Orient and the British West Indies. Some came also from former Vic students, old friends from Morrisburg, and the SCM days, members of the School for Brides and Grooms, and, of course, many of the medical and nursing staff and the Board of Governors at the hospital. Whether the check was for a dollar or a hundred dollars, the donor invariably ended by saying, "I wish it could be more." On monogrammed note paper, business letterheads, ten-cent-store tablet sheets, grateful patients wrote their warm sentiments.

"We want to add our names to those who think she is 'special,'" "She made my two Caesarians the most pleasant experiences of my life," "Another grateful patient and husband chequeing in . . . ," "This is a small down payment on a second chance for life given me by Dr. Hilliard," "I am a student now but would like to pledge ten dollars to be paid in six months when I go to work," "Please accept a widow's mite to help honor a great lady," "I nursed for her for six months . . ."

Until six weeks before the great day the project was kept secret from Marion; then a Christmas note from a former patient living in Japan gave the story away. A few of her medical friends who knew of it were greatly relieved, for they had taken a cautious attitude about it. This was the sort of thing that was done when a doctor retired or died; to allow it while she was still practicing might leave her open to criticism.

Marion made a few inquiries, talked it over with trusted

friends, and came to a typical conclusion: the fund might be a valuable resource for the hospital and she was convinced of her patients' genuine motivation, so what could be wrong about it?

"If it's being done out of love and affection, you must be a gracious receiver," she told her friends. She brushed aside the fact that "some people might think" it was "unfair advertising"; she already had more patients than she could possibly take care of and was doing a rushing referral business.

Knowing it would be, in some ways, an ordeal, she ordered an elegant ice-blue satin formal, replaced her long white evening gloves, and tried to fix her mind on the fun it would be after the presentation was over.

"I know I'm going to bawl," she said resignedly.

The evening started off with a dinner party given by the Macdonalds for a group of Marion's colleagues, family, and friends, including Maryon and Mike Pearson, who were to be star performers on the program. (The young planners had spared no effort in making the presentation a memorable affair. Mike had been Canada's Minister for External Affairs for some time, and had won international fame for his brilliant performance during a term as president of the United Nations General Assembly, and for his "invention" of the United Nations Emergency Force, which in another year was to bring him the Nobel Peace Prize.)

Arriving at the hotel, Marion was nervous as a kitten, but gamely lined up with the three originators of the project and their husbands, a representative of the trust company, and the Pearsons to go onstage after a rousing hula-dance act.

After that things were a blur. Maryon Pearson presented an enormous white-leather volume with "Marion Hilliard, Physician and Friend" beautifully lettered in gold on its cover, containing the signatures of nearly eleven hundred patient contributors. She gave a witty little speech about the years at Vic, including the story of Marion's helping her out and in the window the night of the forbidden dance. Mike made a few remarks to the effect that nobody but Marion Hilliard would get the Pearsons to make an appearance in the middle of a floor show (which was the literal truth). The trust-company representative presented the check (for about seven thousand dollars), telling something about the fund and quoting from some of the letters. The patients' tribute, written by Lois Wilson, Marion's patient and friend, was read from the dedication page of the volume of signatures.

"To Marion Hilliard, Physician and Friend
Whose skillful hands have been the world's first sure strong cradle for thousands of new babies born in her care;
Whose understanding, yet challenging voice has spoken wise counsel, replacing ignorance with knowledge, and fear with courage, for thousands of women who have been her patients;
Whose love of life and of her God has been her freely communicated gift to the men and women of her church, her community and her world."

Marion managed well at first but, true to her prediction, broke down at the touching stories larded through the trust-company-representative's speech, especially when it came to one about a contribution of fifty cents from a poor elderly patient. When Mrs. Wilson's tribute was read she gave up and sat with tears coursing down her cheeks. Then it was her turn to reply.

"How she did it I don't know," her friend "Moody" of the Vic days said later. "Here she was laughing and saying all these witty things, still in tears."

"The tension was so high by that time," said another close friend, "that I didn't know what she'd do. But trust Marion. She did exactly the right thing. Tears and all, she kept her voice steady and struck a humorous note. She recalled that her mother had wanted her to be a missionary, and she had in turn wanted to be a concert pianist, a professional hockey player, and then a doctor. 'But nobody ever told me I'd end up as a trust fund,' she said."

After the program was over, Marion read the telegrams from friends who were out of town or who hadn't been able to come to January Nite, rejoiced over the flowers—from her brother Irwin and his wife; from Marge, her Vic hockey teammate; from the hospital board; from the editors of *Chatelaine*—and one that she treasured particularly, from the teen-age sons of a colleague ("We are very proud of you, Aunt Marion"). Among the letters that came later were one from Uncle Rob and Aunt Clauda ("How proud we were to see your picture in the paper with that fine man Pearson and his wife. . . . The qualities of heart and mind you have shown and kept through the years have made you very precious to us"), and another from a friend of medical-school days who said that though he couldn't qualify as a grateful patient he hoped he could still be listed as a sincere friend and that he had been delighted to see her publicly honored.

"This is a grand remembrance for you," he finished, "and I send you my best wishes, but don't quit work!"

It was a gala evening. After the line of congratulators had thinned out, Marion slipped off with an armful of the party flowers for a visit with Von, who was recovering from an operation at the hospital, then on to a late-late party at the home of one of the patients who had initiated the trust-fund project. There she and her family and close friends ended the evening on a riotous note, for the husbands put on a skit, "Women—Sex's Greatest Hazard," a take-off on one of Marion's more famous titles, the high point of which was a song:

"If your man becomes the type that wants his love on Sundays,
  Let him have his way, for you don't have to wash on Mondays.
  And if you feel that very soon a flush will be your fate,
  Begin at once to gamble on a royal or a straight."

The evening of the presentation was the kickoff for the most eventful year of Marion's career, the year that her great dream for the hospital came true. After nearly nine years of quiet work she saw that the last giant step toward the goal would be taken with the opening of the new hospital wing in the autumn. With its great increase in bed capacity and its new and improved facilities the hospital would meet the technical qualifications for a teaching hospital. Since none of Marion's staff, including herself, was a Fellow of the Royal College, a qualification deemed "desirable" by the college for the chiefs of teaching services and their associates, the problem of personnel would be the thorniest, and she resolved immediately that the best possible use of the trust-fund money would be to subsidize postgraduate training of interns and residents working toward their fellowship examinations.

An enormous amount of Marion's time and energy had gone into recruiting interns for her department. The unique opportunity offered by the hospital to women doctors did not always offset the competition from good teaching hospitals in Canada, England, and the United States. Her plans to train a young woman to follow in her footsteps had had to be abandoned. Most of the possible candidates had married, after which, if they did not give up practice altogether, they switched from obstetrics to a specialty whose hours of work could be controlled. One young protégée who possessed Marion's single-minded devotion to the profession had died tragically when she contracted a fatal disease at a hospital where she was completing postgraduate training.

With the blessings of the Board of Governors, Marion began serious negotiations with the medical faculty at the university. The medical school was growing so fast that additional resources, particularly for teaching obstetrics, were needed, and the professor of obstetrics and gynecology, greeted her proposal with interest.

As spring came on, not only the negotiations, but life in general, gained in momentum. Each year Marion had at least one graduation address to give—to nurses, women doctors, physiotherapists, or some group in which she took an interest; and she tried to be on hand to make the presentations to the year's winners of scholarships from the funds she had set up in honor of her mother at the United Church training school, and in memory of Gwen at the university, as well as the winner of the prize for obstetrical nursing that was her annual gift in memory of Dr. Kerr.

Her eagerness to make the move to Scarborough for the summer was even greater now that the neoclassical cottage had become a gracious contemporary house, under the skilled hand of one of Marion's favorite "fathers," James Murray, the Toronto architect. After nearly a year of large decisions and much poring over blueprints—"A most unusual female to work with," Mr. Murray had said of Marion appreciatively. "Either an idea appeals to her at once or it doesn't appeal at all"—the two householders had taken off in August, 1954, for the return trip to Italy they had promised themselves. Fate had co-operatively set up the opportunity, when Marion was invited to address a meeting of the International Federation of Medical Women at Lake Garda. When they returned to Canada in late September, work was well under way in transforming the erstwhile summer cottage into a year-round house, complete with oil furnace, a kitchen with all electrical appliances, a new bedroom-sitting-room wing angled to frame the best lake views, the old sun porch made into a dining area, and a new screened porch built in breezeway fashion to catch the summer west wind. A structure Poppy had had built to house the bee equipment, known as the Honey House, had been altered to make a small apartment at one end, and Mr. Brown had been installed as full-time gardener and general caretaker of the estate.

Pleasure in the splendid new home was heightened by the fact that the Blatchfords were building a house on their property up the hill, and in another year, when Marion's schedule would permit the final move to Scarborough, they would be year-round neighbors.

Dr. Blatchford announced her retirement as chief of her department. Marion bought a silver box and had it inscribed "To My Favorite Night Rider," in memory of their "fire-horse routine" of earlier days, and put it away in readiness for her friend's retirement party.

What with Poppy's professorial duties and Marion's many

irons in the fire the annual move to Scarborough was not accomplished until early May. Very shortly Dr. Blatchford gave up the idea that the new home on the upper bluffs would be ready for her daughter's wedding to Dr. Edward Sonley in mid-May, and Marion and Poppy offered Birch Point for the reception. With all plans complete for an outdoor affair against a background of spring flowers, members of both households were aghast when, three days before the wedding, the temperature dropped to freezing level and there were snow flurries. For several days the diary at Birch Point was peppered with exclamation marks; then, in the nick of time, the weather changed again, and the forsythia and Chinese cherry trees obligingly bloomed for one of the prettiest wedding receptions Birch Point had yet seen.

In the midst of these pleasantly hectic incidents in her extra-medical life Marion was confronted with a series of major decisions in her arrangements with the medical faculty. It had been agreed that her leadership would be needed during the first year of the teaching program and that she should remain chief of the department for the next year until her retirement. Dr. Geraldine Maloney, an obstetrician and gynecologist on the staff of the Toronto General Hospital, who was a Fellow of the Royal College and had been a consultant to Marion's department for a half dozen years, had been asked to accept the post of associate chief in charge of the teaching program, with the understanding that she would become chief of the department on Marion's retirement, and had accepted.

In an effort to bring the department up to the highest level possible, it was decided that only those who were Fellows of the college would be eligible for the "indoor" staff of the department; all others would retain hospital privileges but would become members of the "outdoor" staff—that is, the staff working in the outpatient clinics.

Having observed the fate of the proposals raised for discussion and brought to a vote several times during her years at the hospital Marion, who saw time growing short, realized that the only way the goal of becoming a teaching hospital could be won was to present it as a *fait accompli*.

She and the officers of the Board of Governors concluded the last agreements with medical-school representatives, and the plan went to the medical faculty for discussion and acceptance or rejection. For several days Marion was on pins and needles; then one evening at a party at Dr. Blatchford's she was called to the telephone. The professor of obstetrics told her that the plan had been approved and accepted.

She came back to the party starry-eyed. It was the greatest moment of her life.

The next day she left town, knowing herself to be unequal to the immediate aftermath—the unavoidable hurt to department staff members who were good doctors, though lacking in the high qualifications that had been set, and the general pandemonium that would be created when the news seeped out. With Poppy she took to the road for a touring holiday through the Adirondacks and up the Maine coast.

In a matter of hours there were impromptu sessions in hospital corridors, the lobby, the locker room, the doctors' lounge, and at the home of a retired staff member. Antiphonal dialogue rose and fell. Why had nobody been told that this was going on? But we were told—we all knew that this was Dr. Hilliard's one goal for the hospital. Why had nobody been warned that the policy would be so stringent? What good would that do—we have less training than is called for and we have rested in a false sense of security. Why were we not encouraged to get our Fellowships? Dr. Hilliard has urged all the younger people to take the exams before they go into practice. Older staff members voiced the fear that it would be the end of the hospital as a women's hospital— men might have to be admitted to the staff to fill the required number of qualified people, and there would probably be male students. Others thought that now the professor of obstetrics "would have too much say in running the hospital." For the first time the staff complained about a ruling Dr. Hilliard had made the year before limiting the freedom of noncertified staff members in using the operating room unless a certified staff member was present. Some thought the chief was "ruthless"; others said, "Not ruthless, just determined." In the heat of the moment it was said that she had "done it for her own glory."

"No," said one defender, "she is not a selfish person. She enjoys success but it is never a goal in itself for her."

As the storm blew itself out, one of Marion's close friends on the staff summed it all up.

"It had to be if the hospital was going to survive. I don't know who would ever have done it if she didn't. The saddest part of it is she didn't have the qualifications to ride the crest of the wave herself. She could have been anything if she had been better prepared. She deserves a lot of credit for standing firm and seeing it through."

Marion returned from her holiday, and on July tenth appeared at a meeting of the Medical Advisory Board to introduce Dr. Maloney as the new associate chief of the department. She announced that she herself would continue as chief and advisory head, and Dr. Maloney would be in charge of teaching and the clinical aspects of department work. She told of special rounds and meetings soon to be scheduled and suggested that the staff hold a dinner party in the fall for her new associate chief.

When Marion asked her friends what had happened while she was away, they told her the truth. When they had finished, she sat quietly for a few minutes, a sober expression on her usually merry face.

Finally she said, "So be it," and changed the subject.

Dr. Maloney, who was, of course, well known to the staff, was welcomed to the fold. Dr. Henrietta Banting, recruited to assist with the teaching, became the first "Hilliard Fellow," since she was paid from the Marion Hilliard Trust Fund. The first students arrived. The staff began speculating about when other departments would be accepted for teaching. (Within the next few years the departments of surgery and medicine both became teaching units.) Hospital life settled down again, and Marion began her last year on the staff.

CHAPTER 21

The Chief Retires

"The year 1957 brings with it the time for me to retire from service on the active staff of the Women's College Hospital," Marion wrote the secretary of the hospital's Board of Governors on March fourth. "I have no hesitation in giving up the position that I have held as chief of the service. I believe the time is exactly right for me to do this. . . . The affiliation of the Obstetrics and Gynaecology Department with the University of Toronto has been a realization of my dreams."

Expressing her gratitude to present and past board members, she added, "The hospital has been the center of my life for these thirty years and I shall certainly miss the association deeply, but I can look forward to new, and to say the least, different experiences on the Honorary Staff. You will probably hear from me."

She finished off her letter of resignation by sending "every good wish for the future of this wonderful hospital."

Even as she wrote it, she was deep in plans with the C.B.C. for a television series that would take a pregnant patient through the whole story of having a baby, from the first interview with the doctor when pregnancy was confirmed, through the various stages, each with its different questions and problems, then to the labor and delivery rooms for the actual birth, and, afterward, her return to her room and the father's first view of the baby in the nursery. The going-home day for mother and baby and the patient's first post-delivery interview with the doctor were the concluding episodes. (Months later, when the tenth floor was invaded by camera and cable, even the loving and loyal Miss

Galbraith was, as she told Marion, "practically crawling the walls," and the hospital corridors echoed with expressions of disapproval of Marion's final brainstorm. All was forgiven when a tape of the series proved to be valuable teaching material both for the obstetrical outpatient clinic and the hospital's nurses' training school.)

As her last year as chief rounded out she received the token honorarium from the university for her year as chief of a teaching department, and a letter from the dean of the medical faculty, thanking her for "your help in this first year of the establishment of teaching in your service . . . [and] your wise leadership and guidance." The president of the university wrote warmly that "not only the Faculty of Medicine but the whole University is in your debt."

The first of a series of parties in her honor was given by her successor, Dr. Maloney, in mid-May. Somehow Marion got the idea that the traditional staff party for retiring members was going to be sprung on her as a surprise, and she decided that she would not be caught lounging around in an old pair of slacks. Craftily she collected all accessories for a dress-up costume ready to slip into in a matter of minutes and put them together in her clothes closet in the handiest spot.

When Poppy announced, the morning of her own birthday, that she would be tied up at the university for dinner and the evening Marion looked wise and said nothing. Surely Poppy would manage not to have to work on her own birthday, she reasoned, so this must be it. She had her hair done between hospital rounds and office hours, rushed home from work, and put on the elegant dinner dress. When nothing had happened by the time she got hungry, she put on an apron and ate dinner. Very late in the evening Poppy arrived home to find her dressed to the nines, sound asleep on the living-room sofa.

The long-awaited event finally took place at Ellen Blatchford's home in late June, after Marion's return from the Canadian Medical Association meetings. Wearing a hyacinth-blue dinner dress and a shoulder bouquet of her favorite red roses, Marion laughed—and once or twice wept a bit—through a heartwarming, hilarious evening with her hospital friends. She was overcome to find that the staff's parting gift to her was something she had wanted all her life—star sapphires; the ring and earring set became her best-loved dress-up jewelry.

Her hostess and "Favorite Night Rider" presented a special gift, a photograph album. There were photos of colleagues at work in the operating room, and on holidays with husbands and children; snapshots of the dedication ceremonies of the new wing of the hospital; picture mementos of the fishing trips to Quebec; close-up shots of Marion's "adopted" nieces and nephews, some of whom she had brought into the world. Marion laughed and then happily mopped at a few tears as she read the inscription on the book's cover: "Medical Picture Gallery, arranged and assembled by Dr. Ellen Blatchford, presented to Dr. Marion Hilliard in appreciation of years of close association and friendship, with the hope that it will recall many pleasant memories. June 1957."

The hospital's Board of Governors gave a party for her, at which she was presented with a suitably inscribed silver coffee server set. Marion made a witty speech, poking fun at herself and her various projects that had periodically stirred up the hospital, but later, replying to the formal notification of her appointment to the honorary medical staff, she wrote the board secretary, "I can never express in words my feelings about the Board. They have made it possible for me to work out my whole life's salvation."

To Gertrude Dearnley she wrote, "You'll be glad to know I have no difficulty in my feeling about leaving the hospital. It really is a great joy to me, and apart from a few gnawing, wistful moments when I realize there are things I want to say and I have no business to say them, I am in fine shape. There are so many pleasant things to look forward to, and life looks very exciting."

The "pleasant things" in the immediate future were her nurse Miss Darlington's wedding to H. A. Wynn, a Toronto businessman, followed by a reception at Birch Point; a holiday trip to the West Coast; the move to the new house at Scarborough—"And from then on," she finished, "I expect to have just a whee of a time."

The happy event that put the finishing touch on the year for Marion was the full-scale family reunion at Christmastime. Everyone was together, from Mrs. Hilliard, then in her eighty-fifth year, to the small sons of Dr. Joe Hilliard and his wife. Out-of-towners were billeted among the Torontonians, with an overflow of Hilliards in a Scarborough motel. The traditional Christmas dinner party at the new house at Birch Point, with the lighted blue spruce, the firelight, and favorite Christmas music for a background, was a warm, gay family affair, memorable for young and old, and deeply satisfying for Marion, who "liked it when everything is merry."

CHAPTER 22

"I Think of the Titles First"

Once Marion confessed that her career as an author came partly because she wanted to earn money for the hospital and partly because she was "beguiled by [her] own titles," which always came to her first.

"Who but me," she chuckled, "would think that the menopause was woman's greatest blessing? A title like that would intrigue me for days, as the ideas and anecdotes fell into place."

In 1956, when arranging with her publishers for the book that would be made of her articles, she pleaded in vain to have it titled *Born to Love*. Of all the phrases that had come to her, she liked this best; to her, it summed up what life was all about; and besides, she thought it most appropriate for a book about sex, marriage, babies, and women. The editors ruled it out in favor of a specifically descriptive, if more pedestrian, title.

Publication day for *A Woman Doctor Looks at Love and Life* came on June sixth, 1957, and found Marion in Vancouver, attending the national convention of the Canadian YWCA, where she made a lively speech.

"Men are the shock troops in the battle of the sexes," she told her audience of four hundred women delegates, "but women are the tacticians. One of the greatest weaknesses in marriage is that women play their hand masterfully in snaring a man, but drop the strategy after marriage."

Midway in the convention, when the book came out, the *Vancouver Sun* reported, "Dr. Hilliard's Book Overnight Sellout," since the small supplies sent to the convention and the Vancouver bookstores were quickly bought up and presented to Marion for autographing. In an issue of the *Toronto Globe and Mail,* which Marion would not see for another month, William Arthur Deacon, dean of Canadian reviewers, headed his review "Pulls No Punches," and told his reading audience that "Frank testimony and good advice is leavened . . . by moments of uninhibited laughter." All Toronto reviewers stressed the fact that the author's Canadian royalties were being donated to the Women's College Hospital.

The convention concluded, Marion was joined by Poppy, and the two fishing enthusiasts disappeared into the wilds of British Columbia to go salmon fishing with the Roderick Haig-Browns, the world-famous angler and nature writer and his wife. They emerged in time to catch the plane for a meeting of the Canadian Medical Association at Edmonton where Marion gave a paper on the psychosomatic aspects of gynecology. In an interview with a reporter from the *Edmonton Journal* she lightheartedly paraphrased her medical title in a Shakespearean quote: "Frailty, thy name is woman."

Back in Scarborough, Marion was notified that two of her chapters would be published by the *Reader's Digest,* and that, serial rights had been sold to a string of newspapers on both sides of the border. After a few months the book had sold so well that, in that peculiar logic understood only by themselves, the publishers began to publicize it. In the *New York Times,* which on June sixth had listed the book in fine print under "Other Books Published Today," full-page advertisements appeared.

To these notifications of the progress of the book's distribution and sales Marion paid scant attention. Then, one crisp fall evening, walking off the grounds of the Canadian National Exhibition, Canada's annual national fair, she saw a delivery truck of the *Toronto Telegram* clip around the corner. Staring at her from the truck's side panel was her own picture blown up to ten times life size, and a splashy legend announcing the first installment of Dr. Marion Hilliard's book. Horrified, she sank down on the nearest bench, weak in the knees and at a loss for words; the possibility of such publicity had never occurred to her. She crept to her car, avoiding the eye of passers-by, then burst into laughter at her own performance.

The fan mail began to filter in.

"I confess I was pained to see your dear lovely face looking up from the baseboard of the Tely news box," wrote a Morrisburg neighbor who had known her all her life, "but I consoled myself it wasn't yet on the front of a street car. Now that I have reached page 108, I don't care where it is if it helps the book reach more people. My dear, I address a courageous and noble woman."

Congratulatory notes came from people she hadn't seen for years: a former ward of the Children's Aid Society, now happily married; one of the Oaklawn roommates, who said she was giving the book for wedding presents; one of the women who had interned with her at the Rotunda, and was now practicing in India; a school friend who said that she felt fortunate to know her, adding, "What you have given the world has been the very best of yourself. So few of us can say that. I hope it brings you great inner contentment."

Women wrote from all parts of Canada, the United States, England, and South America. Some wanted to thank her for expressing what they had always felt: "The way you explain me to myself is almost uncanny"; "Your book has affected my thinking about my marriage for the better"; "Yes, there *is* a relationship a woman feels toward her obstetrician that is different from any other"; "This will help my daughter understand her greatest danger is not her boy friend but herself"; "Truly you seem like a close, understanding parent who has guided me in marriage and motherhood"; "Thank you for your reality, humor and expressing so well that feeling of reverence for the privilege of being a woman"; "My husband and I have hoped and dreamed that we might be lovers all our life, and bless your heart, you certainly encourage that hope."

Other letters came from women and girls who wanted help with troublesome problems: the frigid woman, the woman with an unresponsive husband, the unmarried woman several months pregnant, the girl who wondered about the wisdom of taking an apartment "when you have a boy friend," teen-agers worried about excessive hair, too small breasts (or too large ones), mothers worried about their children's sex education—all poured out their problems on paper, and Marion did her best to answer them.

"It is wise for a girl to make a home for herself, and natural to invite her boy friend into it," she wrote. "The only question is whether she has the wisdom to define the type of behavior which is going to take place."

"Marriages which come from deep and abiding love, even though a marriage does not take place in the situation we have grown up to believe in, so often become enduring marriages and make wonderful homes," she wrote a woman who had got pregnant before marriage and still felt guilty after many years. "It makes no difference to anybody what year you got married and I would never let that come up again. Just skip that year for good and always. And don't get rid of your burden by telling your child—just help him make a happy marriage."

Letters of thanks came from husbands and fathers.

"We shall treasure your book. There is no book like it. You have had the courage to say things a man could not say, or if he did, women would not accept it." "I sent copies to my daughters and daughters-in-law on both sides of the Atlantic, and was so satisfied to learn they so highly valued your spiritual child." One that Marion particularly prized was an unsigned postcard from the Midwest in the States. "Thank you, doll," said the male scrawl, "I imagine I represent a million husbands—sincerely and earnestly."

Another that tickled her came from a husband who warned that she would probably receive an irate letter from his wife.

"You unerringly hit the bull's eye on so many things that it hurt," said the man, who signed himself "A Mere Male." "Some women are imbued with the idea that they are a superior breed.

Parts of your book should be used as a text in common sense for women who want to be happy and aid their family."

"I am grateful for the place you gave the church among the therapeutic institutions," wrote a clergyman. "Some minister ought to say that for the rest of us. God bless you." A Baptist minister praised the chapter on marital love-making because "it is so wholesome." A Catholic seminarian found the chapter "What Women Don't Know about Being Female" "quite revealing and corroborative of Christian principles." "All you say is perfectly true," came from an Episcopal rectory. "Being a priest for some forty years and meeting a lot of people in that time for counseling, I can only add to your sentiments." A Christian Scientist wrote, "Your writing is astounding, sincere, thrilling, and well thought-out."

An educator thought that the book should be required reading on high-school and university curriculum lists.

A source of great amusement to Marion was the repeated query, "How do you, a single woman, know so much about marriage and sex?" She tried to respect the question as a symptom of anxiety in laymen who wanted to know whether or not she really knew her subject. Gravely she would explain, as she told in the book's introduction: "It gives me an objective point of view. A married woman knows only one man."

Among her colleagues she joked about it. All medical people know that the extra understanding which comes to them after experience with thousands of patients having similar difficulties is not usually credited by those outside the profession.

"You can get to know exactly how it feels to a patient to have gallstones without having to have them yourself," one of Marion's old friends told her, "but none of them ever believes it."

For a few months Marion hardly knew what to feel. She glowed at the letters that showed clearly that both women and men had been helped by the book, enjoyed a good laugh at the occasional blast—"What a title for a book! I'm glad I never had a doctor like you," wrote one woman—or the ridiculous query— "Dear Dr. Hilliard, How do we overcome an inferiority complex?" said one postcard—but it soon got back to her that although most of her colleagues thought it was a good book and one worth while writing, many, including some of her closest friends, took the official point of view of medical groups: reputable doctors do not engage in popular writing until they have retired from practice. At a meeting of obstetricians, which Marion did not attend, criticism was expressed, not about what she had to say, but about the ethics of having said it.

Dr. Minerva Reid, under whom Marion had trained as a junior intern, and who was now living in retirement, sent for her. "You have broken my heart and demeaned your gift," she told her sadly.

To a reporter who was writing a profile of her for a Canadian national magazine Marion said stoutly she didn't agree that she had demeaned herself or her profession. "Women have a right to know the truth about themselves. Doctors are not a race apart from their patients," she said.

There were sharp exchanges of opinion. A nurse at the hospital expressed her disapproval and another nurse retorted that it was high time someone got these things out into the open by writing about them. A board member heard the criticism and said that she felt more critical of the conventionally professional doctors than the renegades any day. At a dinner party a patient heard a doctor remark about Dr. Hilliard's self-advertising.

"Hah! Just try and get an appointment with her," she exclaimed to him.

A senior professor on a Canadian medical faculty told a friend, "Very few people who succeed escape the envy of the profession masked by professional disapproval. Sure, it's safe to say a practicing doctor should write only for medical journals. But remember that Dr. Thomas Cullen [of Johns Hopkins Hospital] wrote popular articles about cancer in the days when no one else would, and you can't say that wasn't a good thing."

In the meantime Marion was comforted by grateful letters from doctors, nurses, librarians, and psychologists. One Canadian doctor pointed out two chapters that he thought should be reprinted in a medical journal. Another said that the chapters on sex and the menopause had been especially helpful to him in his own practice. A psychologist in the States said that a half dozen copies of the book were circulating among his patients, and he ventured to guess that the number of women she had helped live a fuller, more satisfying life "is far greater than you perhaps realize."

A "Meds, '27" who was specializing in another city wrote, "You must have had a fine time gradually coming to the conclusions expressed so clearly and forcefully in your book. The fact that you have been able to do so in Toronto makes me feel much happier about Toronto. I have memories of its being a rather strait-laced place, but perhaps it has grown up more than I expected."

"As you probably realize," replied Marion, "I have been embarrassed and wanted to leave town each time an article came out. Now that they are all together in book form, I feel better knowing that, whether good or bad, it contains my philosophy and some of my clinical experience."

To another old school friend she wrote that she would not be in town for the "Meds, '27" thirtieth reunion—and, "I hope the boys won't think I am afraid to turn up because of the teasing I am sure I would get."

To add to the stir created in Toronto's medical world Marion heard that it was being rumored in literary circles that the articles, ergo the book, was "more the work of the collaborator than of Hilliard." She was shocked that anyone would believe she would sign a manuscript that was not essentially hers. At *Chatelaine* the editor who had started the whole project by wheedling Marion into the first article had been succeeded by Doris Anderson, Marion's patient and friend. Mrs. Anderson asked her to write a new series of articles on any subject she chose, and agreed to do the editing herself.

Marion seized the opportunity. Under the title (which gave her great satisfaction) "Man Was Born to Love," she wrote her apologia, for the issue of November, 1957, spilling into it the highlights of her life from the fun on hockey rink at Oak Hall to her "delirious pride" at being a part of the growth of the Women's College Hospital. Referring to her title, she recapitulated her philosophy of life somewhat as she had done in her book, in the last chapter, "The Key Is Faith."

"Let me say in the beginning that I never really wanted to write magazine articles, much less a book," she started off. "I was a doctor and content to do the job and find my satisfaction in the profession for which I had trained."

Even though it had been for a worthy cause, she confessed that she had been "offended by my own creation" and "uncomfortable when it was recognized." Most of all, she felt "real heartbreak that twenty-five years of constant back-breaking endeavor to practice skillfully the art and science of medicine wouldn't compete for recognition with a few articles in a magazine."

She had been comforted to remember that "my simple common-sense pieces" were "the result of years of experience in the observation and care of women," and told of the letters that had come to her from young and old in every Canadian province.

"All I wanted was to help people understand themselves a little better," she concluded. "If I have achieved that, to even the smallest degree, I am happy."

CHAPTER 23

"Wish Something With Me"

"I am starting a new life soon," Marion ended her first book. "Wish something with me. Wish that it will be difficult. And full of laughter."

She had written the words in the fall of 1956. By the time the book was published, in June 1957, plans for the new life were well under way. For five years she had been gradually tapering off her private obstetrical work, and now she had retired from the hospital staff. At last she could fulfill her girlhood dream— as well as others of more recent origin.

"I want to help the pioneer work of women doctors in hospitals in India and China," she wrote. "I hope to live a year or so in Greece or Turkey, where women doctors are involved in exciting pioneering. I want to hear opera in Milan and go salmon fishing in British Columbia. Now that I am fifty-five, I can scarcely wait to get at the future."

Poppy had agreed to retire early from the university faculty so that they could go together as a volunteer doctor-social worker team.

In the spring of 1957, when Marion had attended a session of the United Nations Status of Women Commission as a representative of the YWCA of Canada, she had sought out an old friend in the UN Secretariat to find out about the possibilities of going to India under United Nations auspices.

"I wish you could go tomorrow," said her friend, telling of a team that was indeed leaving the next day. At a *My Fair Lady* theater party Marion excitedly repeated the conversation. Afterward, still chortling over her favorite song from the musical, "Get Me to the Church On Time," which she said reminded her of songs she had heard in London music halls, she burst out happily, "I feel as if we were on our way already."

Through the busy autumn and winter days of 1957 and early 1958 she wrote and presented medical papers on family life and mothers' fatigue for a meeting of the American Medical Women's Association at Dallas, Texas, and on a technical gynecological subject for the College of General Practice at Winnipeg; was double-billed with the American social psychologist Dr. Hadley Cantril at an evening session of the triennial national convention of the YWCA of the United States of America in St. Louis, Missouri; as one of the national vice presidents of the Canadian YWCA agreed to make a series of speeches in "Ys" in Ontario and Quebec; and resumed writing columns for *Chatelaine.*

There were two holiday interludes, one in New York for New Year's, where she lingered a few days to fulfill a commitment to do a radio interview, and ten days in Jamaica in late February with Poppy, who had been asked to consult with leaders planning a new school of social work there.

Through all these activities ran a thread of excitement as plans for the future took shape. Marion became the president-elect of the International Medical Women's Association, so a July visit to England was scheduled, where she would attend the association's meeting and be installed in office.

"I am all ready," she wrote Miss Dearnley in March, in a letter full of plans to rent a car, to meet the Shapiros for a performance in Stratford, and to dine with representatives of Macmillan and Company, her London publishers. "Only one thing more I have to do—get a floor length dress for the opening meeting when the Queen Mother is going to be there. I thought I was all set with cocktail length dresses, but if fashion decrees a floor length dress then I must get it."

In Ottawa to make a speech, she made inquiries about possible Canadian auspices for work in India. When she came back she wrote to an American friend with whom she and Poppy had planned a spring holiday in Italy "sometime."

"Our pots are all boiling like everything. You can start planning for Italy in the spring of 1959."

One day on the street she ran into her old friend and medical-school classmate Dr. William Keith. "Oh, Bill," she exclaimed as she told him that she was going to India in the fall, "I feel that my life has come full circle! You know this is what I've always wanted to do."

From the New York office of Doubleday & Company came a query: Would she like to do another book? Yes, she wrote back, as a matter of fact she would; she felt that there was much more to be said about "woman's greatest enemy," fatigue, than she had been able to get into one chapter in her first book. She would think about whether or not she could do it before she left for India.

Then events began to march swiftly, and what proved to be the last fourteen weeks of Marion's life reeled past quickly, leaving her family, friends, and colleagues stunned, disbelieving, helpless.

Early in 1958 Marion realized that she felt unusually tired, despite the fact that the night calls to the hospital delivery room had now become almost past history. Reveling in the freedom of retirement from the hospital and her tapered-off obstetrical practice, she went off on the Jamaica trip, feeling that it would revive her. But she continued to feel under par after her return, and cut down activities outside her practice except for the speeches she had promised to make.

Finally, in the third week of April, she sought out her friend and colleague Jean Davey, complaining of pain in her chest, and yielded herself up to a complete examination, laboratory tests, and a series of X rays. As they do so many countless times with others, the pictures showed that her chest was affected; but not by what. It could have been several things, including virus pneumonia.

At Dr. Davey's suggestion Marion further curtailed her schedule and began a new regime, allowing for extra rest and sleep and more quiet hours at home, reading and listening to music. She was puzzled and frightened at the way her dependable, robust constitution was letting her down. One night, listening to a favorite Rachmaninoff record, she wept disconsolately and would not be comforted; it was the only time during her illness that she let those close to her see any fear or discouragement she might have felt.

In these hours of enforced leisure she began to think of the proposed new book. Toward the end of April she announced to Poppy, "I'm going down next week and get this thing started. If I don't do it now, I never will."

Whether or not she spoke literally, no one will ever know. At any rate a determined and indefatigable spirit had joined battle with a slowly sickening body. On May second, after her early-morning operations, she flew to New York and spent the day with Ferris Mack, her Doubleday editor-friend. Over a long and gay luncheon they agreed on the rough outline for the book, and laughed over her hastily scrawled list of chapter titles, which, of course, she had "thought of first": "It's Not All in Your Mind"; "Too Tired to Love"; "Trapped by Her Own Adaptability"; "Alas, 'Tis Our Frailty."

At midnight, just home from the airport, she called a New York friend, a writer whom she had tried unsuccessfully to reach all day. "Where in the world have you been?" she asked, and, without waiting for an answer, launched into a breathless description of the new project, ending with an invitation to collaborate on the book. "I never get to finish my sentences, Marianne," she concluded briskly, "and I need help."

A long-time friend of Poppy, frequent Birch Point visitor, and often hostess to Poppy and Marion on their New York visits, Marianne (a nickname adopted to prevent confusion between the two Marions) and Marion had often talked, half seriously, about doing a book together. In five minutes an agreement was concluded. Marianne would do preliminary research on fatigue while finishing current assignments, and they would begin work together in Scarborough when Marion felt well enough.

"There, that's settled," said Marion when she hung up, "and all in one day too!"

A few days later she wrote again to Miss Dearnley. "I've had a virus infection that finally developed into a virus pneumonia. I'm frightfully thrilled about your arranging a trip to Wales for us all. You can't imagine what it means to me when I am on the 'downbeat' to look forward to such a wonderful time.

"Spring is here and I couldn't have picked a lovelier time to stay home. The forsythia, Chinese cherry and Japanese cherry are all out. It's wonderful that in about seven weeks we will be sitting in that lovely garden of yours."

Happily she welcomed her beloved friend Von, who stopped to see her, as always, on her way home to Morrisburg after a winter in Florida; and Maryon Pearson, who dropped in one afternoon for tea. It was Golden Jubilee year for Victoria College; Marion went to the celebration and took part in a skit that had a woman doctor as one of its cast of characters. Miss Galbraith retired as night supervisor on the tenth floor, and Dr. Maloney gave a party for her. Marion asked if she might be the one to send an orchid to the friend with whom she had spent so many "wee small hours" in the tenth-floor delivery rooms, and went to the celebration, because "this is one party I'm going to whether I can make it or not."

The editor of a prominent national women's magazine in the States phoned to ask if she would write an article for him, proposing the title, "Why Premarital Sex Is Always Wrong." She said she would be glad to do an article but not with such a title—it was too "black and white." Choose your own title, he replied, just write the article for us. She dictated the requested number of words into her small tape recorder, made a few changes, and sent it off under her own title, "Modern Variations on the Ancient Theme of Passion."

Marion felt more tranquil in spirit, but her symptoms had

grown more serious. A deeply racking cough developed. The gray look about her face was more noticeable.

On May fifteenth she entered Toronto Western Hospital for further tests, and returned two days later, puzzled, worried, but game. The tests had proved nothing. If it was a virus pneumonia, it would simply have to run its course; she would help it along. She canceled all engagements, including plans for the first week's work on *Fatigue,* as the book was now referred to, and began a "half-day-in-bed-and-asleep-by-nine-p.m." regime.

Alone in her office, the test results before her, Dr. Davey faced the most difficult experience that can befall a member of the profession. The biopsy of lung tissue was negative for carcinoma. In the absence of other symptoms this might have brought happy relief, but the symptom picture, as Marion herself said, "just didn't add up."

There was one dread possibility: a symptomless primary carcinoma somewhere else in the body might have spread through the lymph nodes surrounding the lungs, where it could remain undetected, though suspected. Every known method of revealing the source of illness had yielded nothing.

In anguish of spirit the colleague and friend who had been so close to Marion for twenty years now faced the facts and made a tentative diagnosis: "Secondary carcinoma of the lungs; primary unknown."

In keeping with her belief that "a good doctor never shares fears—only proven knowledge," Dr. Davey kept her own counsel. Quietly she arranged for Marion to be seen by the professor of medicine at the university, by a well-known chest surgeon, by a visiting specialist from England. Conferences were held, ideas and opinions exchanged. They all boiled down to the same thing —a suspicion for which there was no proof.

Now it was June, and the get-well cards and letters arriving in every mail to Birch Point mingled with birthday greetings from friends in seven countries of three continents.

"When I think with what awe I regard you, I wonder at the temerity of your virus," wrote one patient. "You will never know how much it meant to me," came from the new mother of twins whom Marion delivered in May, "just to hear your voice in the delivery room." And from an older patient: "Would that I could do something for *you* now—you have done so much for me."

Messages came from former patients: "Come to see your 'baby' married on the 20th," "You are still the backbone of our lives," "Your name is honored and loved in our home," "I am so grateful to you for your help in my deepest despair"; from colleagues: "I will be glad to get home from vacation. I miss coming out to see you. You always give me a lift," "No one but Sir Winston Churchill could cause such dismay!"; from Vic classmates: "Take care of yourself. You are much too special to be sick."

A young woman doctor whom she had helped to start practice sent birthday greetings. "Thanks for how you have inspired and helped me," and a friend bound for India scrawled, "Don't forget our date to see Kashmir together."

"Get well soon. We have some new drip-drys in," wrote one of Marion's favorite saleswomen; and the young son of a colleague sent a somewhat smudged birthday card bearing a three-line message: "Dear Aunt Marion, We have a new dog. Please come and see him. OOOO XXXX."

Marianne arrived from New York, and a new routine was established. After breakfast Marion crawled back into bed and talked her ideas while the writer took notes. The three friends had lunch, on the lawn if the day was warm enough, and Marion slept in the afternoon while Marianne wrote up the morning's work. The patient arose for a leisurely cocktail and dinner hour and evenings were spent quietly, listening to records and chatting with family or friends who dropped in. Promptly at nine o'clock Marion retired for the night; sometimes she liked to get back in bed to have her after-dinner coffee with Poppy, Marianne, and one or two visitors sitting about the large, pleasant bedroom.

Marion took the lead in creating a business-as-usual, tranquil atmosphere. Beyond Birch Point's grounds her friends and family were anxious and heavyhearted, but here all was quiet and serene. Music filled the house; conversation was lighthearted. To visitors Marion stoutly maintained that she felt better, made jokes about "this blasted old carcass of mine," talked enthusiastically about progress on the new book, gave herself up to enjoyment of a succession of "perfect Scarborough days."

The Doubleday contracts for *Fatigue* arrived to be signed, and, with Poppy, the collaborators gaily built castles in the air about how the book would make a mint of money and they would spend the spring months on one of the Italian lakes; thereafter the morning work sessions were referred to as "earning our villa for today."

Once the sessions began they were concentrated first of all on the physiological basis for Marion's theories on fatigue in women. In her paper for the Dallas medical meeting she had made an exposition of this information; now she set Marianne to studying the paper and writing a summary of it in lay language. The summary went through four drafts, as Marion drilled her writer friend in the medical facts upon which the book would be based.

One morning the mail brought a letter from the magazine editor in the States. He had received Marion's article and was glowing with praise of the style in which it was written and the philosophy of life it expressed; he added a postscript saying that he was sending a check, mentioning a substantial sum.

Marion was pleased with herself, and that night called for a bottle of champagne to celebrate.

"Our first toast," she wrote Mr. Mack in a progress report on *Fatigue*, "was to the magazine editor. Much to my amazement and I am sure to yours, he took my piece with my title and didn't even change any of the words. Since I dictated it straight onto the tape recorder and didn't have much chance to improve it, this did something special for my morale.

"Our second toast was to the book. We felt it was practically finished, as we have the chapters outlined, not only with the headings but with the ideas to go with them."

Clearing away papers to start work the next morning, she crumpled up most of the mail of the day before, including the glowing editorial letter that most writers at least would keep, and some might be tempted to have framed, and threw it in the wastebasket. She was finally persuaded to allow it to be filed away, but it was clear that, for her, yesterday's big event had nothing to do with today!

On his way to and from the meeting of the Canadian Medical Association in eastern Canada, Marion's brother Dr. Irwin visited her. As baffled and worried as her colleagues, he had come from Saskatoon to be with her the month before when she had been in the hospital for tests and had kept closely in touch with his old friend and classmate, Dr. Davey. Now he gently made it clear that Marion must give up her July trip to England, "unless your next X rays are better."

"You will be very unhappy to get this news as I am very unhappy to send it," Marion wrote Miss Dearnley. "I have been told I can't possibly go to England." She told her friend about the development of her symptoms, adding that it seemed this was "one of those diseases which weren't in textbooks when I went to school.

"It is the most amazing thing to be chronically ill after having had fifty-six years of magnificent health. This is the first time in my life I've had to cancel any program because of my health. It is certainly not an experience to cherish."

Thanking her for a book Miss Dearnley had sent, she ended, "Some other day we will have this fun. I am sure there will be another day."

In a few days a loving and sympathetic reply came from Gertrude, saying the officers of the women's medical association "will probably be having fifteen fits" and would likely ask her again to be their president some time in the future. She urged Marion to postpone her trip to India, suggesting, "Why not enjoy life a bit and some leisure?"

Marion's fifty-sixth birthday fell on another "perfect Scarborough day." A final spate of letters, wires, cables, and packages arrived. Marion's bedroom was filled with books, flowers, bottles of wine, enclosures from letters, cartoons ("to give you a good laugh"), pictures of little Hilliard babies, pictures of grown-up Hilliard babies, special prayers. From New York her sister wired: "REMEMBER ONCE YOU SAID HILLIARDS DON'T FAINT WELL. THEY DON'T." From Halifax, where the McNeels had gone for the CMA meeting, Barby sent a gay card, with a short message: "Gosh, *how* we love you." Aunt Luella wrote a long, tender letter, saying how proud of her all the family were, and how they all remembered, "your early years, your blithe and cheerful spirit," and how "your interest, sympathy and inspiration have always been better than a bottle of medicine." From Quebec, where she was studying for the summer, her teen-age niece sent a birthday greeting with the message, "I always say a special prayer for you."

At cocktail time Poppy and Marianne presented their gifts and the three friends had a private celebration. A dozen of Marion's special friends from the hospital came for dessert and coffee, bringing an elegant throw of soft blue mohair. Ellen Blatchford, who had been a daily visitor, brought a cherry-red cashmere sweater that delighted Marion. She told her friends of the birthday check Von had sent, saying that since Marion must spend the summer convalescing, she must do it in style, and the check was to buy "some good-looking gowns and negligees." Marjorie Davis volunteered to pick up some finery on approval and bring it out for Marion's selection.

In the spring Marion had taped for the C.B.C., a radio interview in which she answered some very searching questions about her personal and professional philosophy. The interview had been cut into four parts and slotted into ten-minute spots on four successive evenings. Marion showed no interest in hearing the first three, but on the fourth night she asked to have the program switched through the hi-fi speaker in the bedroom, where she sat drinking her after-dinner coffee, with Poppy, Marianne, and Dr. Davis, who had brought out a large box of gowns and negligees for Marion to choose from.

"I want to see how it sounds," she explained, "because I wanted to do that part over, but the interviewer said it was fine. I'm just going to test my judgment against his."

The program came on. After a few "warm-up" questions the interviewer asked, "As a doctor, are you concerned with the subject of death?"

"In my practice," she replied, her voice low, clear, gentle, "I haven't had very much to do with death, fortunately. I have never been afraid of death, though I have seen it hovering pretty close in some obstetrical cases and the fight has been pretty rugged." She went on to say that "with a patient who is dying of cancer, for instance, you are doing your utmost to make the patient comfortable so she can look at the future with serenity, peace and almost a contentment."

Did she insist on telling the truth to a patient who was dying? She retold a story she had used many times; she had yielded to the entreaties of a young husband and kept the truth from a young woman who subsequently died in an ambulance on the way to the hospital.

"Never again would I submit to such an edict," she said feelingly; but, she added, "I think the most unpardonable thing a doctor can do is to say, 'I *think* you have cancer.' . . . You should only tell the truth when you can give her a cure, if there is one, or you can tell her what kind of treatment is going to be instituted and what the hope is. It's always the hope you have. But if she asks you, I think you must tell the truth.

"I may have a different feeling about death from what some people have. I never worry about the person who is dying, I only worry about the ones who are left behind. . . . I think the person who is going can often comfort the ones who are going to stay."

For the three friends who sat listening with her in the summer twilight it was suddenly a prescient moment. Marion felt the tension and dispelled it instantly.

"My goodness," she said in a casual, half-laughing way, "I didn't realize I'd said all those things about death. Anyway, what I wanted to say *did* come through, so he was right, and it's okay. Well, who besides me is having another cup of coffee?"

En route to Scarborough to check on her patient, Dr. Davey heard the broadcast on her car radio. It appeared to be a clear message. As she had so many times in the past anxious weeks, once more she felt deep appreciation for Marion's complete acceptance of her doctor's judgment, her careful avoidance of putting her "on the spot," and admiration for the enormous courage with which Marion was facing her situation.

Later, her stethoscope on Marion's chest, she said, "You can hear this as well as I can."

"Yes," replied Marion calmly, "I haven't been a clinician all these years for nothing." She paused, then added, "And I'm too good a clinician not to know what questions not to ask."

With her old friend Eva Macdonald she was a bit less veiled. "What does Jean Davey think is wrong with me?" she asked her.

"I guess you know what Jean thinks," replied Eva gently.

"You see, I have to talk over my ideas with you and Irwin," Marion explained, "so then I know how to act." Then she changed the subject.

The first phase of work on *Fatigue* finished, Marianne left for an assignment in New York. Uneasy about leaving her friends, she nevertheless followed Marion's lead in planning for the work they would do together at Scarborough later in the summer.

The "perfect days" gave way before a heat wave. Marion's devoted friend John Hollows fitted out her bedroom with an air conditioner, and for a few days she was comfortable. In spite of increased difficulty in breathing, she dictated material for the book, kept in touch with her editor and her collaborator in New York, talked with the *Chatelaine* editor about a proposed series of articles, and tried to answer some of her mail. She told her friends it was "wonderful to have so much time for reading" and soon she was going to be "the best-read woman in Canada"; described the beauty of her gardens; and said how grateful she was "for the kindness of all my friends."

To a Morrisburg neighbor she wrote a thank-you note for a gift, and mentioned the exciting sight of the new Seaway's being flooded, which dramatic event she had seen televised, adding, "I am glad I knew the River when it was a swift-flowing, exciting part of my life."

It was late on Friday, July eleventh, when she suffered a partial lung collapse. Dr. F. Marguerite Hill hurried out from the hospital with an oxygen mask and stayed to see Marion through the night. Marion awoke feeling better.

"I'm starved," she announced, and with relish downed a breakfast of porridge, toast, and coffee, then asked for seconds. While she ate, the McNeels arrived. There was a brief family conference.

"If I'm going to need oxygen," Marion said to Poppy, "we can't manage. I'd better go to the hospital."

In an ambulance Marion was driven along the road edging her beloved Birch Point acres and up the hill to the upper bluffs. She never looked back.

In the city, traffic was all but at a standstill because of the annual parade of the Orangemen, but a path gave way before the ambulance with its sirens going full blast.

"At last I'm having my innings with those boys," chortled Marion, who was frankly enjoying her first ambulance trip as a patient. "For years I've been held up by that darned parade."

Safely settled in an oxygen tent, with Poppy and Ellen Blatchford established in the next room, Marion was more comfortable and relaxed. She began to think up little things for her closest friends to do to help.

"She arranged for everybody to be able to do things for her, so they would feel better," one of them said later.

There was one exception. When the matter of getting a nurse was discussed, and someone suggested one of Marion's oldest and closest friends on the nursing staff, she said quickly, "No. It would be too hard on her."

In Saskatoon, Dr. Irwin caught an eastbound plane. From holiday spots in northern Ontario, Eva Macdonald, Dorothy Redmond Daley, and Canon John Frank hurried back to town. In Morrisburg, Vonnie got in her car and began the three-hundred-mile drive to Toronto.

Marion rested quietly in her oxygen tent, sleeping under sedation, waking for brief visits with family members and friends. Before she settled down for the night Poppy read the daily lesson from the Anglican prayerbook to her.

From Saturday evening until midnight on Tuesday, Marion's brother, Dr. Davey, Dr. McNeel, Dr. Macdonald, Dr. Daley, and Dr. Blatchford spelled each other at her bedside, doing what they could to make her comfortable.

Von arrived and, bravely squaring her shoulders, went into Marion's room.

"Well, look who's here!" exclaimed Marion joyfully. "Pull up this contraption [the oxygen tent] and get in here with me."

For fifteen minutes the hospital room rang with laughter, while Von told Marion all the Morrisburg gossip and Marion joked about her illness and how her friends were vying with each other to give her attention. Though the older woman knew this was probably the last time she would see the dear friend she had loved through childhood, girlhood, and womanhood—and it is possible that Marion knew it too—this might have been any of the warm, gay, spicy conversations they had enjoyed for nearly four decades. To Poppy, who had always loved to see the way these devoted friends sparked to each other, and who now stood in the background, knowing that, once out of the room, Von would need an arm to lean on, it was, as she told a friend later, "their best performance of all time!"

"What are you doing here?" asked Marion, surprised to see Canon Frank, whom she thought to be out of town on vacation. A friend in the room spoke up quickly, to remark how nice it was that he had had to come back to town, so he could visit her. At the end of their conversation he took her hand.

"Now remember, there is no fear," he said, quietly mentioning Gwen and another dear friend who had died. Marion's eyes seemed to grow bigger and bluer. She said good-by to him quietly.

Very early on Tuesday morning Marion awoke and sat bolt upright in the oxygen tent. "Of all things!" she exclaimed accusingly to Dr. Davey, who sat at the bedside, drinking a cup of coffee.

"Like some coffee?" asked Dr. Davey.

"Of course I would!" she replied emphatically, but before the coffee arrived she had fallen asleep again.

Later she roused to say good morning to Poppy. Then, about ten o'clock, helped by sedation, she drowsed off again, and slept away the rest of this last day of her life.

A few minutes before midnight on Tuesday, July fifteenth, she died, with her brother and Dr. Davey at her bedside.

Early the next morning, July sixteenth, the hospital pathologist returned to Dr. Davey an autopsy report that confirmed her clinical diagnosis.

The lung symptoms had indeed indicated a secondary carcinoma. The source of illness, the primary cancer that had never shown itself in any symptoms, was a small protrusion about the size of a half dollar, located in the center of the large intestine. It could not have been detected by any means now known to medicine. Even if, by some chance, it had been discovered, it would have been inoperable.

Later, speaking to a mutual friend about the "diagnostic nightmare" of this rare cancer illness, Marion's doctor said sadly, "It was an act of God in the sense that it was far beyond present medical knowledge and power. We were beaten even before we started."

CHAPTER 24

"Go Forth Upon Thy Journey"

As the noon news broadcast came over a local station on July sixteenth a businessman got into a taxi in downtown Toronto. The husband of one of Marion's colleague-friends, he had done business for Marion, danced with her at staff parties, joked with her about the problems of being married to a woman doctor. From her, he had heard the glad news of his son's birth; with her, he and his family had shared their highest and lowest moments.

Now he sat silently in the taxi, listening to the news he had heard earlier in the day and still couldn't quite believe.

As the broadcast went off the air and they pulled up at their destination the driver said, staring straight ahead, "This is sure a sad day for Toronto, mister."

Unable to speak, Marion's friend handed over a bill, then leaned across to shake hands with the driver, who saluted as he drove away. Whether he was a "father," a patient's husband or brother, or one of Marion's readers, no one knows; but that day he was one with many hundreds of other people.

By early afternoon cables began to arrive from European cities, and telegrams from scores of places on both sides of the Canadian–United States border, as wire services, radio, and television carried the news around the world.

A former patient put her feelings into a short newspaper article, printed because, said the editors, "it expresses the feelings of thousands of women whose lives Marion Hilliard has touched in her too-brief career." Under the title, "Thank You, Dr. Hilliard," the writer told of her experiences as a patient, concluding,

"I know that if you could talk to us now you would tell us not to mourn for you. You would tell us briskly to carry on with living. . . . I know you are still very much alive in this world. You are living through all the thousands of babies you brought into the world, and through all the thousands of adults you have influenced, steadied, helped. . . . For all you've done for so many of us, I think it will make everyone feel a little comforted if we can say once more . . . Thank you, Dr. Hilliard."

At Suite 716 at the Medical Arts Building the telephone rang incessantly, and tearful patients crowded into the waiting room, some keeping afternoon appointments, but many driven by the pathetic hope that the news had been wrong and some terrible mistake had been made. Tearful themselves, the nurse and secretary, Dr. Hilliard's proud "team," did their best to help the young obstetrician, Dr. Marjorie Kuck, the second Hilliard Fellow at Women's College Hospital, who was caring for Marion's patients. Somehow the three shaken young women got through the afternoon, then, by mutual consent, closed the office for thirty-six hours.

Through the long day Marion's brother and Poppy, whom Marion had chosen as her executors, met with family members and Canon Frank to make the sad arrangements. It was agreed that there should be a church funeral, although Holy Trinity was then closed for renovations; Marion's will directed that she be cremated. The burial would be in the family plot in Fairview Cemetery at Morrisburg.

At the hospital, staff doctors met and appointed two of their members to compose a tribute to be read at the funeral service.

Out at Birch Point preparations were made for the sorrowful homecoming. The faithful Mrs. Paterson put the house in order. Mr. Brown, with the help of Mr. Blatchford, trimmed the lawns and gardens. Ellen Blatchford and Marianne, who had come from New York, dismantled the sick room, packing away gifts, sorting the mountains of mail, removing Marion's tape recorder and other mute and painful reminders of her last days at home; and wrote down telephoned cables and wires, as well as the many messages of friends, offering, begging, to be allowed to "do something."

Early the next morning Canon Frank held a special communion service in Holy Trinity's chapel, and a small group of Marion's friends gathered for the comfort of worship in the little chapel she had loved and of the clergyman's prayers of thanksgiving for Marion Hilliard's life and work.

Marion always had had a horror of the impersonal atmosphere of a funeral home. Years before, she had asked Poppy and her brother, if such a decision were to fall to them, to see to it that she would be brought "home to Scarborough." These arrangements made, and notices sent to the newspapers, in the late morning of Thursday, July seventeenth, the gravel drive that had always crackled briskly as swiftly driven cars came and went at Birch Point now crunched under the slow, heavy wheels of quite a different kind of car.

"I wish you could have been here," one of the small group of family and friends in residence at Birch Point wrote a grieving friend in a distant city, "to share the odd little comforts we have had. The weather has been beautiful and benign. The flower gardens and trees never looked lovelier. Marion wore a blue dress—that kind of sky-blue she liked best—and her favorite jewelry, the star sapphires her friends at the hospital gave her, and one perfect red rose—from Poppy, who knew it was her favorite flower. She looked so happy, so peaceful and (I know this will sound just out of this world but we all felt it) so *vital*. You kept expecting her to open her eyes and issue one of those brisk, salty phrases of hers.

"Hundreds of people came in and out, of course. It was all an atmosphere she would have approved of—sad and grieving, but sooner or later, people would dry their eyes and begin to talk of happy, funny, gay memories, all in a quite natural way.

"Her family asked that people contribute to the Marion Hilliard Trust Fund instead of sending flowers, but we have coped with fifty-some baskets and wreaths, and been glad after all, that there were some. The last word from the Trust Fund is that nearly a hundred contributions of greatly varying amounts have been received."

Marion's brothers and sisters had agreed that the old folks on Lonsdale Road should be spared the funeral and the tiring trip to Morrisburg. Other visitors tactfully moved out onto the lawns when, in the late afternoon, Mrs. Hilliard and her sister, brother, and sister-in-law were brought to the house.

"Oh, you dear little thing!" cried Mrs. Hilliard, clasping her hands and bending tenderly over her child. After a few minutes the little party was led into another room, where they could have a cup of tea in privacy. Mercifully Mrs. Hilliard's memory was such that Marion's death was not quite real to her.

The living Marion who always dreaded being alone in the dark still seemed so real that no one felt comfortable about leaving her for her last, long night in her home. In a kind of night watch, in twos and threes, Poppy and her friends, Ellen and Douglas Blatchford, Dr. and Mrs. Hilliard, and Dr. and Mrs. McNeel sat with her until daylight, talking quietly.

Long before two o'clock on the warm, clear afternoon of Friday, July eighteenth, St. James' Cathedral, set like a great jewel in a well-tended churchyard in downtown Toronto, had filled; of its one thousand seats, all but those reserved for the bereaved family and the pallbearers were occupied, and another hundred people stood in the aisles at either side of the great church. As the service began, many others stood in the churchyard beneath the open windows.

The rich red velvet robe over the casket at the foot of the chancel echoed and blended with the deep colors of the windows at the back of the sanctuary that depict the Ascension and the Last Supper, as painted by Leonardo da Vinci.

The service began with Marion's favorite Bible passages—the thirteenth chapter of First Corinthians.

"Though I speak with the tongues of men and angels . . ." Canon Frank's voice rang out, clear, deep, melodious. ". . . and now abideth faith, hope and love, these three, but the greatest of these is love."

After a hymn, "The King of Love My Shepherd Is," the clergyman read the doctors' tribute.

"The thoughts of the doctors who have worked with her over the years have centered quickly on the way in which the strength of friendship and the give and take of professional partnership have been wonderfully mingled," it began. "This quality of staunch and spontaneous support has had in it both great loyalty to others and humility in the face of all life that she found so adventurous."

It spoke of "her unique and radiant secret," by which she conveyed courage to so many women, "helping them to start on careers and to do good medicine," how her practice of medicine was "an art as well as a science," and how she always gave to a question "an answer both convinced and convincing."

"She had outstanding ability and faithfully acquired knowledge," the tribute concluded, "yet she walked and worked in the presence of a higher power. She gave leadership to leaders, yet she was completely at home with the lowly. Her smile was the natural expression of the joy and grace that she found in life, and which she possessed so abundantly."

Once again the patients' tribute, written for the presentation of the Marion Hilliard Trust Fund, was read.

The summer sunshine slanted through the windows onto the faces of the choirboys as their matchless young voices soared through the stillness, in the song Marion had loved for so many years.

> "In the bleak mid-winter
> Frosty wind made moan,
> Earth stood hard as iron,
> Water like a stone;
> Snow had fallen, snow on snow,
> Snow on snow,
> In the bleak mid-winter,
> Long ago.

What can I give him,
Poor as I am?
If I were a shepherd
I would give a lamb;
If I were a wise man
I would do my part;
Yet what can I give him—
Give my heart."

The service drew to a close.

"Go forth upon thy journey from this world, O Christian soul . . . may thy portion this day be in peace, and thy dwelling in the heavenly Jerusalem."

After the benediction the congregation sang together, "Unto the Hills Around Do I Lift Up My Longing Eyes."

As Canon Frank left the chancel the great bell, rich and mellow, began to toll. At the usher's signal the honorary pallbearers rose and, two by two, walked slowly down the aisle: Dr. Evelyn Bateman, Dr. Ellen Blatchford, Dr. Dorothy Daley, Dr. Jean Davey, Dr. Marjorie Davis, Dr. Jessie Gray, Dr. Eva Macdonald, Dr. Geraldine Maloney, Dr. Margaret McEachern, Dr. Marjorie McIntyre, Dr. Elizabeth Stewart, Dr. Elizabeth Wiley.

A single thought dominated the minds of those who had known Marion well, at the sight of these twelve fine-looking women walking in dignity from the cathedral: These women *are* the hospital she loved so well. How proud she would be to see them!

The pallbearers moved into place and slowly wheeled the robe-covered casket toward the great doors: Marion's nephews, Dr. Joe Hilliard and "Young Went" Myers; Eva and Charlie Macdonald's two sons, stalwart young men whom Marion had brought into the world; Ellen and Douglas Blatchford's son, Bob; and "Wake" Wynn, the husband of Marion's office nurse and friend. At the door they lifted the casket to their shoulders and bore it to the waiting car between the double line formed by the women doctors.

As family members and Poppy emerged from the church they

moved quietly down the line of doctors who stood under the great churchyard trees, shaking hands with each and expressing appreciation for their share in the service. Then, from the small chapel of the cathedral, after the brief service preceding cremation, they returned to the McNeels' apartment, where the older family members joined them for tea. There they began the painful process of closing ranks, as a family must do when a beloved member has gone.

It had rained on Saturday night and the morning of Sunday, July twentieth, was cloudy and damp. At nine o'clock a small group of Marion's family, close friends, and a few Morrisburg neighbors gathered at Fairview Cemetery. The brief committal service was shared by Marion's elder brother, Reverend Foster Hilliard, and Canon Frank.

("The final scene was so much in keeping with her life," Canon Frank wrote later. "The cemetery is close to the scenes of her girlhood. It is also close to the mighty seaway project, which will stand for many a year to come as a symbol of Canadian adventure and achievement. It is right that such should be the abiding place of the mortal part of one of the great Canadians of our generation.")

As the benediction was pronounced, the sun broke through the clouds to the southeast and light fell across the calm waters of the Seaway, the pale, sorrowing faces of the little group gathered around the Hilliard family plot, the blue-green tips of the row of blue spruce trees.

Turning back to the gates, one paused under a great willow tree, struck with the soft, graceful skyline of Morrisburg homes and trees in the distance. Then the eye was drawn to the little cove next to the point of land on which the cemetery stands. The sandy beach, old tree trunks to lean against, the little red canoe and jaunty blue rowboat rocking on the gentle waves—all gave proof that this was a spot the children had made their own. There was comfort in knowing that tomorrow the air would be full of the sound of their laughter.

Acknowledgments

A great deal of generous help—and, in many cases, warm hospitality—went into the making of this book. It was a rare experience to meet old friends and make new ones in the many talks I had with Dr. Hilliard's family, colleagues, patients, and friends; to them all I offer heartfelt thanks.

Chief among these are my partners in this undertaking. Miss Opal V. Boynton and Dr. Irwin M. Hilliard collaborated with me in the interviewing and other research, took responsibility with me in the choice of materials to tell the story of Marion Hilliard's life, read all drafts of the manuscript, and, as Dr. Hilliard's executors, made available her letters and private papers. Their wholehearted sharing of the ups and downs of the three years in which the book was in preparation, no less than their working collaboration, made the book possible.

We are particularly grateful to Dr. Marion's sister, Mrs. Burdett McNeel, for her help in shaping the chapters dealing with childhood years in Morrisburg; and our thanks go also to these other members of the family: Mrs. James Warner, Reverend Foster Hilliard, Mrs. Wentworth Myers, Sr., Dr. Burdett McNeel, Mrs. Irwin M. Hilliard, and Mrs. David Bowes.

For their interesting recollections of Dr. Marion's childhood and early background we are indebted to her cousins, Mrs. David Countryman, the Misses Sadie and Jane Dillen, Mrs. Fred Winters, and the Misses Mary and Blanche Van Allen, as well as Mr. Foster Hilliard, who gave us access to the Hilliard family Bible.

We are especially grateful to Dr. Marion's lifelong friends, Miss Georgeanna Von Doran and Mrs. Clifford Hare, for their picture of her as a child and young girl, and to the editor of the *Morrisburg Leader*, Mr. Arthur Laurin, for opening the files of the newspaper to us and giving us other valuable assistance. For their warm welcome and generous help we owe much to these other present and former residents of Morrisburg: Reverend and Mrs. Maxwell Allen, Miss Sadie Bush, Mr. George Challies, Mrs. George Clark, Miss Marion Coligan, the late Miss Isabelle Farlinger, Mr. Clinton Fetterly, Mr. Arthur Hickey, Mrs. Parker Locke, Mrs. Elisha McIntyre, Mrs. David Morgan, Mrs. Henry Randall, the Misses Minnie and Frances Smith, Mr. Gordon Thom, Miss M. Joy Wallace, and Mr. William Weegar.

Classmates and other associates, particularly those in the Student Christian Movement, during Dr. Hilliard's years in Victoria College and the University of Toronto's medical school gave us helpful information and loaned us letters, yearbooks, and scrapbooks. Our warm thanks to: Mrs. Brian Barrett, Dr. Douglas E. Cannell, Bishop F. A. Cockin, Mrs. John Davidson, Miss Marjorie M. Fenwick, Dr. R. E. Haist, Mr. F. A. Hare, Mrs. Lorne J. Henry, Professor S. H. Hooke, Mrs. J. D. H. Hutchinson, Dr. W. S. Keith, Dr. Jessie Macpherson, Miss Helen Nichol (to whom we are also indebted for a lively description of a visit to the Hilliard cottage at Iroquois Point), Mrs. Lester Pearson, Miss Olive Russell, and Mrs. Clifford Weber.

For firsthand information to supplement Dr. Hilliard's diary and letters during her year of postgraduate work in the British Isles we are greatly indebted to her English friends, Miss Gertrude Dearnley of Surrey and Dr. Margaret Read of London; and for special information about the Polyklinic in Budapest, where Dr. Hilliard did additional work later, we want to thank Dr. Michael Balkany of Toronto Western Hospital.

For their generous help, by way of personal and professional information and reminiscences, we owe much to these colleagues and others with whom Dr. Hilliard was associated as a junior intern and later as a staff member of the Women's College Hospital: Dr. Ellen Blatchford, Mrs. Ernest Bogart, Dr. Dorothy Daley, Dr. Jean Davey, Dr. Marjorie Davis, Clara Dixon, R.N., Dr. Mary Elizabeth Forbes, Evelyn Galbraith, R.N., Dr. Jessie Gray, Dr. Marjorie Kuck, Dr. Marjorie McIntyre, Dr. Eva Macdonald, Miss Dorothy Macham, Dr. Geraldine Maloney, Mrs. Peter Sandiford, Dr. Elizabeth Stewart, and Dr. Elizabeth Wiley.

Dr. Hilliard's office nurses, the late Mrs. Winifred DeGruchy and Mrs. H. A. Wynn, and her secretary, Mrs. Richard Carrick, gave invaluable assistance in helping us shape the sections on Dr. Hilliard's professional life.

We are indebted to Dr. Joe V. Meigs, Mrs. Gladys Mabey, and Mary Ross, R.N., for information about Dr. Hilliard's association with Vincent Memorial Hospital, the gynecologic service of Massachusetts General Hospital, Boston, Massachusetts.

Toronto and Scarborough friends, neighbors, and associates in Dr. Hilliard's extraprofessional activities gave us information and shared personal memories with us. For this help we are indebted to Mrs. Ross Anderson, Mr. Maurice Brown, Mrs. Harry Cassidy, Mrs. John Coleman, the late Miss Eva Coon, Reverend and Mrs. John Frank, Miss E. Ray Godfrey, Mr. and Mrs. Leslie Hancock, Mrs. J. A. Harrison, Miss Nora Lea, Mrs. James Lewtas, Miss Marjorie Macdonald, Mr. and Mrs. F. W. C. Mayor, Mr. and Mrs. James A. Murray, Mrs. Helen Paterson, Mrs. Gilbert deB. Robinson, Miss Marion Royce, the late Mrs. Harold Taber, Mr. Charles Tugwell, Dr. Alice Turner, and Mrs. J. R. M. Wilson.

We want to express warm appreciation to the many women patients, and their husbands, who described for us their experiences and feelings about Dr. Hilliard. With one exception, these are told anonymously; to Mrs. Pauline Shapiro and her family, especially Mr. Jonathan Hilliard Shapiro, of Birmingham, England, we are grateful for permission to quote from her letters to her husband from Canada in the summer of 1940.

Dr. Hilliard's neighbor, friend, and patient, Mrs. E. J. Wylie, typed all drafts of the manuscript. Mr. George Nelson, president,

Doubleday of Canada, and Mr. Ferris Mack, editor, Doubleday & Company, New York, Dr. Hilliard's great friends, gave us much appreciated advice and assistance.

Finally I want to thank my teacher and friend, Miss Ola Elizabeth Winslow of Sheepscot, Maine, for reading and commenting on the manuscript.

MARION O. ROBINSON

Scarborough, Ontario, 1960
New York City, 1963

Index